KU-022-120

GARDENING AT EDEN

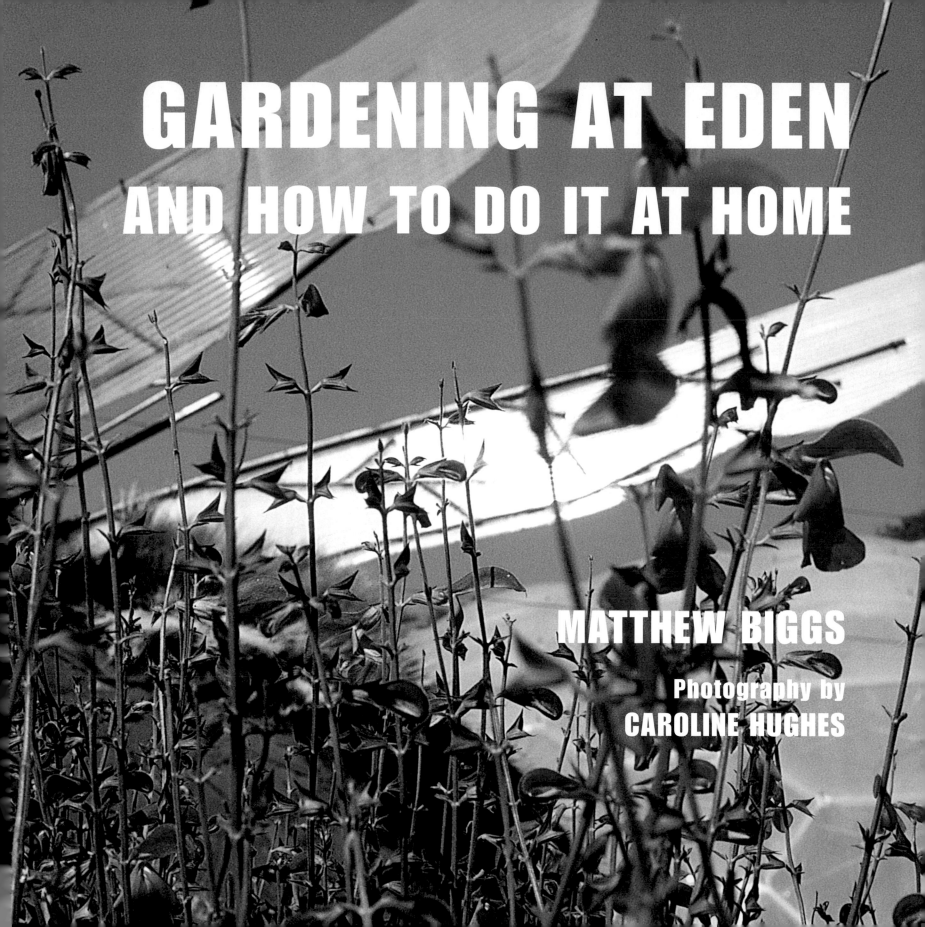

GARDENING AT EDEN
AND HOW TO DO IT AT HOME

MATTHEW BIGGS

Photography by
CAROLINE HUGHES

TRANSWORLD PUBLISHERS
61–63 Uxbridge Road, London W5 5SA
a division of The Random House Group Ltd

RANDOM HOUSE AUSTRALIA (PTY) LTD
20 Alfred Street, Milsons Point, Sydney,
New South Wales 2061, Australia

RANDOM HOUSE NEW ZEALAND LTD
18 Poland Road, Glenfield, Auckland 10, New Zealand

RANDOM HOUSE SOUTH AFRICA (PTY) LTD
Isle of Houghton, Corner of Boundary Road & Carse O'Gowrie,
Houghton 2198, South Africa

Published 2006 by Eden Project Books
a division of Transworld Publishers

Published by arrangement with The Eden Project Ltd

Text copyright © Matthew Biggs 2006
Foreword copyright © Tim Smit 2006
Concept copyright © The Eden Project Ltd

All pictures copyright © Caroline Hughes 2006 except
page 68, Stephen Bedser; page 98, Tim Grigg; page 200, Garden Picture
Library/Tony Howell; pages 212 and 213, Andrew Ormerod; page 270,
Edward Parker/Images Everything Ltd.; page 279, Charles Francis

Design by Isobel Gillan

The right of Matthew Biggs to be identified as the author of this
work has been asserted in accordance with sections 77 and 78
of the Copyright, Designs and Patents Act 1988.

A catalogue record for this book is available from the British Library.
ISBN 9781903919736 (from Jan 07)
ISBN 1903919738

All rights reserved. No part of this publication may be reproduced,
stored in a retrieval system, or transmitted in any form or by any means,
electronic, mechanical, photocopying, recording, or otherwise,
without the prior permission of the publishers.

Typeset in Helvetica

Printed in Germany

1 3 5 7 9 10 8 6 4 2

Papers used by Eden Project Books are made from wood grown
in sustainable forests. The manufacturing processes conform to the
environmental regulations of the country of origin.

CONTENTS

IMAGINE BEING ASKED to grow plants from almost anywhere in the world – and most of the world's crops too – in a waterlogged hole in the ground, with no soil. That was the challenge that faced Eden's horticulturists back in 1998. The old adage, 'They didn't know that it couldn't be done, so they just got on and did it', could not be more true of what has since been achieved. Matthew Biggs, a Kew-trained horticulturist, has captured the essence of their trials as well as the benefits of their errors in this enormously useful book for all gardeners.

Eden is cutting-edge stuff, full of things that have never been done before: one day soon it will probably be listed by English Heritage as a significant twenty-first-century landscape. From the start, the Project has been lucky enough to be showered with good advice from an army of well-wishing experts – from university researchers to botanic gardeners to retired tea and coffee growers, not to mention international gene banks. All of this, combined with an ever-resourceful horticultural team and sound scientific backing, has led to seemingly insoluble problems being solved and new approaches found.

I have no doubt that you will be inspired by the sheer horticultural professionalism of this book, and glean from it many ideas to suit your own plot, however large or small.

SUE MINTER,
Former Director of Horticulture, Eden Project

FOREWORD BY TIM SMIT

All is still. As dark blue turns to the grey of dawn there is a tension in the air. The ghostly outline of the glass pyramids rises from the desert, glistening with dew. This is Biosphere 2 outside Phoenix, Arizona, the controversial closed-system ecology centre where they are researching the possibility of constructing life-support systems for living on Mars. Whatever its successes or failures, something is about to happen this morning that will change the perceptions of all who will see it for the first time, for ever. On the external wall of the entrance is a meter to measure the oxygen being generated inside. As the first rays of the sun break the horizon the dials go crazy. The numbers go round faster than the eye can see, as three acres of plants begin to photosynthesize all at once. Silent power beyond imagining. And while we have known since our schooldays that without plants there is no life on earth, this is the first time that understanding has transcended belief. From now on, wherever you are, whether it be walking down country lanes, through woodland or field, on moor or valley, you will see greenery and know you are in the presence of something fundamental.

I am not a plantsman, nor even a gardener of the roughest sort. My involvement with horticulture both at the Lost Gardens of Heligan and here at Eden has been based on deep admiration for those who do it and on acting as a champion for the stories they inspire – as interpreter, if you like.

At Heligan my office was a garden shed, from which John Nelson and I plotted the restoration of one of the most romantic and mysterious gardens in the country. Its fate sealed by the loss of most of its gardeners during the First World War, it slowly went to sleep, buried under mountains of overgrowth. Entranced by its tale of loss as well as by the art of the Victorian gardener, we seized the opportunity to tell for the first time the story of the ordinary people who had once worked here. The project could not have been undertaken without first the help of Philip McMillan Browse, the former Director of RHS Wisley, who came initially to help and advise, and also of Peter Thoday, who as the presenter of the BBC programmes *The Victorian Kitchen Garden* and *The Victorian Flower Garden* was a huge source of expertise. Both these men were deeply interested in the Productive Gardens (those that provide fruit, vegetables and flowers for gathering in) and the emerging technologies that saw Heligan move from manure-heated pineapple pits to fancy boiler systems that powered the assortment of glass and stove houses that were a feature here in the four walled gardens. Exotic fruits and flowers, jungle gardens and ornamental herbaceous borders, follies and woodlands, introduced the adventures of the great plant-hunters to me. Philip and Peter were full of it, and from this we launched into conversations that explored the plants that had changed the world.

We decided to create an exhibition in a glasshouse. But it was a shock to realize that once Philip's list of plants was complete it would barely have fitted into Heligan as a whole, let alone into a humble lean-to greenhouse. An idea was evolving, and many days ruminating in a garden shed were followed by a visit to Peter Thoday's house in Somerset, where we drank lots of whisky and talked into the early hours. The idea was not only born now, but growing. Peter and Philip became joint horticultural directors and drew on all their old colleagues, friends and former students for advice and good conversation. These were heady days. No one was paid, yet people came from all over the country to meet in private houses, hotels, pubs and motorway service stations, excited at the idea of being in at the start of something special.

The story of how we went about creating the Eden Project is told at length elsewhere, but the potted history is as follows.

We had the idea to build three giant conservatories which would tell the story of human dependence on plants from three climatic areas: the humid tropics, including Oceania; the warm temperate or mediterranean regions, and the dry tropics. Temperate zones would be represented in the outside landscape, because Cornwall's unusually mild climate allows for the growing of plants across as wide a spectrum of habitats as can be found anywhere in the world, ranging from subtropical valleys to moorland. As the project progressed we would find that we could afford only two conservatories (or Biomes, as they came to be called), so dropped the dry tropics in the hope that, once successfully open, we could raise the money to complete the set.

These Biomes had to be the biggest in the world – for who would wish to visit the second-largest? – and their setting had to be magnificent, such that the greatest of cynics would, if only for a moment, be dumbstruck. The picture that played in our minds was the famous woodcut of David Livingstone discovering the Victoria Falls, where he is pictured right at their edge staring down into the abyss. To this was added the image of Conan Doyle's 'lost worlds' hidden in the craters of volcanoes. The two merged in our imagination into the notion of creating a tiny civilization in an old clay pit.

We searched everywhere for the right kind of hole in the ground, until we finally found it at Bodelva, three miles east of St Austell in Cornwall. It had no soil, but it had water (in abundance), was south-facing and had a distinctive rim that passed admirably for a crater. It was thirty-four acres in area and two hundred feet deep at its south face. The architects, Grimshaws, worked with Dominic Cole, the landscape architect, in creating the setting. This was to be the most challenging work of their professional lives, as they battled to make the pit feel like the natural home for the structures that would be built there. Dominic's brief was to develop a design that saw Picasso meet the Aztecs at wow factor 11. This he achieved with his magnificent scimitar-shaped beds, sensuously zigzagging footpaths, and his overarching master aesthetic that saw themes carry from one side of the pit to the other. Inside the Biomes the planting is a technical and aesthetic masterpiece, as the paths wind through the plantings to give the effect of great distance and size while in fact all is held in fairly confined spaces and on slopes that are at best challenging, at worst plantable only by abseilers.

The particular Biomes were chosen because of their ability to tell particular stories. The Humid Tropics enables us to talk about the first human adaptation to the wild in its early domestication, and thereafter the impact of the Industrial Revolution in

RIGHT: *Striking sculptures provide strong focal points at Eden. Always view a sculpture from every angle before securing it in place.*

the development of mono-cropping with the aim of feeding the now global markets for coffee, sugar cane, oil and rubber palm, cocoa and bananas as well as many other crops. The Warm Temperate is a place to tell the stories relevant to the birth of Western civilization, as well as exploring the amazingly floristically rich regions of the Fynbos in South Africa, the Chaparral of California and, of course, the Mediterranean itself. The underlying themes of livelihoods and survival are never far from the surface, but our intent was to interpret what wildness looks like and then to explore its domestication. 'Eden' as a name was always intended to be ironic, alluding in one breath to a wild paradise dripping with produce of every kind – a cornucopia – while at the same time playing on the conceit that if humans were thrown from paradise for eating from the tree of knowledge, perhaps only by eating much, much more could we ever hope to return there. It is important to say that the overtly religious association was one we never made.

Even before we opened, the public voted with their feet to come and see the building of Eden, then returned to see it completed. Over eight million people have visited since 17 March 2001, opening day.

People come because, though gardening is supposed to be a hobby, anyone who gets hooked on it soon realizes that there is something far more important going on. There is a spiritual dimension to it, an acknowledgement of some time deep in the past when our hunter-gathering instincts appreciated the discovery of edible fruits, berries and nuts, when flowers provided the seasonal roadmap and marked moments of celebration or rites of passage, and

more recently, when we sought to demonstrate that we were lords of all we surveyed and could bend Nature herself to our will. Plants remind us of our origins and can bring us back, if only dimly, to a remembrance of our total dependence on them. They can also, like a rumour, hint at senses lost in urban background noise, and provide a palette with which we can paint our gardens in our own image of the world, as a place we can control – or perhaps more accurately, let be – as much as we want.

Garden sheds seem to be a constant. First the one at Heligan and then, when we started Eden proper, we moved to Watering Lane Nursery at Pentewan where the office was another shed, popularly known as the Wendy Hut. The five-acre site had three long glasshouses and a range of polytunnels and hard-standing areas, and boasted a bungalow where we held our meetings and where Philip brought his library, to become a common resource for all of us. The big shed that had been the nursery shop was where the horticultural team set up base alongside the finance team. It felt like the start of a military campaign, as week after week new faces would appear, skilled in one horticultural art or another.

The autumn of 1998 was extraordinary, as we built an acre of huge glasshouses six metres in height to take the tropical plants. Financial years and seasons do not mix, and we had to start heavy-duty propagation and assembling the collections then, or else we would miss the deadline of 2000, the Millennium. Tom Keay and Robin Lock (Warm Temperate and Humid Tropics curators, respectively) travelled like lunatics to other botanic gardens around the UK and in Europe, mainly Holland and Italy with a bit of Spain thrown in. Many came as volunteers who eventually turned into staff, as the glasshouses filled up and soon were bursting at the seams. The core nursery team were established by that autumn, working all hours propagating, doing pest and disease analysis, washing the roots of the imported plants and instituting quarantine protocols (we had by now also built a quarantine greenhouse).

The giant greenhouses now became our marketing tool, to sell the vision of what Eden would become. Even in one acre, the humidity and dense ranks of plants created the feeling of jungle. Ian Martin, who was managing the nursery at the time, became our secret weapon, beguiling visitors with his stories and his certainty of our success.

All the time the deadline of early autumn 2000 loomed as the moment when construction in the pit had to be completed. The constructors had never faced such a challenge; late delivery would result in the probable deaths of all the really big plants that were due to be trucked in from Italy. Any time after the end of September and the Alps were too cold, and the trucks couldn't insulate the palms. It concentrated minds most wonderfully: on 25 September 2000 the planting began, with large cranes set up in the Humid Tropics Biome swinging their cargo off the backs of pantechnicons through the giant void to be lovingly planted and then guyed. It is hard to convey the excitement of the team, working eighteen-hour days as the empty hangar-like structure was gradually transformed into a jungle while at the same time the constructors were completing the paths and drainage features around

them. In a month it felt populated; in three, the team were already working on the detailed under-storey.

Simultaneously, the largest soil-creation project in the world was being managed in a pit a mile from the site. Eighty-five thousand tonnes of soil were made, using a mixture of china clay waste and a range of composts. As if it wasn't hard enough planting thirty-four acres to an immensely detailed brief, it all had to be planted in a medium that had never been grown in before. Add to that the facts that many of the slopes both inside and outside were at 45° angles or worse and we were suffering the worst winter in Cornwall's history (over 100 consecutive days of rain), and you get the horticultural equivalent of the Somme. Some days the slopes would get waterlogged and slide down into a messy heap and have to be shovelled back by mass labour, then pinned down under acres of hessian or coir matting (which would eventually rot out after the plant roots had taken over the job of slope stabilization). Then, in the wild parts where the rockfaces were crumbling, a grass mulch was pressure-hosed on to chicken-wire surfaces and hey presto, green hillsides.

In March 2001 we opened the Biomes in a quiet ceremony attended only by the Eden team, the constructors and our one guest Bill Ind, the Bishop of Truro, who said a few ecumenical words and we all felt a little bit weepy. As I looked up at the huge slopes in the Humid Tropics Biome and saw the thousands of small plants poking out through the hessian and thought of the hundreds of man hours spent at the end of a rope making it possible, I was awestruck. When later in the season we started to

Prior to the opening of the Eden Project, 80,000 plants jostled for space in the Watering Lane Nursery.

RIGHT: *The Eden Project is a form of educational theatre designed to instil in its visitors a sense of the importance of plants.*

see the plants fruiting and took in the sheer vigour of the pioneer species reaching for the sun, we realized that the Green Team had created the first rainforest in captivity. As the plants grew to full height, we would eventually have to consider aerial walkways, and as I write today the joke that the plants wouldn't touch the roof is wearing thin as large numbers of species are outperforming what was expected of them from experience in the wild.

The Eden horticultural team today I would measure against any anywhere in the world, and in what follows Matthew Biggs has distilled their knowledge, their skills and their practices brilliantly. The challenges they have faced and then overcome, the powerful aesthetic they've instilled into everything they do, and their flexibility in collaboration with artists, performers and the education team make them our greatest asset. We are all hugely proud of them. The horticultural tradition is rooted in the great botanic gardens, and the Eden team's greatest achievement has been to realize that Eden *isn't* a botanical garden. It isn't a collection of plants, it's a

form of educational theatre designed to instil in visitors a sense of the importance of plants, and of wonder at what they do and are. Just as importantly, plants provide the backcloth against which we tell our human stories, and it is here in the world of livelihoods and living on the edge that education and understanding are most necessary, and where new opportunities can be found. Issues such as Fair Trading and equity, water shortage and the fight for natural resources, are addressed here. Eden is a big story, and they have mastered it.

There are more than two million acres of private garden in Britain, and gardens occupy 20 per cent of the area of London. We use them as a canvas on which to paint our horticultural pictures, as a space in which to reflect our private attitudes to the environment and our focus on beauty, food and wildlife; to reflect on what civilization really might mean, to live with the grain of Nature – and perhaps of our own natures? All of us with gardens in this country, whether we obsessively tend our prize-winning dahlias or just keep a pot of supermarket chives watered, share responsibility for a very sizeable chunk of the landscape, one that is as much a part of the natural world as the Amazon rainforest. Eden is ultimately not only a visitor attraction gardened to extremes with a fine set of stories to tell, it is also a powerful symbol of connection: between us and Nature and of us to each other, where through the metaphor of plants we can see that what we share is far greater than what divides us. Funny things, plants...

INTRODUCTION

In Africa you hear the dull rhythmic thud as the well-worn blade of an ancient mattock bites into the dusty soil, preparing a seedbed for sowing millet; in Manchester a new-generation allotment enthusiast harvests the first of the season's lettuce; and in Asia you hear a gentle splashing as a man's hand repeatedly ripples the water as he plants his field of rice. Wherever there is the sound of tilling, tending or harvesting, the vibrations echo around the globe, through history, gender and generations.

Mankind has worked the soil for survival for over ten thousand years. The most precious substance on this planet allows us to grow plants that feed, heal, clothe and protect us; without plants, we would not survive. Early humans harvested food from the surrounding vegetation, and the first settlements were established where food was plentiful, soils were rich and the best plants could be selected and cultivated. These early communities developed an understanding of the earth, a spiritual relationship with it, and learned to value the plants that it provided for them. In the developed world many of us forget, or don't realize, how dependent we are on plants and think of food as coming from the supermarket. Our lifestyle has detached us from its source but now times are changing.

In recent years, and for the first time in history, millions of gardeners in the developed world have enjoyed gardening for pleasure, rather than necessity. The Industrial Revolution, offering the promise of a better life, brought past generations to settle in the towns, but now many of their early-twenty-first-century descendants are returning to the land. Gardening has never been so popular. For many years ornamental gardening predominated, but recently sales of vegetable seeds have overtaken flowers and in some areas the waiting lists for allotments are over ten years long. The new kid on the plot is more likely to be a mother with pre-school children who is concerned about pesticides and wants to grow organically, or a member of an ethnic group who wants a regular supply of a favourite vegetable that is not always available in the shops. Everybody's doing it, and gardening at Eden brings together history and cultures, vegetables and ornamentals, in the search for a sustainable future.

I spent a year watching and talking to Eden's expert gardeners at work, as they nurtured plants both familiar and unusual from around the globe, reflecting climates and environments in all their diversity. Many of these plants, such as our rainforest 'houseplants' and Mediterranean herbs, have been grown in Britain for some time, but now gardeners can further spice up their plot by growing tropical crops like sweet potato and yard-long beans outdoors, without the help of a Biome. Such homegrown additions to our diet are likely to become even more appropriate if predictions of global warming are fulfilled. Visit Eden and you'll begin to understand that gardeners around the globe have much in common. East and West already share many crops – tea, okra, bananas, oriental greens – and staples like potatoes are grown in over 150 countries. Wherever we live, we all aim for the finest crops, battle with pests and diseases such as whitefly and blight, and use similar tools and techniques.

One of Eden's aims is 'to promote the understanding and responsible management of the vital relationship between plants, people and resources, leading to a sustainable future for all'. With a view to achieving this, a living theatre of plants and people has been created; the message is conveyed through exhibitions, art, storytelling, workshops, lectures, displays and events. And every zone in every Biome is a stage on which some remarkable stories unfold.

But why focus on natural habitats such as rainforest, Mediterranean scrub and deserts? The answer is that the origins of all the plants we depend on for our survival are found in the wild; destroy those habitats, and we lose the plants that have provided for our needs in the past as well as those yet undiscovered that could influence our future.

It's time to cultivate a greater awareness of the world around us, to get out and garden the Eden way. Most gardeners have already started by reducing their reliance on chemicals, but there is so much more that we can do to make domestic gardening sustainable. This book offers information, practical ideas, gardening tips and solutions to problems. Above all it invites you to take a fresh look at the plant world. The whole world is a garden, and we are merely the custodians for those who follow. Let us enjoy it, and cultivate it with care.

LEFT: *One of the most flamboyant plants in the Humid Tropics Biome, the torch ginger is native to Indonesia, Thailand and Malaysia.*

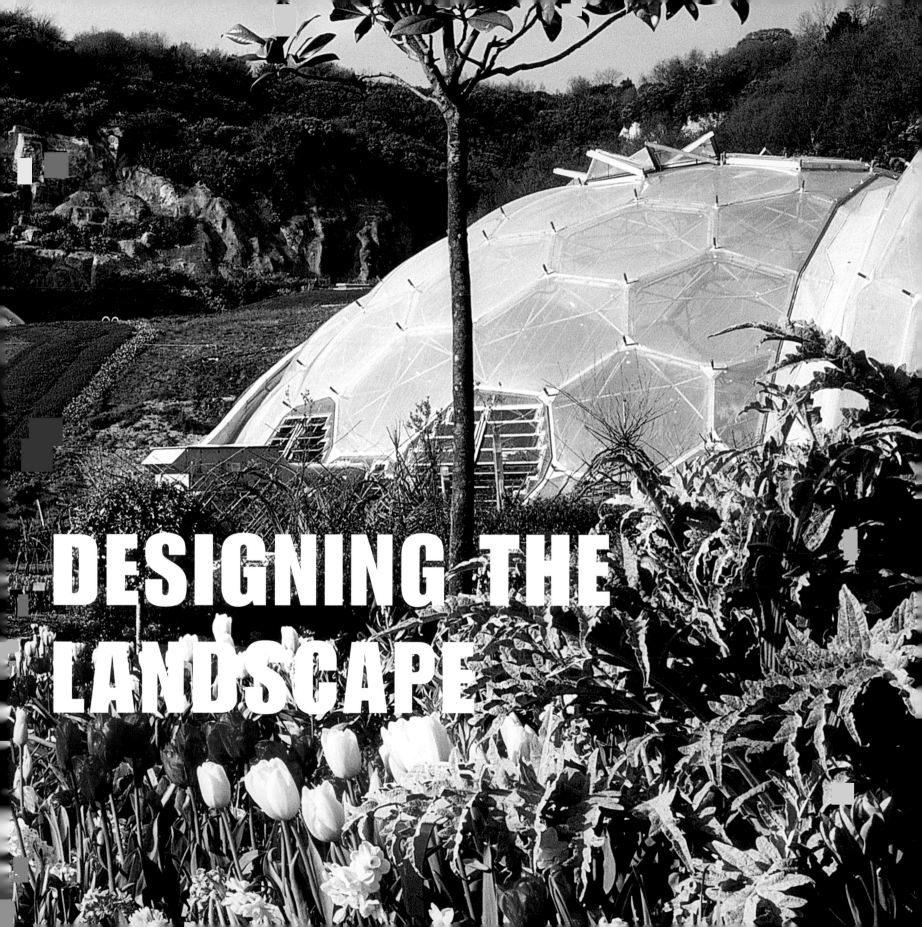

DESIGNING THE LANDSCAPE

IN THE BEGINNING

As the Biomes emerged like giant bubbles from the mud, a landscape was being created around them. Although the project developed from a collaboration between horticulturists, botanists, soil scientists, designers, engineers and constructors, who all had their own perspectives to contribute, creative responsibility lay ultimately with Dominic Cole, a landscape architect at Land Use Consultants, who specialize in planning, design and ecology. In most landscape projects the designer's hand is invisible, but there was no chance of that at Eden: the design had to be bold as well as beautiful. Dominic sculpted the land so that it flowed around the Biomes and reflected the contours of the pit to form a timeless masterpiece that more than met the 'Picasso meets the Aztecs' brief.

The landscape needed a robust and striking form so as to create an impact when viewed from

At Eden bold brushstrokes of colour turn the landscape into contemporary art.

the pit edge above, yet be intimate enough for visitors to feel comfortable. Everything to do with Eden has been designed: from the moment you arrive at the site and park the car, then begin your walk through the sculpted landscape of the pit towards the Biomes – it's as if you are passing through a sequence of pictures. Here, the design rule that says you must incorporate elements of surprise – at Eden, by revealing the garden little by little and stage by stage – comes into play. One of the main challenges was to screen the view so as to obscure the pit until that breathtaking moment when you step from the Visitors' Centre. This effect is achieved using a clever mix of distraction and concealment: any views that you might catch from the approach road, which follows the route of one of the old haulage roads, are screened by grass mounds and carefully placed trees and shrubs.

PLANTING THE PIT

In July 2000, after several weeks of viewing the site from above, Eden's horticultural supervisors hitched a ride down into the pit for the first time. They made their way through the Humid Tropics Biome, then bristling with pipes and cables protruding from the roughly sculpted land, and into the landscape beyond; it was intimidating, exciting and surreal. Surrounded by white clay spoil but with no paths, no plants, no soil, it was no place for a gardener! But the transformation was about to begin.

The floor of the pit had been torn up by diggers and ploughed, and the contours of the outdoor landscape were being sculpted and graded. A chisel-like implement attached to an excavator ripped through the spoil at 45 degrees, in two directions, across the slopes, creating a lattice pattern and breaking up the subsoil. By September that year, endless lorryloads of Eden's homemade soil (see page 40) were dumped around the site, then transferred into dumper trucks before being tipped on to the slopes and levelled with massive excavators. It might have been expected that 'traditional' terracing would be used on such a steep site, but instead strong, level, crescent-shaped 'fields' were created with a series of even steeper sloping terraces in between.

Some of the pit's slopes are so steep that the Eden gardeners need to choose plants that will flourish in shallow or unstable soils.

Stabilizing the soil on the steep terraces proved to be a massive challenge; eco-engineering, harnessing the amazing power of plants, turned out to be the answer. Grass and gorse, dogwood and willow, came to the rescue. Planting groups of willow and dogwood was the perfect way to stabilize the steepest slopes because their dense intertwining roots bind the soil together. Although you may not realize it, plants are doing just this in your garden: their canopies prevent the soil, especially light soils, from being blown or washed away by wind and rain and the roots bind the soil together like a 'green glue'. If you have a slope in your garden, try this technique – if the plants manage to hold the surface of the soil together, their roots will also promote stability lower down.

As well as being of practical use in situations such as the one faced at Eden, coloured-stemmed dogwoods are stunning plants for any garden. Available in a range of cultivars from the yellow and orange of 'Midwinter Fire' to the chocolate-coloured 'Kesselringii', they offer truly dramatic winter interest. Willow is often used for weaving 'living hedges' and other garden structures; but beware when planting the more vigorous types of willows in your garden, as they are liable to block leaking drains in their search for water and can damage foundations. The kinds of willow that are cut back annually in the same way as dogwoods (known as 'coppicing') to show off their brightly coloured stems, or smaller species such as *Salix caprea* 'Pendula', are less likely to cause such problems.

The Eden site was landscaped during one of the wettest winters for years – there were over 100 consecutive days of torrential rain. Water from

The pit's dramatic contours create an ideal backdrop for the displays.

previously undiscovered underground springs swept down the slopes, creating gullies and landslips on already saturated soil. Landslips often happened overnight, and staff would arrive the following morning to find huge sections of terrace and new plantings completely washed away. So extra drains were added and coir matting pegged over the entire surface of the site like a giant carpet. This matting broke the flow of the water and stabilized the soil surface, then gradually rotted away as the roots of the plants became established. Whatever the scale of the challenge, nothing is impossible at Eden!

Newly laid turf sliding down the slopes gave a further cause for concern. The problem was solved by the practicality of the horticulturists, who created narrow terraces of scaffolding planks, 60cm wide, held in place with tree stakes 7.5cm in diameter. These were split in half and knocked into the ground until they were completely buried, their tops just below the surface. In areas like the amphitheatre, where the banks are particularly steep, the turf, like the coir, was secured with metal pegs. It proved to be a master stroke. Despite the weather, within three weeks the turf had firmly rooted and the pegs were removed.

Twelve people worked outside during the first winter spreading manufactured soil, preparing the planting areas, incorporating green waste (see p. 41) into the china clay, and planting and mulching the new borders. Over one-third of the pit was to be cultivated, including the steep upper slopes. Preparing the soil on extreme gradients and in these conditions called for hard graft and ingenuity, so several labour-saving techniques were developed to assist large-scale planting. One was to cover the

slopes with a 5–10cm blanket of green waste, adding a little extra where there were planting holes, rather than painstakingly incorporating it into the individual holes. Planting on slopes on heavy soil was particularly difficult – sometimes it took up to twenty minutes to dig a hole for one of the larger plants.

Because of the terrible weather, the difficult location and the tight schedule, many traditional planting principles had to be ignored: it was impossible not to walk on the wet soil; the planting holes could rarely be much larger than the rootball, as is recommended, and they constantly filled with water. Also, the traditional technique of leaving a small gap between the stem and the mulch to stop the plant's bark from rotting was only a priority where it was likely to cause problems, at the top of the steepest slopes where the mulch was likely to slip and build up against the back of the stem. But despite breaking so many rules, a staggering 95 per cent success rate was achieved, proving that even in seemingly impossible conditions anything is worth a try. The choice of tough plants like willow, dogwood and cotoneaster to stabilize the soil increased the chances of success, but there were also plants whose performance surprised everyone: *Olearia macrodonta* and *Olearia traversii*, two New Zealand tree daisies that have been grown in Cornwall for centuries, both flourished, as did several roses.

Summer drought followed the wettest winter on record, but constant irrigation with harvested water and mulching with coarse bark chips to a depth of up to 10cm ensured that newly planted trees and shrubs survived. Competition from weeds was minimal, mainly because the manufactured soil was sterile and

The living willow spiral in the Children's Garden just after planting. It needs regular pruning to keep growth under control.

LEFT: *Flexible willow stems woven into extraordinary structures are just some of the many organic shapes and forms that are dotted around the Eden landscape.*

therefore free of weed seeds. This was one of the most important reasons why manufactured soil was used – without it Eden would have been forced to employ twice as many gardening staff. Using a wheelbarrow was impossible on such terrain, so instead 75-litre bags were delivered on pallets and the gardeners carried them on their backs up the long, steep slopes; they devised a system whereby the sacks of mulch were spaced so that when the contents were spread, the areas covered just overlapped each other.

Systems and planning are always of the essence when you are creating a garden – it saves time and effort if you can work out the most efficient method of completing the job before you actually start on it. If you are laying a path or building a wall, for instance, stack the materials at several places along the route so you don't have too far to walk. If your garden is large and on a steep slope, or terraced, install several taps so you don't have to climb the slope to the house each time you need water, and have a watering-can by each one – or simply place water butts around the garden. It is also helpful to have a small shed or tool cabinet in the middle or at the bottom of the slope – again, so that you don't have too far to walk.

The Eden Green Team are now gaining a greater understanding of how to care for plants in these conditions, yet there are still underlying problems with drainage on this site that was compacted by heavy machinery in waterlogged conditions for over two years. Creating a garden in the bottom of a disused clay pit had never been attempted before, and the knowledge and experience gained by the staff of subjects ranging from soil management to large-scale recycling have exciting implications for the future.

LEFT: *Simple repeated shapes and bold colours create a strong impact.*

PLANNING AND DESIGN

Whenever you inherit a clear plot or decide to make over an existing garden, it is a good idea to create a master plan before getting to work. You should first think about how exactly you would like the space to be used and then draw up a wish list of new features, as well as existing features or plants to be retained. Your list may include such diverse items as a patio, a barbecue, a greenhouse, a shed, a lawn, a rock garden, perhaps a herbaceous and shrub border, to be made now or added to the garden over several years. Your finished master plan should show the completed garden structure and all main features and, even though the garden may be built in phases, it should avoid lots of unnecessary work.

First, work out how you are going to use the space: small sites are cosy and intimate, but if you want to make them feel larger you can do so by putting in curved paths, thus momentarily obscuring what lies beyond and slowing your walk through the garden, or by placing here and there tall structures that are impossible to see over. Collect design inspiration from books, visit gardens and shows, take photographs, consider other people's experiences and recommendations. Don't just look – observe, record then create. Think about your plans carefully before you put any of them into practice: it is better, and cheaper, to make your mistakes on paper than on the ground.

The next step is to plot the locations of the features you want, bearing in mind the horticultural and practical considerations that go with them.

DRAWING UP YOUR GARDEN PLAN

THE ADVANTAGE of drawing a plan, on paper or using a computer program, is that you can make mistakes and modify your ideas without any difficulty. You can work out the size of the spaces you need for play, paths, sheds or greenhouses and make templates to see how they can be combined to be practical, while at the same time making the best use of the space available.

Modify a single plan, or draw several different designs and discuss them with your family or friends. There is never just one solution to a problem, and it's by a process of elimination and consensus that good decisions are usually made.

Ponds and greenhouses should be sited away from overhanging trees so as to maximize light and avoid having leaves blowing into the water in autumn; a barbecue is usually best near the kitchen so that you have food and utensils nearby; and the compost heap and any other less attractive features should be screened from view using trellis, climbers or shrubs. Of course, at this stage it is also important to take into consideration any natural views within the garden or beyond that you can incorporate into your design, and any existing entrances and exits. If you

ALTHOUGH NO ONE will be *intentionally* swimming in the pond at Eden, the idea of a natural swimming pool is not new; some of our oldest swimming ponds, such as those on Hampstead Heath in London, have been in use since the 1860s. However, the idea of a 'swimming pond' rather than a conventional pool is a new concept for domestic gardens in Britain. A pond for swimming in looks just like a natural garden pond but uses plants and micro-organisms to keep the water clear; usually half the pond is designed for swimming and the other half is a shallow planting area which acts like a solar panel, keeping the water warm. Such ponds are environmentally friendly and can provide a habitat for wildlife – so if you have the space for one, be prepared to swim with frogs.

NATURAL PONDS

THE 'CORE' AT EDEN

THE EDUCATIONAL CENTRE, or 'Core', which opened in 2005, is inspired by the spiral shapes found in Nature – from the seeds in a sunflower head to the spirals on a snail shell. These patterns follow what is known as the Fibonacci sequence. Leonardo Fibonacci (1170–1250), after whom it was named, was the first person to introduce the Hindu-Arabic number system into Europe. His formula follows a sequence in which each number is the sum of the previous two – 0, 1, 1, 2, 3, 5, 8, 13, 21, 34. This pattern is found extensively in plants: many have petals following the Fibonacci numbers sequence. Count the florets in a cauliflower, the leaves on a lettuce or the sides of a banana and you'll find it's a Fibonacci number! Another feature is that if you divide any number in the sequence by the one preceding it, the answer will always be close to 1.618. The 'golden ratio' 1:1.618 is used in art, architecture (the Parthenon, for example) and landscape. It creates a perfectly proportioned form.

want to plant trees, ensure there is sufficient space for them to grow – outwards, but upwards too – don't plant them under telephone lines!

At Eden, the designers and horticulturists endeavour to maintain the integrity and spirit of the master plan – vital when it comes to maintaining that wow factor and coherence when you step out from the Visitors' Centre. The eye is drawn immediately to the Biomes and most people take the most direct route towards them, the walk heightening the sense of anticipation. Others who have been before or who know the Biomes well may want to visit the latest attraction, and often approach the Biomes with less urgency. One aspect of the subtle design ensures that the buildings at Eden don't always have their entrances in the most obvious places, which makes visitors think more about the landscape and the view. Main paths through domestic gardens should be subtle and meandering, taking you through its different areas rather than directly leading you to the end point.

■ Making the best of what you have

Once you've thought about how you are going to use the garden, you need to consider any features or details that are likely to affect plant growth and landscaping. So take into account cultural and practical considerations when assessing your site, and don't be dismayed if they don't tally with the optimum gardening conditions.

Ask yourself some basic questions: When does the sun shine on the garden? In the morning? After midday? All day? Not at all? Where are the shady corners? What is the drainage like? Are there damp or waterlogged areas? Are they present all year round or only in winter? What is the microclimate like? Sheltered? Windy? Is it a frost pocket? Where are such things as gas and electricity conduits – you don't want to cut through a cable or be hindered by overhead electricity wires.

You may have a plot that seems impossible: for instance, one that is roughly triangular, about 350–400 sqm, say, north-facing and shady. At Eden, a small, north-facing, unusually shaped space behind the Core, not unlike the one just described, has become a Children's Spiral Garden: here was the perfect opportunity to prove that, far from being a problem, a plot like this offers potential. Dark corners are not ideal for sitting out, unless you are looking for summer shade, but when packed with vibrant colour, textures and interesting activities, a patch like this can entice children outside, whatever the weather. With a little planning and positive thinking, constraints can be turned into assets.

Shade doesn't have to limit your design. You can make shady corners or whole gardens interesting by planting shade-loving cultivars of plants such as ferns and hostas; or you can reflect any light you do have using mirrors or white paint. Add a splash of artificial colour too, by introducing murals, mosaics or statuary. Shade need not be a problem, just another challenge!

If your garden needs to incorporate practical hard surfaces but you are worried about how you can make them interesting, forget concrete and similar uninspiring substances and try bark, wooden boardwalk, stepping-stones, coloured gravel, brick, even recycled-rubber safety surfaces. For the Spiral

Wine bottles make excellent edging and this is a great way to recycle. Leaving the labels on adds an element of fun – can you read them upside down?

GARDEN MOSAICS

E DEN'S ON-SITE DESIGNERS and makers have been entrusted with beautifying the Children's Garden. This involves decorating the basic design, and here they're working in particular on mosaics of a delightful giant daisy at each entrance. There are many books about mosaic making, and the method is simple. First of all, buy your decorative tiles from a DIY centre, specialist craft or tile supplier, or a website. Then overlay a 15cm hardcore base with a 10cm layer of concrete (the specification will vary according to location and should be modified in a frost-prone area by increasing the depth of the hardcore and concrete layers). Then mark your pattern with string or draw it with chalk and set the tiles in place. Allow the mortar to dry before grouting. It goes without saying that you will have drawn up your design plan, on paper or computer, beforehand.

Garden at Eden a plea went out to the staff: 'Bring us your bricks and broken plates, your copper piping, slabs and slates …'. Piece by piece things arrived and were incorporated into the design. The finished feature wall is a recycler's dream: cob blocks rendered with lime plaster, bricks, old chestnut fencing, recycled decking, plant pots, handprints in the mortar, tin cans and wine bottles – all topped with shingle coping and a copper ridge. It's a vibrant work of art in its own right. And it just shows that when it comes to building your garden, almost anything goes! Complex designs can be especially stunning. The only criteria are that a garden has to be both practical and aesthetically pleasing – and must have that X factor.

ADDITIONS

Gardens constantly evolve, and Eden is no exception. Creating a building such as the Core has an impact on the site and any such additions have to be located carefully so as to respect the master plan and the spirit of Eden. As with any new garden, it takes time before some of the plants are established enough to play their part in the grand vision. During these early stages, most of the structure of Eden comes from the buildings, paths and shrubs, but in fifty to a hundred years' time trees and hedges will play the major structural role. So even seemingly insignificant actions taken now, such as removing a tree, may have a long-term impact on the original design concept. Consequently, any changes have to be made with consideration and care.

Changes made to an original design can affect landscapes and gardens in different ways. In some, such as the gardens at Hidcote, Gloucestershire, designed by Lawrence Johnston, it is easy to make major changes within the 'rooms', as the different parts of a garden are sometimes called, without affecting the whole garden. In contrast, Capability Brown, who was renowned for his grand designs, saw change as an opportunity to give the landscape a new identity, destroying in the process what had gone before – he thought nothing of digging out lakes or moving or creating hills. It is generally agreed, today, that when new elements are added to a design they should usually relate to the existing forms. Quite often the garden will be viewed from above as well as from ground level – from the top of the pit at Eden, or from an upstairs window in a domestic setting.

In front of the Core, the planting areas are designed for year-round interest and to link the building, particularly its colours, with its surrounding

Clipped evergreens create a strong structure that becomes prominent in winter and reflects the shape of the Biomes.

COLOUR-THEMING

THE BED in front of the Core is strongly colour-themed with 'hot' and contrasting colours, but it also features spiky architectural plants with bold shapes to complement the radical contemporary design of the building.

Plants include golden-yellow daisy flowers with a deep-brown centre (*Rudbeckia fulgida* var. *deamii*), *Helenium* 'Moerheim Beauty', a classic mid-summer herbaceous plant with brownish-red flowers, and the angular-leaved red-hot poker that has pinkish-red flowers (*Kniphofia* 'Nancy's Red').

Among the purples are two trees with deep-purple foliage: the maple *Acer palmatum* 'Bloodgood' and a relative of the Judas tree, *Cercis canadensis* 'Forest Pansy'. Then there is the *Agapanthus* 'Purple Cloud' with its globes of nodding blue-purple flowers, *Euphorbia dulcis* 'Chameleon' with burgundy leaves and stems, and *Phormium* 'Platt's Black' with dark foliage. Among the spiky plants are the cardoon (*Cynara cardunculus*) with its jagged grey foliage, and the extraordinary spurge *Euphorbia griffithii* 'Dixter', with its striking flowerheads and leaf mid-ribs, both orange.

landscape. Here the 'blue border', which runs in front of the Warm Temperate Biome, has been extended to include foliage and flowers in bright yellows, reds, oranges, and purples which contrast with the building's black-stained timber cladding and complement the copper roof. At Eden it has been proved that planting huge drifts of agapanthus and cannas, for instance, and making unusual combinations of familiar plants has considerable impact. Bulbs don't have to be planted in blocks – they can look wonderful set out in abstract shapes, in streaks or in blobs. Any new ideas for what was originally the 'blue border' will maintain that principle, whenever possible using familiar plants that you could find in garden centres or nurseries. Of course, Eden's large scale permits it also to make bold use of plants that are usually found only in small numbers in the home garden.

■ Themed displays

Among the themed plant exhibits surrounding the Core building there will be a display of plants for construction with trees including larch, cedar and chestnut planted in rows as if they are in plantations. Red spruce (*Picea rubens*), which is uncommon in Britain but has been used in the framework of the Core's roof, has also been planted next to the building. The 'Plants for Colours and Dyes' exhibit will be located opposite 'Plants for Paper' with most of the 'Crops for Health' exhibit nearby. The exhibits will all reflect the strong geometry of the building, which is also present in the shapes and forms in the hard landscaping and 'structure' planting from trees,

so, although it takes a lead from the shapes of the new building, the landscape design is also in harmony with its surroundings.

Plants for Paper

Paper, in the form of newspapers, wallpaper, wrapping paper and so on, is an integral part of our daily lives; it also records our history, through books and letters, and is our link with the past. The Plants for Paper exhibit will pay homage to this material with a display of plants used for paper manufacture at different times and places, ranging from the paper mulberry (*Broussonetia papyrifera*) to papyrus (*Cyperus papyrus*) and the architectural rice paper plant (*Tetrapanax papyrifera*). Also included will be the fabulous late winter-flowering *Edgeworthia chrysantha*, a choice garden plant that is grown in Japan for its bark, from which is made high-quality paper used for banknotes. There are also ambitious plans for a 'paper pavilion', to be decorated with origami, paper sculpture, wallpaper, writing – whatever may illustrate the value of paper and its place in cultures past and present.

The Children's Spiral Garden

Another important factor when designing a garden is to take into account any special needs of the people using it most. The Children's Spiral Garden at Eden, situated at the back of the Core, was designed in conjunction with Eden's Schools Team, who develop the educational programmes, and the brief was that it should be innovative, attractive and creative, made from natural or recycled materials, and provide year-round interest for children aged between five and

Almost anything can be recycled, as this old bath in the Children's Garden proves.

The Eden Project buildings demonstrate an impressive use of materials – the copper of the Core roof will eventually turn an eye-catching green.

eleven. If you are designing for a family, or with any specific person in mind, try to imagine their needs so they will feel that the space has been created especially for them. In this case, designing a space on a child's rather than an adult's scale was essential and an area has been created that is inspiring, magical, rich in texture and rich in potential. Children's areas should inspire creative play and interaction and offer new experiences. Let them be quirky and a bit untidy, but structured, so that they exercise the mind as much as the body.

Representatives from the group Transforming Violence, who promote peace through the creation of gardens, were part of the design team. They helped make the conscious decision not to turn the children's patch into a curriculum-based education area with the usual slides and swings, but to focus on stimulating their imagination instead. The garden gives them things to absorb, a busy discovery space with hidden corners and places to hide, and is

packed with bright colours, movement, textures, and lots of details such as the mosaics. Areas have also been set aside for birds and beasties in the wildlife area. Just the inspiration that children need to encourage them to become the next generation of gardeners and environmentalists!

The classrooms in the Core lead out into 'school yards', where the children can congregate before going into their garden. Each of the yards will have planters for practical work, plus a selection of edible plants such as peas that can be picked and eaten by the children. All of the plants featured can be easily replaced.

The centrepiece of the garden is a living willow spiral built by Environmental Art, a team who have worked with willow extensively in schools and at Eden. The design of the Children's Garden is a collaboration between them, the Schools Team and Jane Knight, Eden's landscape architect and project manager. The spiral tunnel was created from bare-root willow, pushed into the ground in early spring before any leaves appeared, and is 2m at the highest point. The shape was laid out by eye, using string as markers. It took three days to construct, and the stems are interwoven in a diamond pattern so that they are self-supporting. It should last indefinitely and the longest new growth only needs trimming or weaving back into the structure a few times each year.

Textures feature strongly in this garden. As well as mosaics, there are rocks of all shapes and sizes, soft tactile foliage, gnarled logs and smooth paths, the glorious, versatile willow, and spiralling ammonites set into the hard surfaces. Fibreglass

CARNIVOROUS PLANTS

CARNIVOROUS PLANTS are a main attraction in the children's bog garden. They are grown in a mix of equal parts coir, pine needles, pine chippings, grit and masses of moss in a hole lined with pierced pond-liner and watered with Eden's rain water (see p. 49) through a drip line. (Don't use tap water – chlorine kills!) Among those in the display are several trumpet pitcher plants such as the giant form of *Sarracenia flava*, with red traps, the white-topped *S. leucophylla* (there are also several by the water-storage pond), the round-leaved sundew (*Drosera rotundifolia*) and the fork-leaved sundew (*Drosera binata*). All are hardy except *S. leucophylla* which is slightly tender, but happy in the Cornish climate.

ammonites were used to demonstrate a 'Fibonacci spiral' (see p. 28) to visitors before the Core was built; other ammonites were cast in concrete from rubber moulds bought on eBay.

The Children's Garden is a quiet and peaceful place: banging, clanking and whistling may be fun, but not for those in the classroom nearby. Instead, as a soundtrack to the site, there are soft tinkling bells, wind chimes and natural sounds. Among the plants there are wonderful touchy-feely grasses, plants to please insects, plants for eating and for fragrance, plants for butterflies and birds, and bulbs to put the zing into spring. But there are no sunflowers because they bloom in the summer holidays, and anyway they come into their full glory in the main displays. As well as the bog garden with its insect-eaters, there are also storytelling trees including holly, rowan and hawthorn under which children sit to hear tales of magic and mystery. And if you visit in the summer there's a mass of dancing daisies showing the diversity of flowers in this plant family. Among these are the 'Chocolate Cosmos'

THE RAINBOW PATH

THE RAINBOW PATH in the Children's Garden is surfaced with bouncy rubber from recycled tyres, and the borders nearby feature the colours of the rainbow – yellow, red, green, orange, blue, violet – bringing both fun and education into the garden.

RED includes Japanese bloodgrass (*Imperata cylindrica* 'Rubra') with crimson-tipped leaves; the bold architectural form and dark-red leaves of the poisonous castor oil plant (*Ricinus communis* 'Impala') set well away from the path, and the red-stemmed dogwood (*Cornus alba* 'Sibirica').

ORANGE is displayed in the climbing honeysuckle (*Lonicera* × *tellmanniana*), the funky *Dahlia* 'Orange Nugget', the bold Barberton daisy (*Gerbera jamesonii*) and the double-flowered day-lily (*Hemerocallis fulva* 'Flore Pleno').

YELLOW includes the lemon-yellow Mexican orange blossom *Choisya* Sundance, the bright Chartreuse-yellow-leaved *Hosta* 'Lemon Lime', the yellow-to-olive-stemmed dogwood (*Cornus sericea* 'Faviramea'), and the delicate climber *Dicentra scandens* with its bright-yellow locket-like flowers.

GREEN gives a chance to show off unusual plants like the late-winter/early-spring-flowering *Hacquetia epipactis* with its dense clusters of yellow flowers set in green 'petals', the green-flowered arum lily (*Zantedeschia aethiopica* 'Green Goddess'), and the dainty green-flowered tobacco plant (*Nicotiana langsdorffii*).

BLUE includes the exquisite *Gentiana* × *macaulayi* 'Kingfisher',', bluebells (*Hyacinthoides non-scripta*), the globe thistle (*Echinops bannaticus* 'Taplow Blue') with its metallic-blue flowers, and the mid-blue crocus (*Crocus speciosus* 'Oxonian').

VIOLET'S dark delights include an elderflower with pink-tinted flowers and deep burgundy-black leaves that turn red in autumn (*Sambucus nigra* 'Guincho Purple'), the low-growing dark-purple-leaved *Heuchera micrantha* var. *diversifolia* 'Palace Purple', and mid-purple-flowered *Clematis* 'Jackmanii'.

(*Cosmos atrosanguineus*) with its warm, almost edible fragrance, the vibrant *Dahlia* 'Moonfire', the spiky architectural sea holly (*Eryngium variifolium*), the South African blue marguerite (*Felicia amelloides*) with its mid-blue flowers, and the *Osteospermum* 'Lemon Symphony'.

A particular challenge was how to manage the flow of rainwater that runs off the Core's copper roof in wet weather so as to make it a feature rather than an eyesore. The solution arrived at was to drain it into hoppers filled with limestone; where copper residues are neutralised. The water then flows into a storage pond, thereby preventing flooding during heavy rain. Later, the water runs down into the bottom of the site and is then pumped into a series of settling lakes before it is discharged off-site. So, from being a problem area, the space around the pond became the perfect place to display marginal and bog plants.

In summer the garden is alive with brightly coloured plants and lush foliage, including bold blocks of red-stemmed, crimson-flowered *Lobelia cardinalis*, sweeps of hostas, primulas such as *Primula bulleyana* with its red buds and orange flowers, *Primula florindae* sporting yellow candelabras and *Primula japonica* with its purple-red flowers; glossy yellow kingcups (*Caltha palustris*) add the finishing touch.

EDEN'S FUTURE PLANS

Development within the pit is finite because of the nature of the space, and soon there will only be scope to add extra 'layers of richness' to the existing framework. This will include such activities as food trails radiating from the restaurant and 'Plants for Taste' displays; or clue-based games that lead you up and down the pit in a Snakes and Ladders style.

A growing number of ideas have to be packed into the space as people returning to Eden expect to see something new. Balance is always needed between those who see Eden as a source of educational enlightenment starring the plants, and those who, while not neglecting this aspect, also that see attracting visitors is essential to the economic stability of Eden. It's a tightrope to be walked, while maintaining one of the most exciting landscapes on earth.

The Garden at Eden

At the time of writing, the Garden is still at the early planning stage. Current notions indicate that it will be a place to relax, yet will also be stimulating to the senses and full of ideas that people can use in their own gardens in a contemporary but crafted style. Like the rest of Eden, it will also demonstrate sustainable gardening practice. The Garden may include a family-sized 'garden room', miniature gardens, and tiny natural worlds on pedestals at eye level. It may offer opportunities for unusual encounters, possibly through reflections. The Design Team are also considering innovations that will permit the visitor to experience Eden and the world in other unconventional ways, perhaps by lying down and looking up, making imaginative use of mirrors.

Garden sculptures need not be expensive – here pieces of mirror have been simply stuck on to gnarled, weathered branches.

GOOD
GROUNDWORK

Gardening at Eden is a 'hands-on' experience and ancient practices like hoeing and hand weeding still play a vital part in a twenty-first-century garden.

FACT!

With six specific compost mixes made up to suit the specialist areas, 85,000 tonnes of soil were transported into the pit over a period of ten months from May 2000 to February 2001. The average depth of manufactured soil across the pit is 60–90cm, but look at the range and size of the plants they've managed to grow!

THE RIGHT SOIL

Once you've determined your basic garden design, or simply cut out a new bed or border, you can either choose plants that will enjoy the existing soil or improve it so that you can grow a wider range. A good soil means healthy plants, and you'll want to give them the best start you can.

Eden's soil

At Eden the staff were faced with the kind of dilemma that confronts people creating a garden at a newly built property, where the soil has been compacted by heavy machinery or there's nothing but builder's rubble under the turf. With no natural soil in the bottom of the old pit and the idea of importing topsoil having been ruled out because of transport costs (there being no building projects of sufficient size in Cornwall at the time) and the difficulty of achieving the necessary consistency, it was decided that the soil should be created from composted 'green waste', mixed with the existing china clay waste – still freely available in the area – which contains a high percentage of sand and a smaller amount of lignitic clay. Using these ingredients, soil scientists from the University of Reading designed simple recipes that could be modified according to the needs of individual plants or groups.

There are two main types of substrate in the pit: the original china clay spoil and man-made soil. The manufactured soil was mixed two miles away on the edge of a spoil heap, using heavy machinery. Green waste was added for use outdoors and composted bark was added to the soil to be used in the Biomes. The only problem with using bark in the soil is that it causes soil levels to sink as it rots.

The mix being used outdoors is growing plants successfully, and organic matter and nutrients from sustainable sources are continually being added. No problems have been encountered in mixing and adding new soil. Staff have found that the fine structure makes it easy to dig and to create a good seedbed; one great advantage is that this soil has no stones and few weeds. The disadvantages are that there are no soil-dwelling creatures such as worms or microbes to develop the structure naturally, so it tends to compact on the surface and at lower levels impede drainage; and it is very poor in nutrients at manufacture, particularly nitrogen, and rapidly loses the little it has. Continual applications of organic matter and fertilizers are necessary to maintain fertility, and to keep the structure open and free-draining. But any new soil takes time to develop – it has taken thousands of years to create the soils found naturally, so staff do not expect it to be perfect immediately! The artificially created soil will improve in time; until then, the quality of the displays at Eden is a testament to the tolerance of plants and to the skills of the horticulturists.

Altering soil quality

Some plants tolerate a range of soils, while others have specific requirements. You can deal with this situation by turning conditions to your advantage: first, by growing plants that thrive in your soil and climate; second, by improving the soil with organic matter or other materials to create a better structure suitable for a wider range of plants; third, by growing plants with distinct needs in raised beds or pots containing specialist compost mixes – an ericaceous compost, for example, for camellias and rhododendrons, if your garden has alkaline soil.

At Eden, the soil requirements vary from one part of the site to another, and a multitude of plants has to be catered for. The compost for the Humid Tropics Biome was the most difficult to create because high temperatures and moisture levels break down organic matter quickly. Forest bark, though expensive, turned out to be the ideal solution. It was vital that the soil structure should include a range of particle sizes, the different-sized pores thus achieved allowing excess water to drain away yet retaining enough moisture and air for healthy root growth. Fertility and the soil pH – its measure of acidity and alkalinity – could be controlled once the compost was in place.

EDEN'S GREEN WASTE

EDEN'S COMPOSTED green waste is made from organic material collected from domestic gardens around Plymouth, then processed on a large scale using giant shredders and heap-turners. Eden still uses 500 cubic metres of 16mm-screened compost a year as a mulch and soil improver – the same stuff is sold in bags for domestic users. Many local authorities now offer similar products, and of course, many people prefer to have their own compost heaps. Beware, composting is addictive!

The basic compost in the Warm Temperate Biome contains about 60 per cent sand. This was the first time the Reading University compost-makers had been asked to create a compost that would restrict plants' growth! The free-draining mixture they produced encourages natural compact growth, ensuring that the displays look just like their real Mediterranean counterparts. Around twelve 'special recipes' were created too, for areas like the Fynbos (see p. 156) that need low-fertility compost.

The greatest volume of compost was made for the Outdoor Biome, to be laid on top of a spoil that has a very poor structure.

Making compost is a serious business, and an important one for the well-being of the plants, whether at Eden or in your own garden, so it's worth getting it right.

COMPOSTING

Making your own compost has several benefits for the gardener. Homemade compost offers you a soil improver that is environmentally friendly and 100 per cent natural, eliminates transport costs, and takes advantage of another of Nature's remarkable recycling processes. Fresh compost creates healthy soil and healthy plants, so home composting is common sense for Eden and for small-scale gardeners alike.

As Eden is a new garden, at the start there were few weeds or prunings to compost, and even now, six years after its inception, it still does not produce enough compost to be self-sufficient. At the time of writing only about 150 tonnes of plant waste are produced annually. This will slowly increase as the plants become more established – already the volume of material coming out of the Humid Tropics Biome has suddenly grown to about two trailer-loads every week. But for now, Eden buys in high-specification green-waste compost made from the city of Plymouth's household waste – which makes a compost of a higher quality than could be produced on site. The project's weeds and prunings collected during regular maintenance are either taken in a utility buggy directly to the composting site at Vounder Farm near the perimeter of the pit, or are put into large trailers behind the Biomes, then taken to the composting site when filled – a much more time- and energy-efficient system saving a 5- to 10-minute buggy trip.

LEFT: *The rich, organic, man-made soil in the pit is easy to dig but still demands a good technique from the gardeners in order to turn the soil effectively.*

BELOW: *A compost mixed especially for the Humid Tropics Biome and containing a high-level of organic matter ensures that Eden's tropical plants thrive.*

Whether mixing with a tractor at Eden or using a shovel at home, the ultimate aim of turning the heap is always the same – to provide rich, crumbly compost for the garden.

■ How it's made

Eden makes compost by two different methods. One is the traditional composting of plant waste in large heaps; the other involves an innovative system using an 'in-vessel' composter (see pp. 46–7) that primarily recycles food waste from the restaurant.

The traditional composting site at Vounder Farm is like a giant garden compost heap. High-quality composting on the scale required at Eden relies on good facilities, good equipment and a considerable financial investment – which will not be made until a permanent composting site is decided upon. Like an ideal home-compost patch, the site will need a concrete hard-standing area, controlled drainage

and space to 'turn' the heap, but the composting yard at Eden also requires storage space for machinery such as a shredder and chipper to process different types of waste; producing greater volumes in future years will help create a more balanced and productive mix.

The material for composting is first stacked in separate piles – at least two, one of hard and the other of soft stuff. Once there is enough of it, woody waste is shredded or chipped and soft waste such as grass cuttings and weeds is passed through a pulverizer. Semi-woody material such as palm leaves is too soft to be chipped and does not pulverize easily either, so specialist equipment is hired in to shred it.

The treated piles are then mixed into one huge heap; at any one time there are several of these mixed heaps at various stages of decomposition in the yard. Another essential piece of equipment on Eden's shopping list is the screener: rather like a large industrial sieve, it removes pieces of unrotted wood and other coarse material that has not rotted down, thereby improving the quality of the compost.

The Eden method follows the traditional composting principles of mixing materials that rot slowly, such as wood shavings and shredded prunings, with materials that rot rapidly, ensuring they don't dry out and become difficult to re-wet, or clump together in sodden layers. Wood decays slowly, but adds substance to the finished compost; the smaller the particles, the more rapid the decomposition, so shred prunings to speed up the process.

If you are making a 'cool' heap – the sort that's left out in the open rather than in a bin – mix slow- and fast-rotting materials together in a bucket and build up the heap in layers, or make alternate layers of fast and slow materials. If you run short of slow-rotting stuff, tear up cardboard such as cereal boxes or loo-roll tubes. Check your heap regularly; if the lower layers have rotted down nicely, this organic matter can be used and the remainder returned to the heap, then new material added on top.

The temperature in the heap needs to be high in order to destroy plant diseases and weed seeds. Ideally it should be 60°C for two days if powdery and downy mildew, potato blight, seeds of weeds such as groundsel and bitter-cress and roots of perennial weeds are to be killed. Not all pests and diseases can be destroyed in this way. As part of a DEFRA

order, vines in the Warm Temperate Biome at Eden affected by phylloxera had to be buried 3–4m deep on a site that must not be disturbed for seven years.

You can create a 'hot heap' in a bin by mixing a mass of chopped-up hard and soft material together and putting it all in in one go, watering as you fill the bin up. The mixture will heat up, then cool down, so you will need to mix it again, adding more water if it's dry or dry material such as newspaper if it's too wet. You'll need to continue this process until the bin is filled with well rotted organic matter.

You are not trying to replicate the performance of the ultra-efficient in-vessel composter at Eden, so don't add fish, bones or meat (raw or cooked) to your compost heap, as it will only attract rats, flies and foxes and accumulate animal waste that may harbour disease. Don't add plastic or glass or

HOT HEAPS

At Eden, the temperature of active heaps is tested once a month and is usually about 50–60°C; this is slightly cool – a constant 65°C is the perfect temperature for making compost. A common system used for commercial composting involves using 'windrows' – these are piles of compost about 4m high by 2m wide and from 10 to 40m long, the ideal volume for heat to build up and provide enough oxygen to feed the bacteria.

Seed potatoes planted in early spring are guaranteed to produce good early crops in Eden's crumbly, moisture-retentive soil.

diseased potato tubers, for instance, and do chop brassica stems so they rot rapidly. Wood ash, shredded newspapers, kitchen towels, natural fabrics like wool and cotton, hair and feathers, and rhubarb leaves (which are not to be eaten!) are safe to compost, and you can also add rabbit, gerbil and hamster bedding and straw from the chicken-house (high-nitrogen chicken manure is like rocket fuel to a compost heap!). Activators that can be added to a heap to kick-start the process include dried blood, seaweed and nettles. Both comfrey leaves and urine are high in nitrogen and potassium; if you do use urine, dilute it 1:3 with water – otherwise, the salt levels will be too high for the brandling worms that feed on decaying plant material and pass it through their gut, adding microbes and improving the soil structure. Other usable soft materials include grass mowings, weed seedlings and young shoots.

The minimum volume for efficient composting is a cubic metre, and, depending on the volume of raw material your household and garden produce, two or three composters of this size may be needed for a workable system. If you don't have enough space for one or two large heaps, you can still successfully produce compost on a small scale in bins. The bins can be purpose-built of timber or made by recycling old pallets, large pieces of polystyrene or plastic. They should have a cover or lid to prevent the compost from becoming too wet and to provide insulation. And make sure that you'll be able to move the bin, and that the front detaches so it's easy to turn the heap. Look in the back of gardening magazines and newspapers, where you'll usually find a range of designs and prices to choose from; or contact your local council – many now offer cheap bins in a drive to encourage people to recycle kitchen waste and reduce the landfill problem.

COMPOSTING WEEDS

'IF YOU HOE when there are no weeds, you won't get any' – this is a traditional gardeners' saying, and it's true. Hoeing disturbs germinating seedlings before they become established and prevents later problems. Keeping the garden weed-free is essential because they compete with plants for moisture, nutrients and light and they can harbour pests and diseases too. Weeds are easier to remove when small but easier to see when in flower, and should always be removed before they set seed. Put perennial weeds in a separate bucket, then dry the roots in the sun before adding them to the compost heap, or put them in a bin-liner to rot down. Remember to keep a separate bucket for stones and plants infected with pests and diseases, as neither are welcome in the compost heap.

■ Maintaining a compost heap

At Eden, the heaps are turned every one or two months, to ensure the material is thoroughly mixed and is all decomposing at the same rate; the same frequency is recommended for home gardens.

If the correct mix of woody and soft materials is used, a large volume should rot down and be ready for use in a short time. It takes about six months before the compost at Eden is ready; the greatest activity within the heap happens in the first two or three months, and after that it slowly 'matures'.

Eden's giant Swedish-made in-vessel composter in the recycling compound is the first of its size in

Britain, and is being trialled there for food-waste disposal to see how it performs and whether it is cost-effective. It has considerable potential for use in the catering industry, in hotels, schools and hospitals and on housing estates, saving transport costs, reducing pollution and the volume of food waste currently having to be dumped in landfill sites. The composter produces a much higher-quality compost than most of that produced in Britain at the moment. Controlling the temperature and the mix of materials in this huge piece of machinery takes some skill. If there is too much moisture the temperature drops, but with the right proportions of the different types of green waste it is possible to control the quality of the end product. After just a few months of the trial the Eden staff are impressed.

Although food is the main material fuelling the composter, semi-woody material, wood shavings, pieces of wood and sawdust are added to balance the input. The 6m cylinder, a more sophisticated version of the rotating compost drums that can be bought for the domestic garden, rotates 10 degrees every twenty minutes (producing a full rotation every twelve hours); a fan blows air through the mix to keep it well oxygenated and, as mentioned earlier, temperatures can be monitored and controlled so that they remain around the required 60–65°C. Providing it does not become too wet, the material composts quickly and naturally, flowing smoothly through the cylinder to emerge as the desired product. When the machine is working to its full potential, the volume of compost created is 10–20 per cent of that of the original material. With a carefully controlled system such as this, composting is rapid: in goes the raw material, and about sixty days later out comes the compost.

FACT!

At the time of writing, trials are being undertaken using the compost from the in-vessel composter when it is only two weeks old. Tomatoes and lettuce have been potted up in it and its nutrients have been analyzed, and so far the results appear promising. The same material is also being used as a mulch. The Science Team will be undertaking a series of experiments to see how it can be adapted or improved.

RECYCLE IT!

Because of uncertainty about its quality and about whether it is disease-free, Eden's homemade compost is used for mulching and planting around the rim of the pit in the carparking areas. If you are disposing of badly diseased plants, put them in your local authority green-waste bin rather than your own compost heap – the council will compost at high enough temperatures to destroy any pathogens such as unwanted spores.

Eden is trying to balance input and output so as to become waste-neutral. The policy is to reduce waste: to reuse items wherever practicable and source remaining items, wherever possible, from materials that can be recycled. Another policy at Eden is to purchase items made from recycled materials, for use on site or for sale in the shop. In come plants, compost and food and out go bottles, cardboard and plastics. There are lots of ways you can recycle within your garden: for instance fork old compost into borders, add cardboard to your compost heap, cut the base from plastic bottles and bury them vertically upside down into borders for watering at the roots. To save compost, you can also put broken-up pieces of polystyrene or upside-down plant trays in the bottoms of taller pots to serve as a drainage layer. See p. 73 for biodegradable flower pots.

Many local authorities operate recycling schemes for plastics, tins and glass. Do take advantage of this service, but you may also be able to think of ways of using salvage with style: for instance, plant up old water tanks, or use lavatory cisterns or chimney pots as planters. Old fertilizer sacks can be cut up as liners for hanging baskets, and with a few holes pierced in the base, old paint tins can become novelty plant containers. Growing-bags can be reused for strawberries or French beans the following year, or the growing-bag compost used as mulch.

WATER CONSERVATION

In these days of changing climate and water shortages, we are all aware of the need to conserve water and make the best use of what we have. At Eden, excess water is collected from the Biomes for re-use, and in the Warm Temperate Biome there is a 'Growing Systems' display demonstrating water-saving techniques for container plants. For the gardener, a hosepipe ban always comes as a real blow, but there are many water conservation techniques practised at Eden that can be used by the home gardener.

■ Water-saving gardening

As the soil at Eden is so shallow, the outdoor soil dries out after two or three weeks without water, and so plants tend to be surface-rooting. Watering early in the morning or in the evening to reduce evaporation, and mulching and applying water around the roots where it is needed rather than over the plants, are part of the daily routine in the effort to conserve water. Irrigation systems are the most efficient way of using water, and drip lines like those used at Eden are easy to install. Constant dripping means there is never any excess water to run off the soil – what there is soaks in steadily. Or you can use a leaky-pipe system around the roots in shrub borders, which again reduces loss by evaporation. If you live in an area affected by a hosepipe ban, do check which watering methods you can use.

Even in warm weather, you need only water established trees and shrubs that are showing signs of stress, so concentrate your resources and effort on newly planted specimens. And don't be tempted to water the lawn – most of the world's grasslands become parched and brown in the dry season, then recover at the first sign of rain. Letting the grass grow longer by taking the blade height of your mower up a notch to about 3cm helps reduce the potential for scorch and stress – yours as well as the grass's!

Small touches such as mixing water-retaining gel in container composts before planting up, using plastic pots instead of terracotta ones, and putting planted containers below hanging baskets to catch the water that drains through, all help to reduce the amount of water you need to use. Collect water in butts, placing them, if you can, at strategic points to catch run-off from the roof of the shed, the greenhouse, the garage and the house too, and reuse it around the garden. Ensure the water butt is on a secure platform of timber, stone or concrete slabs or a purpose-built stand – not on standard bricks, which crumble – and make sure there is enough space for the watering-can to fit underneath the tap. If you have the space, you can even join several water butts together with a plastic pipe so when one is full the overflow is fed into the others. Do fit a lid so that small children and pets don't fall in.

If you can use less detergent in your household water, then that can be recycled too; washing-up water is fine for shrubs and ornamental plants providing it is not too greasy. Don't use it on vegetables as there's a slight risk of salmonella. And use all such 'grey' water within seven days of collection.

If you want more advice on water conservation, all the water authorities will have water-saving tips for gardeners on their websites.

The Californian poppy, seen here surrounded by spiky opuntias, is an ideal annual for the water-conscious gardener

■ Planting for drought conditions

Another message coming through loud and clear to gardeners in these times of water shortages is the desirability of planting a garden with more drought-tolerant varieties. The Warm Temperate Biome at Eden can give gardeners inspiration for schemes and displays that will look beautiful and interesting, while also helping them to cut down on watering.

There is a huge variety of plants to choose from: acacias and olearias (tree daisies), for instance, can be happily planted in drier areas – in fact, they are renowned for their drought tolerance. The Garrigue and Maquis displays at Eden demonstrate a wonderful collection of drought-tolerant plants that will thrive in British gardens; and many of the South African bulbs and Californian plants, such as ceanothus, do too. The key to the survival of such plants is to position them in free-draining soil so that they don't become water-logged in winter. Excellent herbaceous plants include New Zealand flax, euphorbias, globe thistles, sedums, bear's breeches and cardoons. And for good drought-tolerant bedding and patio plants go for petunias, *Helichrysum petiolare*, pelargoniums, the trailing and yellow-flowering *Bidens ferulifolia*, marguerites, the pink- and apricot-flowering diascias and osteospermum.

Good gardening is about the careful management of resources: improve the soil, recycle, save water – it's a strategy that is used around the globe to ensure a continuous supply of food and all other essential plant products.

ALTERNATIVE WATER SOURCES

A T EDEN there is a water surplus around the pit. It pours in from surrounding springs and causes drainage problems, disrupts plants, and creates poor patches in crops and parts of hedges. The pit itself would fill up to a depth of 15m if the several special pumps stopped working during heavy rain. The pumps between the Warm Temperate Biome and the stage areas move water up to the Middle Lake, above the Core and onwards to the top lake, where it supplies a small stream called Bodelva Brook. Eden's water is of a very good quality, having been filtered through the rocks rather than coming from rivers or deep boreholes whose high mineral content would cause blockages in the pipework, produce deposits on leaves and affect the pH of the soil. You may never have thought of having a well in your garden, but it may be worth considering. Check with your local water authority for details about drilling for water. A well could answer the water needs of your garden, and provide an extra supply for your home too.

WATERING LANE
NURSERY

The rapidly expanding cacti and succulents collection at Watering Lane will move into the spotlight when the Dry Tropics Biome is completed.

The purchase of Watering Lane Nursery in October 1997 as the first stop for plants bought in or needing to be nurtured before becoming part of the displays at Eden was a first sign that the dream of a 'world of plants' was becoming a reality. This holding bay for a growing collection of exotica became the focus of much media attention in those early days. Plants were dispatched from botanic gardens and private collections around the globe and from nurseries throughout Europe and the United States, to be brought together at Watering Lane's revamped tomato nursery. At one point, before their journey of a lifetime ended at the Biomes, there were around 80,000 plants of 4,000 varieties all jostling for space there.

Most were huge specimen plants that created an instant impact when the Eden Project was opened to the public. Others, such as fast-growing balsa, were grown from seed. It was essential that all the plants destined for Eden came from legitimate sources.

Most were crop plants, or plants cultivated in the public domain, and therefore not rare or endangered. When rare seeds did arrive, all legal requirements were met.

Watering Lane Nursery, situated a few miles from the main site, covers 6 hectares of damp ground with natural springs. After the site was purchased, a 0.5 hectare block of new greenhouses was erected. This has a heating system powerful enough to keep plants at tropical temperatures, and computer-controlled automatic ventilation systems to promote optimum plant growth. The site is divided into three areas, which reflect the Biomes: there are two warm temperate glasshouses, two for the humid tropics, plus many polythene tunnels and open areas for the plants destined for the Outdoor Biome. There is also a collection of arid-zone plants, mainly cacti and succulents, in another glasshouse that is awaiting its new home in the Dry Tropics Biome, currently under construction.

A simple shade bench protects delicate cuttings and newly potted-up plants from scorching, ensuring a stress-free start to life.

A T WATERING LANE NURSERY, horticulturists and scientists combine their knowledge and enthusiasm to find solutions to Eden's unique challenges. Projects in progress include researching plants' uptake of nutrients from the manufactured soil, developing composts to promote root systems that will be successful in the Biomes, and looking into the effect of post-propagation techniques on tree stability on the site. All their research and experiments are geared towards one goal: to produce healthy plants that will thrive in the Biomes.

Eden is also sponsoring and nurturing a link with Chang Mai University's Forest Restoration Research Unit (FORRU), who are developing techniques for forestry restoration on degraded sites in Thailand and sharing their experiences of developing new rainforests on inhospitable sites.

A SEEDBED OF SOLUTIONS

A RAPIDLY EXPANDING collection of cacti and succulents – there are now well over eight hundred – is waiting in the nursery ready for the completion of the Dry Tropics Biome.

Cacti can be propagated either from cuttings or by sowing seed, using clean, sterilized pots. The seed is sown in a tray in a fine, moist seed compost mix, given a bottom heat of 18–30°C (depending on the species), then the tray is put in a closed case and the compost kept moist. Around seven to ten days later most seeds will have germinated, so the covering is removed and the temperature set at 20–21°C. If this were not done, there would not be enough root growth to support the stem and the seedlings would be liable to rot off and die. Low light levels do not unduly affect plant growth.

Alternatively, cuttings are taken from sections of stem as well as, in the case of plants such as opuntias, from the 'pads'. The cut end is allowed to air-dry for several weeks until a 'callus' has formed – the callus will produce roots and protect the cutting when it comes into contact with moisture. The cutting is then potted up.

When potting up cacti the staff wear thick gloves, and to lift smaller plants they wrap a strip of folded newspaper around each, then pop it into a free-draining mix of 4 parts peat-free compost to 2 parts each of bark, fine grit and vermiculite. The vermiculite enables easier re-wetting after winter dormancy and ensures that nutrients are properly taken up. Finally, a layer of grit up to 5cm deep is laid over the surface to prevent neck rot and suppress weeds.

Any repotting should be done when the medium is quite dry: cacti and succulents are two of the few plant types that are not watered after potting. Even careful repotting damages some of the roots, and moisture increases the chance of infection in the damaged area, so wait a few days for the roots to recover before watering. At Eden, most of the smaller plants are left to stand on metal grids to ensure that they don't become waterlogged and to improve air flow around them. This is important for good growth – deserts, their natural habitat, are windy places where hot air is continually circulating. Most cacti open their stomata, or breathing pores, during the night when it is cool to reduce moisture loss, and take in and store carbon dioxide for use in photosynthesis the following day.

Most cacti also have two dormant periods: one from late autumn through winter when light levels and temperatures are low and they should be kept at around 6–8°C; the other during very hot periods in the summer when the temperature rises to over 30°C – at these times watering should be drastically reduced. During the growing season feeding encourages flowering and promotes good health, so use general liquid fertilizer every ten days at a quarter of the strength indicated on the container.

THE SEED BANK

The Eden Project houses its own seed bank at Watering Lane Nursery. It contains 3,400 seeds from 2,000 different species, all saved in individual batches and stored at specific temperatures and humidity levels so as to prolong their lifespan. Half the plants growing at the main site originate from seed that was collected, donated or bought. Some of these seeds came from specialist commercial suppliers and some came from botanic gardens in Gibraltar, Jerusalem, the Seychelles, Spain, Hawaii and many other countries around the globe who operate an *index seminum*, or seed index, in which seeds are listed for donation or exchange amongst horticulturists and horticultural institutions.

The seed bank holds many common species too: there are samples of 66 different types of sunflower; 72 types of brassica, including cabbages and sprouts – most destined for the ornamental vegetable display; 63 types of sweet and chilli pepper and 26 types of carrot in a multitude of colours; plus 56 types of lettuce. Rice is also well represented, with 122 varieties: 64 come from the International Rice Research Institute (IRRI) based in the Philippines. Others were added by Andrew Ormerod, head of exhibit research at Eden, who bought Chinese imperial green rice, Nanjing black rice and Camargue red rice from his local supermarket, ate some of it, and donated the rest to the seed bank! Very little of it germinated, but what did was grown on to maturity and the resultant seed was used to bulk up Eden's seed collection.

Eden's stock of seed that is rare or in short supply is often increased in the same way. Andrew visited Spain, and returned from one of the few places in Europe where it is still grown with a small amount of einkorn wheat, one of the nine original crops domesticated in the Fertile Crescent – the ancient region stretching from the eastern Mediterranean to the Persian Gulf – around eleven thousand years ago. The sample contained not only the corn seed but priceless ancient cornfield weed seeds too, which are now a valuable part of the collection. Another ancient variety, emmer wheat, donated by the National Institute of Agricultural Botany in Cambridge, was a sample left over from an experiment to recreate an ancient Egyptian beer!

Each seed batch is given a unique accession number so that it can be identified. This number stays with the seeds for life.

Eden occasionally commissions staff to go on trips throughout the world, making local contacts who ensure that seeds are collected in the spirit of the Convention on Botanical Diversity (CBD) and Convention on International Trade in Endangered Species (CITES) regulations. They also ensure that, if required, consignments arrive with phytosanitary certificates, which guarantee that they do not harbour pests or diseases, and that all other legal requirements of the country of origin have been met. Some seed types have a naturally high infestation rate, with up to 50 per cent containing insect larvae. Seed that can be dried to low moisture content can be frozen at –18°C in a domestic freezer for a month to kill any insect pests, although any seed-borne viruses may survive even this treatment. Seeds that need to be sown immediately do not undergo this treatment so any pests and diseases they may be carrying could become a problem.

Rice seedlings from the Philippines, which germinated in the nursery, are planted out for display in the Humid Tropics Biome.

To counter these and other problems, Eden has its own plant health team and isolation unit (see p. 272). Sometimes members of the public offer seed collected abroad, but because of conservation legislation and potential pest and disease problems, Eden declines their offer politely.

■ Storing seed

It is vital that seed is collected in perfect condition and completely ripe; collected too early it may germinate if sown immediately but it will not survive long in storage. The storage life of seeds kept by home gardeners in unsealed containers in a cool room varies considerably. Lettuce and onion seed will last up to three years, carrot up to six and tomato and radish reach ten. The secret is to keep them cool and dry. Any left in a hot, humid room may fail to germinate even after a few weeks; leave them on the shelf in the shed, and poor germination may result later. The best solution is to store them in a glass jar with silica gel or a pinch of rice, both of which absorb moisture. Coloured silica gel is particularly effective. Put the sachet in the jar until it is moist – it will turn blue – take it out and dry it in the oven, then put it back into the container with the seeds. Repeat this process until all available moisture has been removed.

Once they arrive at Eden, seeds are assessed and sorted according to their type. Some need more attention than others. Seeds that have not been cleaned will undergo various treatments: those with papery coats are riddled through a series of brass sieves, and if there is still a lot of chaff left Maureen

Newton, the seed bank manager, sits on the step of her Portakabin and drops the seed and accompanying chaff from the greatest height she can manage on to a white tray, so that the wind (hopefully) blows the chaff away. Berries with fleshy seedcases are lightly crushed, then put in a beaker of water; after a week or two the seeds can easily be separated from the detritus and mouldy scum on the surface. The extracted seeds are left on paper towels for a few days to dry, then moved to the seed-drying room where a dehumidifier keeps the relative humidity (RH) at about 45 per cent (ideally it should be 15 per cent, but that requires expensive specialist equipment – which is on Eden's long-term 'wants' list). After about a week the seeds are put into air-tight containers with silica gel for around four weeks to bring the moisture content down to about 10 per cent, before being packaged for long-term storage.

Total accuracy here is essential; too dry and they are killed, too moist and the seeds rot in storage. At Eden, the moisture content is checked using a specialist piece of equipment that measures the moisture without destroying the seed. Once checked, the seeds are hermetically sealed in foil sachets or placed in air-tight containers, which are labelled and stored at −18°C in a freezer or 9°C in a fridge, depending on the species. (A seed's water mass can be measured by weighing it, drying it in the oven, weighing it again, then subtracting the 'dry' weight from the 'moist' weight. You must bear in mind, however, that the individual seed tested would not survive this process.)

Periodically, seed is tested for viability: a few seeds from the collection are germinated in agar

Any unwanted material such as pods and 'parachutes' is removed before the seeds are put into storage. Smaller seeds are cleaned through a sieve.

EDEN'S SEED STORES

VERY SMALL SEED packages are stored in air-tight containers in domestic fridges; one-kilogram hermetically sealed packages are kept in a chest freezer; and 10kg sacks or larger are stored in the cool seed-drying room at 17°C and 45 per cent relative humidity (RH); most of the grains for the outdoor Biome arrive in 25kg sacks. However, not all arrive in such large quantities. In 2004 Eden was the proud recipient of three seeds of the rare *Euphorbia origanoides*, presented by the Conservation Officer of Ascension Island in the South Atlantic. The seeds germinated rapidly in one of the greenhouses at the nursery, and the plants then produced their own seeds – hundreds of them! *Euphorbia origanoides* disperses its seeds from explosive capsules, which fire them up to a range of 2.4m. Now there is a forest of seedlings coming up in every conceivable nook and cranny in the glasshouse – not bad for an endangered endemic!

ABOVE LEFT: *Rice seeds are sown on agar in a Petri dish; those that germinate are later transferred into pots of compost for growing on.*

ABOVE RIGHT: *Coffee is one of Eden's more frustrating plants. Its seed germinates freely around the parent plants in the Humid Tropics Biome but is short-lived in storage.*

(a nutrient gel) in Petri dishes under carefully controlled conditions, and the percentage of seeds germinating is recorded. If this percentage falls below 70, new seeds are produced by growing a plant in the nursery and collecting its seed, or a replacement batch is ordered from the suppliers. All seeds are kept under conditions that aim to preserve their viability; most will survive for decades or even hundreds of years if kept dry and cold.

Not all seeds can be dried or stored for long periods, of course – some will die if not sown shortly after harvesting. These are known as 'recalcitrant' seeds, and the main plants in this category are the double coconut (*Lodoicea maldivica*) and the giant

water lily (*Victoria* species) that grow in the Humid Tropics Biome. Water lily seeds are either saved from Eden's plants or ordered from the Victoria Conservancy in America. Around ten seeds arrive in a film canister filled with water to prevent them from drying out, and are sown immediately. Other plant seeds such as coffee (*Coffea* species) cannot withstand drying, so these 'intermediates' are stored on open shelves in a cool room (about 15°C); they have a limited shelf life – usually between six months and two years. Fortunately, most seeds stored at Eden are what are called 'orthodox': once dried to about 10 per cent moisture content, they can be kept at −18°C for decades.

WHY KEEP SEEDS?

SEEDS ARE KEPT for conservation, for sowing in the nursery, for display purposes and for use by Eden's tour guides: raw cotton (*Gossypium hirsutum*) is one that particularly fascinates visitors. In spring the seed bank is deluged with hundreds of parcels containing seeds of all sorts. They are all recorded, sorted and stored – it's a monumental task! Saving seed saves money: it is easier to store seeds rather than plants, and pests and diseases are less of a problem. And, of course, from the conservation perspective, seeds are the future.

PROPAGATING AND NURTURING

Seeds in all shapes and sizes are stored under carefully controlled conditions to ensure their survival.

Although the nursery was created initially to store the plants for the new Eden Project, since then it has become an invaluable resource for propagating and caring for new plants before they are introduced to the main site. The scale of the nursery's work is huge: it produces anything from rainforest trees, to plants for temporary exhibits such as capsicums, maize and tomatoes, to specimens for the display beds. Plants are also produced for the guides and education teams, so that visiting schoolchildren and other groups can handle exotic plant material such as cotton bolls, gourds, papyrus, grains and sugar cane. The nursery also maintains plant collections for staff studying for PhDs.

■ Propagation by seed

Seed-sowing at Eden is at its busiest from January to the end of June, and cuttings are taken from the end of February to the end of September. Around 45,000 plants are grown each year from seed sown in trays in a standard commercial compost containing 20 per cent perlite (an inert, porous material widely available in small volumes for the domestic gardener from garden centres), which improves drainage. Others, particularly those that resent root disturbance, are sensitive or rare, or have a taproot, are sown in modules to increase the chance of success.

Preparation

Most pre-sowing treatment is carried out in the seed store or laboratory before the seeds are sent for propagation. 'Chitting', or sprouting, is a technique by which germination is started before the seeds are sown, thereby eliminating the effects of weather and soil at this early stage; it also saves time with crops such as parsnips and carrots that germinate slowly and advances plants such as cucumber and marrow. With tomatoes, growth is advanced so much by this process that it is possible to produce outdoor crops in areas where the season is usually thought to be too short. Although tubers rather than actual seed, seed potatoes too, particularly 'earlies' (see p. 208), are 'chitted' so as to advance growth.

Chitting is an especially useful trick if used early in the season when the soil is cold, because it avoids uneven germination. Seeds are then 'fluid-sown' to protect them from damage. This is a simple process: put a layer of tissue paper or similar in the base of a plastic container such as a sandwich box, cover the tissue with a piece of kitchen towel, sprinkle water over the surface until it is wet, then pour away the excess. Sprinkle the seeds evenly over this surface, put the lid on and keep the whole thing at around 21°C – this is appropriate for most vegetables, but some, like celery, need to be kept in the light. When most have germinated and the roots are about 5mm long – slightly less for lettuce – wash them through a plastic kitchen strainer. Mix them into a gel of fungicide-free wallpaper paste (to act as a carrier) in a plastic bag, cut one corner from the bottom as if making an icing bag, and squeeze them through into moist soil. Finally, cover with a thin layer of fine soil.

This method gives higher yields of early carrots, better germination of lettuce when ground temperatures are high, and earlier parsley crops.

If a seed is rare, or only a small quantity is available, then it may be sown on agar in a Petri dish to test its viability; this germinated or 'chitted' seed is then lifted from the Petri dish with a bit of agar attached and the jelly mass sown in conventional compost.

Across cooler parts of Britain, fleshy seeds should be 'stratified' – this means leaving them in hessian bags full of moist peat substitute or in pots in a cold frame to be chilled over winter. However, warm winters in mild climates like those in Cornwall make this method unreliable, so the seeds are usually put in the refrigerator to be sure of breaking their dormancy when the time comes.

Unless instructions suggest otherwise, seeds with hard coats are germinated without any pre-treatment, especially if they are collected straight from the plant. However, at Eden, if there are no signs of life within two weeks, they are removed from the compost and soaked overnight on the mist bench (see p. 66) or encouraged to germinate using other techniques. Other methods that can be used to encourage the germination of hard-coated seeds include putting a sheet of sandpaper in the bottom of a tray, tipping the seeds over it, then rubbing another sheet of sand paper over the top to wear away the seedcoat; putting the seeds in a sealed container or plastic bag with a handful of grit and giving them a good shake; or nicking a hole in the seedcoat with a sharp knife, taking care not to damage the inside. Some South African and Californian plants that, in their natural habitat,

An open, free-draining compost will ensure good root development from the moment the seeds germinate.

ABOVE: *Sweetcorn seedlings are sown in pots in spring and planted outdoors when the weather has improved.*

BELOW: *High-tech rolling benches ensure that maximum space in the greenhouse can be used for growing plants.*

germinate after fire at the end of the dry season can be heated in a pan or soaked in water with a disc impregnated with the same chemicals as are contained in smoke. When the chemicals are released, the seeds respond by rapidly germinating.

Sowing seeds

Sowing in seed trays is cheaper than using modules, as the trays are less expensive to buy and can produce more plants. Seed is sown into moist compost at a range of depths: small, dust-like seed can be scattered over the surface; large seeds can be planted up to 5cm deep in pots. Seeds larger than a peanut are planted in potting compost rather than seed compost because it doesn't become waterlogged in the larger volumes needed for bigger

seed. Tree seeds that develop a taproot need as much compost as possible below the seed; one successful technique used at Eden is to cut the bottom out of a pot, then tape it on top of another to get a double depth of compost.

The surface of the soil is covered with a layer of grit to prevent algae growing on the compost when it is on the mist bench; for seeds that need light to germinate, perlite is used instead. Just as in many domestic greenhouses, after sowing, the seed trays are put on the propagating benches where the heating cables warm the compost.

Not all seeds needing light to germinate are welcome – many of the impatiens have become a weed that is almost as prolific as bitter-cress. Seeds of plants such as *Tradescantia spathacea* actually

germinate while on the plant, so spent flowerheads are removed at the first signs of germination, broken apart and the seeds scattered over the compost (if covered, they tend to rot).

■ Propagation by cuttings

Another cheap way for gardeners to propagate herbaceous plants at home is to take cuttings, as we saw when looking at cacti and succulents. This is generally a faster process than growing such plants straight from seed; it is a simple and popular way of propagating many garden plants including woody herbs, weigela, mock orange, deutzia, flowering currant, forsythia, ceanothus, elaeagnus, hebe and pittosporum.

About 95 per cent of the 10,000 cuttings taken annually at Eden are semi-ripe, and taken from mid-summer onwards using material that has begun to ripen at the base. A standard technique is used. Cuttings 7–10cm long are taken from healthy material and the leaves are trimmed off from the lower half; they are then planted in free-draining compost, and kept in a warm, humid environment until they root.

Although semi-ripe cuttings are the most popular method for propagation, nodal, internodal and stem cuttings are taken too.

Internodal cuttings are taken using stem sections. These are cut from between the leaf joints (the nodes) and are only used for tropical plants such as philodendrons (*Philodendron* species) and cheeseplants (*Monstera* species). When the stems of the mature plants trail on the ground, they grow roots

PROPAGATING PLANTS

A RANGE OF PLANTS are propagated at Watering Lane Nursery, from the critically endangered jellyfish tree (*Medusagyne oppositifolia*) from the Seychelles, to bananas and bedding plants that are sold in Eden's shop. Most of the non-woody plants grow so rapidly that they are propagated regularly so as always to have a stock of small ones. This is necessary for ease of maintenance, as well as ensuring that plants are of a suitable size for establishing in the Biomes. Larger plants are used for temporary display off site at shows, before being discarded.

between the nodes (stems growing upwards usually send out roots from the leaf joints). A length of stem with roots already on it and at least one leaf or leaf bud should be removed and planted in peat-free compost, watered with tepid water and set on a bench with a bottom heat of around 18°C and no mist. The same technique is used for banana 'offsets', which usually produce roots at the base.

Nodal cuttings are usually used for rapid-rooting plants that have roots forming around the leaf joints already. Many of the creeping grasses, trailers and climbers, most bamboos and sugar cane fall into this category. The cutting is made from a length of stem with at least one, and preferably two, 'joints', and is pushed horizontally into the compost, then left to root on the mist bench.

Soft-tip cuttings can be taken from plants such as fuchsias, chrysanthemums, climbing honeysuckle, deciduous azalea, deciduous

FACT!

Staff at Eden have their own effective cutting-compost recipes. Sue Reeve, one of the skilled propagators, uses 2 parts of peat-free compost to 1 part seed compost to 1 of perlite to 1 of grit (washed china clay waste, a rough gravel with particles ranging from 3mm to dust).

SIMPLE CUTTINGS

SOFT-TIP CUTTINGS are taken from new shoots early in the year (these can be just a few centimetres long). They are fast-growing.

SEMI-RIPE CUTTINGS are taken from July until September, as stems start to mature – ideal for conifers and herbs.

HARDWOOD CUTTINGS, unlike the others, which are propagated in the greenhouse, are taken from wood that has developed over the previous year. Most should be cut pencil-thick. Plant them outdoors.

Some plants that feel more at home when clinging to a tree are grown on the absorbent, fissured bark of the cork oak.

magnolia, winter-sweet, begonias and impatiens (such as 'Ray of Hope'). Because they are soft and have no roots, soft-tip cuttings call for specific growing conditions and are more demanding than the more resilient woody cuttings. Soft-tip cuttings are collected with secateurs, then prepared using a sharp knife (Eden's propagators have their own propagating knives, but a craft knife is equally effective – use it with care, though). A sharp knife is essential for taking cuttings: a sharp edge guarantees a clean cut. Blunt knives bruise and tear the tissue, making it liable to rot. When taking cuttings, never cut towards yourself. Put the base of the cutting against your thumb and draw the knife through the tissue so that it slices – don't just push it through, as this damages the plant cells. Put a plaster over the end of your thumb as protection before you start!

Taking cuttings

Except with the internodal kind, cuttings should be taken just below a leaf joint, or you can cut off a small sideshoot with a wedge of main stem attached. Then put them straight into the compost, water them and put them in the greenhouse. At Eden they are placed on the misting benches with a bottom heat of 25°C and with misting timed at 15–30-minute intervals, depending on the general humidity, the heat and the amount of direct sunlight on the glasshouse. The cuttings are covered with netting and white polythene to provide shade and to create 100 per cent humidity.

Mist units are the most successful way of reducing evaporation from the plant, and offer a simple and effective way of rooting cuttings. The leaf surface is constantly covered with a fine layer of water and is never stressed by water loss. Soft-tip cuttings have the greatest rooting potential of all cuttings and spend less time in the mist unit, so more can be taken each season. Soft-tip weigela cuttings, for instance, take three weeks – as hardwood cuttings they would take three months.

The mist unit at Watering Lane Nursery is located at ground level, because this made it cheaper to construct; its fixed benches hold the heat better than free-standing benches would. The base is a layer of polystyrene about 2.5cm deep, over which a layer of silver foil is sometimes placed as extra insulation and to reflect heat from the heat mat and cables. The latter are laid in a serpentine fashion about 2.5cm apart, right up to the layer of sharp sand containing the cuttings. A thermostat in the sand measures the temperature at the base of the cuttings where the roots will form. Nozzles set at intervals mist the cuttings with fine droplets of water while an electronic meter constantly measures the humidity. Many larger propagating units use hot-water pipes linked to their glasshouse heating system. These are cheaper to run than those currently in use at Watering Lane, and this type of system may be installed there at some point in the future. If you are keen on growing plants from cuttings, a mist bench can be installed at home using the same technique. Alternatively, simpler, small-scale propagators using a polystyrene layer and a heating mat with a plastic cover to maintain humidity are available for domestic use.

Wilting reduces the chance of success, so if you are using trays or pots of compost, prepare these beforehand. Cuttings should always be collected in small batches and put straight into the trays or pots. However, cuttings rooted in trays of compost or directly into sharp sand suffer some root disturbance when they are transplanted, and growing time is lost if they take a week or more to recover. For this reason they are often rooted instead in moist, preformed

All plants are quarantined before they are used for propagation.

IMPATIENS 'RAY OF HOPE'

IMPATIENS 'RAY OF HOPE' is a hybrid between the common busy lizzie (*Impatiens walleriana*) and *Impatiens gordonii*, an endangered species with only 120 plants left in the wild. As part of his PhD, Alistair Griffiths, scientific curator, is working on impatiens species recovery in the Seychelles – both these species of impatiens grow there. Alistair's concern was that they might hybridize, thereby posing a threat to the genetic purity of the endangered plant. If they did, the busy lizzie, an introduced weed, would have to be removed from the area where its rare relative is found. The plants were indeed hybridized at Eden, and 'Ray of Hope', with its soft pale-pink flowers, was the offspring of just two plants. It is sold in the shop at Eden and is a popular plant for containers; the money raised goes to a conservation project to save *Impatiens gordonii*.

modules of varying sizes made from a mixture of peat and perlite. When transplanted into pots, they don't suffer from root disturbance and will start growing immediately. Cuttings rooted in modules are not watered until they reach the mist bench. At Watering Lane they buy in preformed module trays, but for home gardeners compost module-makers are often sold in catalogues or at garden centres.

Once roots start to show and the cutting is firmly established in its module – pull gently on a leaf to see if the roots are starting to show on the outside – the module should be transplanted. The size of the destination pot depends on the size of the module. Small modules should go into a 7cm pot, and larger ones into a 16.5cm pot. These should be filled almost to the top with compost, then lightly firmed. The first watering settles the compost to the required depth. This method saves time but needs practice before you can judge how much compost to put in each pot.

The newly potted cuttings are then moved into a weaning unit, where for two to three weeks only a third of the amount of water hitherto used is sprayed on the leaves. They then progress to an uncontrolled environment in the glasshouse to 'harden off', or acclimatize. Here they are given a very weak general feed at 1:200 dilution – roughly a teaspoon per litre twice weekly in the growing season. It is essential that new plants are not allowed to dry out as they are still vulnerable, but they shouldn't receive too much moisture either; and they should be shaded and protected from draughts.

Once new upper growth appears, showing that the cuttings have rooted, and providing it is not too cold, plants for outdoors should be hardened off in a sheltered spot for ten to fourteen days. Before going outside at Eden they are transplanted into pots with drainage holes in the base and slits in the sides. This design provides efficient drainage: if a pot is standing directly on a hard surface, then the water can drain through the sides, preventing new roots from rotting. If you don't have pots with slits in the sides, put a layer of horticultural grit in the base of your usual pots or stand them on a layer of gravel in a tray. Stand larger pots with permanent plantings on 'feet' – these can be ornamental or simply bricks or blocks of wood, depending on where you are siting the pots.

It is impossible to take cuttings early in the year without supplying extra, artificial, light; most gardeners have to wait until late March or April to take soft-tip cuttings, when day length and light intensity are naturally increasing. If you want to take lots of cuttings, you need to force the parent plant into growth by increasing the temperature to 15–16°C and increasing day length and light intensity by means of supplementary sodium lights. (These are used, along with fluorescent lighting, over early cuttings too.) Metal-halide lights are the second most efficient kind, providing plants with the most usable light and also producing heat; fluorescent are the least efficient, but produce cool light and can be placed nearer the plant material. Metal-halide lamps can be used on strawberries in December and January to encourage the production of plantlets for early propagation, but they are expensive. Sodium lights are the most economical, producing maximum light using the least energy and giving off heat, but they do include 'red light', which can cause stem elongation.

Preparing cuttings quickly is essential for their survival. All secateurs and knives should be clean and sharp.

Once the cuttings are taken, they should be labelled with the plant name and date, then moved to the mist bench. In the case of plants that need high humidity, such as *Medinilla magnifica*, the container is put in a plastic bag or a bag is placed over the cuttings and tied on to the pot so that the compost can still take up moisture from the capillary matting on the mist bench.

■ Soil and nutrition

Plants that are grown in containers for the whole of their life are 'top-dressed' in the years that they are not repotted by removing the top 7.5cm of compost with a hand fork, a trowel or by hand. To give them a boost, slow-release fertilizer at 3g per litre of the pot size is then sprinkled over the surface and covered with fresh compost; this is normally done every fifteen months at Eden and annually at home.

Most plants at Eden are grown in the Project's own standard acidic, peat-free compost, modified to the plant's individual requirements. The standard mix is 4 parts bark to 6 parts composted wood fibre, plus granular clay and general fertilizer, which remains active for four to six weeks. Slow-release fertilizer is added in the nursery if the compost is going to be used by plants potted for a long period of time. If Eden relied on the compost suppliers to add this themselves, the fertilizer would be released long before the plants were able to use it, and wasted, creating a high concentration of fertilizer solution in the soil water which would scorch the developing roots. Because it holds nutrients then slowly releases them, clay is also added to the potting compost for any plants destined to stay in their pots – otherwise, an open free-draining compost like Eden's would soon become impoverished. Compost should always be bought in small batches as required and used rapidly, as it deteriorates when stored for long periods or in the sunshine.

Plants waiting to be moved to permanent display at Eden's main site are fed with slow-release fertilizer and in summer topped up with a general liquid feed that is slightly high in nitrogen so as to encourage leaf growth. At the other end of the lifecycle, once plants become too large to handle they are either pruned or re-propagated; any not needed are composted. Plants have a limited life during which they can be replanted, too; once pot-bound, they

ROOTING POWDER

MOST TROPICAL PLANTS **are so eager to grow that rooting hormone powders or liquid are not needed. The only plants at Eden that these are used for are dwarf ebony (***Trochetiopsis melanoxylon***), St Helena ebony (***Trochetiopsis ebenus***) species and one hybrid from the two,** *Trochetiopsis* × *benjaminii* **from St Helena, which are very reluctant to root from cuttings and have never set viable seed to ensure genetic variation. When powder is used the success rate is around 10 per cent. It is used more often on temperate woody cuttings because it contains fungicide that prevents infection.**

don't adapt well to being planted in the ground – as Eden's experiences in the Biomes have already proved. Now that the borders in the Biomes are established and packed full of plants, planting in a confined space is much more difficult, and smaller plants that are likely to develop better root systems are preferred. From here on, the aim is to grow plants that have been supplied on request, to ensure they spend as little time as possible in pots.

Potting on

In many respects, the aims of Watering Lane Nursery are much like those of a domestic greenhouse or garden. It is a place where seedlings are sown and plants are grown and maintained until they are ready to be planted out. However, the nursery also has to deal with problems that are less common in smaller-scale gardens and it has had to develop its own solutions to deal with them.

Lorry loads of plants, used to create displays at regional shows, are returned to the nursery and placed in quarantine.

The gardeners at Eden have encountered many problems with transplanted pot-bound trees – poor growth and instability, in particular – and many replacements are now being grown in recyclable 'Airpots'. In these revolutionary containers, rather than spiralling around the inside of the pot, roots grow out *through* the pot and dry up – a process known as 'air pruning' – which in turn initiates further root growth, creating dense, fibrous root systems that develop naturally when planted out, rather than continuing to grow in a spiral. The aim is to have huge trees in the Humid Tropics Biome that flower and produce seed, just as they would in nature, so root systems must be well developed from the start.

Although seedlings are still started in traditional plastic pots, they are repotted into Airpots as soon as possible and before they risk becoming pot-bound. This technique has been so successful that shrubs as well as trees are grown in these pots, and at Eden palms have been particularly successful. The process is similar to what happens when you grow seedlings in the peat pots you can buy from the garden centre, the roots simply grow through the sides.

Plastic pots are cheaper to buy and lighter to transport, and require less watering than clay ones. They also don't break when dropped. However, some gardeners believe that plants prefer clay pots because they are porous, allowing roots to 'breathe' and moisture to evaporate as it would in the ground; their weight certainly provides extra stability. The plastic pots in which the Eden gardeners grow their plants are washed and reused. Over 25,000 are washed by hand all year round in a cold 1:50 solution of disinfectant, rinsed, then left to dry under cover. Washing in cold water with only rubber gloves as protection may seem brutal, but warm water makes the disinfectant more volatile, which can create nasty fumes. At home you can pot-wash in the sink with a dishwashing brush – preferably not the same one you use for washing up!

Biodegradable pots made from maize oil, that can be composted after use, are currently being assessed at Eden for future use – providing their lifespan increases and their price goes down. There are already several types of compostable pot available, which are made from raw materials such as rice-husk fibre, coconut shells, plant starches and oils. When they reach the end of their productive life, these pots can be crushed to break the protective glaze, then put on the compost heap to rot down. Perhaps the most unusual recyclable pots are those made from chicken feathers, which are said to repel mould and algae, and contain 10 per cent slow-release nitrogen, making them ideal for fast-growing plants such as tomatoes; when the time comes for recycling, they break down rapidly in the soil.

Plants that are long-term residents of the greenhouse or are intended to be container-grown should be checked in spring just before they start into growth to see if they need repotting. When around 75 per cent of the surface of the rootball is covered with roots, plants should be transferred into a pot one or two sizes larger; if fewer roots are visible, you can leave the plants until the following year or later.

Staff at Eden offer a good tip: make sure that the rootball is wet before repotting. Watering first makes things easier, you are less likely to damage the roots, and dry rootballs take longer to re-wet when they have been repotted. The pot is knocked off – or cut off – and the old compost then removed from the roots by hand, or using a pressure washer if it is tightly packed. Always place a layer of drainage material such as perlite or broken polystyrene pieces in the base of the new pot before filling it with compost.

At Watering Lane, once plants have reached the size when repotting in a larger pot would make them difficult to handle, they are moved to a clean pot of the same size. This is because, for hygiene reasons, it is better to transfer to a new pot – though you could wash the existing pot and return the plant to it. This repotting is done every two to three years when the structure of the compost and the nutrient levels start to decline. Some plants are also root-pruned before being repotted, to regenerate the root system and reduce plant growth. Palms that are 3m or taller have about 15–22cm cut from the base of the rootball with a saw. Palms, oleanders and drimyses are happy to be root-pruned; those that dislike this type of pruning, including indigofera, peonies and acacia, are left undisturbed. Because so many unusual plants are grown at the nursery, a plant's response to root-pruning often has to be learned by trial and error.

FACT!

It takes up to four people to repot large plants at Eden. The greatest challenges of all are spiny ones such as certain acacias and large cacti, which can be dangerous to handle as well as difficult. The staff's solution is to wrap sacking around the stem then lift the plant with a padded canvas strap and a telescopic hoist. The largest potted plant is the giant arum (*Amorphophallus titanum*), which is kept in a 113cm × 80cm pot.

PLANT RECORDS

Many plants, like these Impatiens gordonii, *begin their lives as seeds in Watering Lane Nursery.*

RIGHT: Lobelia tupa – *a sculptural Chilean perennial – is available from specialist nurseries and could be growing in your garden.*

Details of all nursery work, both successes and failures, are entered into the BG-BASE computer plant-record database for future reference. It is an old format but one that stores vast volumes of information, and it is widely used in over 120 botanic gardens throughout the world. It is essential that these records are constantly maintained – particularly when plants are new to cultivation – as they will benefit staff at Eden in the future, and indeed other gardeners too.

When a plant first arrives, the botanical name is checked, the type of material (tuber, bulb, seed, cutting and so on) and the date of receipt are recorded; also noted are the condition, height and spread, and where the plant comes from. In addition, all ongoing cultural information is continually documented and updated. Every time a plant is repotted or pruned, and when it flowers or fruits, the horticulturists record the date and the details. All this provides important cultural information, not only for Eden but also for other botanical gardens and organizations. From this information bank it is possible to discover, for example, the number of plants in a border at any given time, which is the tallest, which the smallest, or how many cultivars there are in the entire Eden collection.

A plant's accession number (see p. 57) permits it to be monitored throughout its life; this, and its label, enable the Green Team to recognize it instantly and to link it to the database. Details of the thousands of packets of seeds and cuttings are also recorded, including where (in the case of seeds) they are stored (fridge, freezer, coolroom or cupboard) and how (in

the case of cuttings) they were propagated. Once seeds have been germinated or cuttings rooted, they are classed as a plant and transferred to the living collections database.

The information in the database also plays an important role in international research projects. Some of the plants collected from the wild, like those in the Chile collection, are part of a combined conservation project being undertaken with the Royal Botanic Garden Edinburgh, who run the International Conifer Conservation Programme in collaboration with the University of Valdivia in Chile. It is crucial that Eden monitors in detail the conditions and progress of the invaluable plants in its care, so that the fullest possible data can be shared with these, and other, organizations.

Within these records there is also a plant health database containing observations on pests and their controls which have been kept since the Biomes were first planted; plant diseases and their treatment have also been included in the data.

The universal power of the internet means that it is now possible to inform and educate online, and so Eden is currently developing this potential by uploading information on the plants that can be found in the Biomes. Prepare to be amazed!

The nursery, there from the beginning of Eden's creation, remains the hub of the Project. Without propagation work, few species, whether common, rare or endangered, can be guaranteed to survive. The nursery is set to sustain Eden, as well as some of the world's most valuable species, for many generations to come.

THE HUMID TROPICS BIOME

WELCOME TO THE TROPICS

Staff in the Humid Tropics Biome access the canopy by using an air balloon designed for research in the rainforest.

The Humid Tropics Biome at the Eden Project is an impressive piece of engineering. Covering some 26,400sqm, it is 240m long, 110m wide and 50m high. It contains nearly 5,500 plants from the main rainforest regions: South-East Asia, West Africa, South America and the tropical oceanic islands – particularly the Seychelles and St Helena. Within this massive structure there are twenty-one different displays, from the Malaysian Garden to a banana plantation – plenty of inspiration for the British gardener keen on bringing a touch of the exotic to their own outdoor space!

Covering barely 6 per cent of the earth's surface, the rainforest is home to 50 per cent of the world's species; just one hectare may contain up to 300 tree species and 40,000 kinds of insect. It is not a random 'jungle', but an exquisite, delicately structured ecosystem comprising four different layers, scaling up from the forest floor to the trees of the canopy, and home to an incredible range of accompanying fauna. We marvel at its intricacy, yet this most complex, productive, dynamic and diverse habitat on earth is currently facing destruction – as a result of human activity: primarily, the removal of trees for logging and the clearing of sites for agricultural use. In time this will prove a short-sighted move, because the growing conditions make grazing land unsustainable, and because the secondary rainforest that colonizes derelict pastures contains different species, so that the many undiscovered species of the original rainforest may be lost. In turn, destruction of the original landscape denies us the opportunity to exploit the real treasures of the rainforest, such as food and medicine, through the use of more environmentally friendly and sustainable methods. Some plants, such as cocoa and rubber, have been bred as crops, but fewer than 1 per cent of the plants in the rainforests have as yet been tested for their medicinal properties (the figure is fewer than 5 per cent for plants worldwide).

The rainforest displays at Eden feature plants from the world's three principal regions, which lie on either side of the Equator between the tropics of Cancer and Capricorn – in particular their predominant plants. The forests in South-East Asia are dominated by one family, the *Dipterocarpaceae*, which includes a variety of timber trees and many conifers (by contrast, there are only two of this family in tropical America, and one in Africa) as well as rattans, used for furniture-making. Tropical Africa has experienced fewer geological upheavals than South-East Asia and, as a result, the forest is less diverse with fewer palms. It actually contains many plants, such as *Dracaena,* that we would commonly grow as houseplants. In tropical America the pea family is dominant; the region is also home to over two thousand species of bromeliads, and to epiphytic cacti (see p. 90).

A bird's-eye view from the balloon shows the incredible diversity of shape and form in the foliage of Eden's 'rainforest'.

CREATING THE CLIMATE

THE HUMID TROPICS BIOME is heated by a warm-air system from twenty-four climate-control units, which maintain an average temperature of 19–26°C; at 26° the vents open automatically. Humidity is maintained at 70–90 per cent by spray nozzles from a computer-controlled, high-pressure fogging system.

Think about a hot conservatory, the air heavy with moisture, and you'd be on your way to summoning up the essence of rainforest conditions. The rainforests are hot and wet: it rains virtually every day – that's a minimum of 2,000mm per annum. Day-length scarcely varies, with approximately twelve hours' daylight all year round, and temperatures range from 23 to 31°C.

Lowland plants are happiest when the surrounding temperature is consistent, but the problem that gardeners, both at home and at Eden, face is controlling temperature fluctuations in the winter because it is difficult to ventilate when it is cold outside. At Eden, night-time minimum temperatures are set to 19°C with a daytime temperature of anything up to 33–35°C on the top path; this might sound extreme, and unlikely in a domestic environment, but it bears similarities to central heating, reflecting the temperature at which it may be set and our habits of switching it off for periods of time.

In winter, always move plants away from the windowsill at night, as the temperature in the space between the curtains and the glass plummets on cold nights. Central heating also makes the air desert-dry, so plants from tropical rainforests such as rubber plants or weeping figs should be lightly misted two to three times daily using tepid water, or stood in groups on pebble-filled trays of water in order to increase the humidity around them. Avoid standing plants in draughts, and keep the central heating on low overnight when it is very cold outdoors.

Over winter, the growth rate of plants naturally slows, even in Eden's controlled environments; then when light levels and temperatures increase in spring, there's a burst of growth. In the Humid Tropics Biome at Eden, only about 55 per cent of available light enters the dome throughout the year, so the gardeners reduce feeding levels and prune the tree canopy regularly to allow as much light as possible to reach the ground.

Soil

As a result of leaching and high temperatures, the soils that are found in rainforests are generally very low in nutrients. The reason the rainforest fauna and flora can survive on such poor soils is that any available nutrients are held within the vegetation and efficiently recycled. The forest naturally feeds itself from the masses of organic material that settles and decomposes on the ground, and which is then turned into liquid fertilizer by high rainfall. At Eden these conditions are carefully recreated as far as they can be in the Humid Tropics Biome, but without the complex ecosystem of the natural rainforest to recycle the nutrients, the shallow soil rapidly runs out of food. So nutrient levels in the soil are constantly monitored by staff to avoid deficiencies.

Good, healthy, productive soils are not solid: they contain spaces between the particles for air, drainage and root growth. Ideally, any soil to be used for growing plants should not be walked on at all. Vegetable gardeners worldwide use the 'no-dig' method on raised beds like those in Eden's Malaysian Garden; once they have been dug over as part of the initial soil preparation they are never walked on or disturbed again. Organic matter is added annually, and it is the activity of the resident soil organisms that improves and maintains the structure without the need for further human intervention.

Light, airy soil is important for healthy plant development; if the soil becomes compacted, leaves become yellow, growth is poor and stems die back. The predominantly sand-based soil mix at Eden has a high organic content because of the green waste

The boldly colourful flower of the Clerodendrum paniculatum *is perfect for attracting pollinators and stands out against the dark foliage.*

used. The high sand content means that the soil settles and compacts easily, which in turn creates poor drainage and aeration, so water cannot drain away and the soil becomes too acid. As a result of all this, the soil surface can become very dry in summer and needs mulching to help it retain moisture. Because of the steep slopes in the Biome, a lot of water drains down to the lowest point. From time to time this leads to problems with waterlogging in certain locations, particularly in areas that were not well drained when the beds were first created. Watering and pruning, when the soil has to be

walked on, inevitably exacerbate the compaction tendencies of Eden's clay soils; compaction is also a problem during the 'Time of Gifts' (part of the winter season's celebrations) when the lighting engineers have to tramp over the beds to illuminate the plants.

Lightly forking over compacted areas does help to open up the soil, but if your soil already suffers from poor structure just ordinary wear and tear will cause compaction and affect plant growth. Incorporating organic manure and grit will help to open up dense soil and improve the structure, and it's well worth the time and often back-breaking

effort to keep your plants hale and hearty. An obvious way to keep compaction to a minimum is not to walk on the soil when it's wet or when it sticks to your boots. Also, where there is compaction around trees planted in grass, try boring into the ground with an auger to make breathing holes; and don't lay concrete or tarmac right up to the base of established trees. In the Humid Tropics Biome, borders are regularly topped up with green waste to help improve the soil structure. It is also hoped that adding more well-composted bark will improve the soil.

Supplementary feeding

Plants in the Biome are fed monthly with organic slow-release fertilizer; this diet is topped up every two weeks in summer and once a month in winter with a liquid seaweed foliar feed, to compensate for any shortfall.

Foliar feeds are rapidly absorbed through the leaves and are the ideal fast-acting tonic for any house or garden plants that are sickly or need a boost. They are widely available for the domestic gardener in garden centres, DIY stores and gardening catalogues. If you are using such a feed on your houseplants, move them away from direct sunshine before spraying,

In the tropics bamboo has a multitude of uses from scaffolding and fencing to containers for carrying water.

Vibrant Passiflora coccinea *can be seen in tropical gardens and will grow in a heated conservatory in cooler climates.*

then apply the liquid food over the whole of each plant, lightly covering the leaves. For long-term success, improve your plants' cultivation and growing conditions by feeding them with a slow-release fertilizer in spring, and implement a regular feeding programme.

Nitrogen helps plants to produce rich green leaves and shoots, and is found in most plant feeds. Use high-nitrogen feeds from time to time through the year but apply it sparingly, particularly towards the end of the growing season. In the Humid Tropics Biome in winter, over-use encourages rapid growth: fast-growing stems are drawn upwards by a combination of low light and high temperatures, increasing the need for pruning, particularly among climbers that quickly outgrow their supporting trees. Too much nitrogen also encourages excessive soft growth, which is liable to break, vulnerable to pests and diseases, and can discourage flowering and fruiting.

■ Planting the Biome

The desire for instant displays sometimes leads people to plant up a new garden with large specimen trees. Out of necessity, this was the case at Eden, so that a true picture of the rainforests could be created without delay. But while buying mature specimens can solve some problems, it can also create many more, not least the risk of introducing pests and diseases. Such a dilemma faced Eden's team in the early years: the public expected, understandably, to see high-quality displays and 'instant' landscapes, while the gardeners wanted to take it more slowly, creating a balanced landscape filled with happy, healthy plants.

It takes time to produce good-quality plants, and you are, of course, buying years of established growth when you buy a large one. But if much of this growth has been put on while the plant was in a pot rather than in the ground, specimens can become 'pot-bound'. The roots of plants that arrive in this condition can be quite impossible to tease out, and the plants may fail to put on new growth and establish themselves properly in their new home; and often, as at Eden, they won't grow well afterwards. This in turn brings more problems: large, top-heavy trees with poor root systems growing on steep slopes are liable to fall – and this is exactly what has happened, with some specimens, in the Humid Tropics Biome!

Another factor affecting the stability of the larger, pot-bound plants is the lack of air movement within the Biome. In nature, tree trunks flex as the wind blows, encouraging roots and stems to grow faster than the crown so that the plants never become top-heavy. In the Biome, winter dimness draws plants towards the roof, and those with large leaves or densely packed small foliage become top heavy. Then, because the undeveloped root system is unable to support them in the artificial soil, some inevitably fall. This is often prompted by the sudden rush of air that sweeps through the Biome when the vents are opened, making the foliage act like a sail in a squall.

This problem is, of course, worse outdoors, as we witnessed during the great storms of 1987 and 2000, when some trees couldn't cope with the full impact of the winds, and succumbed because their root systems were undeveloped. One way to avoid this problem with trees in your garden is to plant smaller specimens (about 1m tall) as they do at Eden.

MAKING IT ALL LOOK NATURAL

THERE ARE considerable challenges in creating a natural-looking habitat artificially. It has to be fed and watered, and gardened to control plant growth. Irregular spacing is the key to forming natural landscapes; it's a matter of selecting the correct species and setting the plants in clumps, in varying densities. And you have to leave falling branches and foliage to rot. Employees are encouraged to visit the habitats on which Eden's are based: experiencing a habitat first hand is of the greatest aid in creating one under artificial conditions.

POT-BOUND PLANTS

IF PLANTS REMAIN in their pots for too long, the roots have nowhere to go. Unable to grow outwards, they spiral round and round, eventually creating an impenetrable mass. Then, when planted out in the ground, they continue spiralling, unable to spread outwards. This leads to a poor root system, instability, drought stress and weak growth. Don't buy plants that are severely pot-bound unless they are very cheap and you like a challenge.

The signs to look out for are roots growing from the drainage holes and small, yellowing leaves. Before buying, carefully knock a plant from its pot and look at the root system. Some roots should appear on the outside of the rootball, and if there is slight congestion, can be teased out with your fingers; but if what you see is one thick mass of root, the same shape as the pot, don't buy it. There is also the option to buy 'bare-root' plants during the winter – these are exactly as their name suggests, they are sold without any soil on them at all.

One way to lessen the likelihood of problems with a pot-bound plant is to dig square planting holes within which the spiralling roots may eventually reach the sides and break out from the planting pit. But even that cannot save a severely pot-bound specimen – it will always be prone to falling and will never make a mature, long-lived plant.

Although you may find this frustrating because they lack immediate impact, smaller plants usually grow rapidly (depending to an extent on the species you choose), and in the long term they will become better specimens. Alternatively, if you're determined to plant larger trees, spread out their roots as well as you can, then stake their trunks on the windward side to a third of the trees' full height. This ensures that the roots are secured but also that the roots, trunk and branches can still move and develop in the correct proportions.

Of course, another restricting factor in importing more mature specimens into your garden is cost. The price of paying for many years of growth is usually high. By all means allow yourself the odd treat or two, if your budget will allow, but when buying for the garden, money is often better spent on things other than extra-large trees.

Making exotics feel at home

Ideally, you should treat exotics as you would all plants, and 'sow where they grow'. In nature, trees and shrubs mature in harmony with their habitat and their root systems are never disturbed. In the rainforest in particular, the roots of hundreds of seedlings and mature plants are interwoven, binding them all to the soil.

At Eden, it is almost impossible to sow seeds among the larger plants in the Biome, so seeds for tropical plants are sown at Watering Lane and planted when they reach around 1m tall; this guarantees well-developed roots and rapid establishment, so that the new plants will be able to compete with the others around them. Homegrown plants destined for borders or for use as specimens are normally started off in a cold frame, a greenhouse or on a warm windowsill to give them a good start. At Eden, once the seedlings have put on a bit of height, they are planted alongside fast-growing plants which act as gap-fillers. These plants are removed once the slower growing plants are established. Two rainforest species that are used as fillers at Eden will be familiar to many as popular houseplants. One, *Ficus elastica*, the rubber plant, grows up to 30m tall in its native habitat; the other is the delicate-looking *Ficus benjamina*, or weeping fig. Take a second look at the specimens in the Humid Tropics Biome when you visit – since they are substantially larger than most houseplants, they may not be instantly recognizable!

In their natural habitat, the sticky seeds of the weeping fig are dispersed by fruit-eating bats or birds and germinate among the branches of other rainforest trees. Slowly the fig seedling spreads out a network of roots that wraps round the trunk and branches of its host like a webbed straitjacket, gradually crushing it as would a boa constrictor. The host trunk, of course, is expanding as it grows, which hastens the strangulation that, together with root competition and the effects of shading, will eventually kill the host. Once dead, the decaying remains of the host plant provide food for the weeping fig, which then takes its place in the rainforest.

If you grow the tropical *Ficus* in pots at home you will know that they can grow like conventional trees too. A common problem with these plants is leaf loss. This mostly occurs in the winter, and can be avoided by standing the pot by a bright window and rotating it half a turn daily to ensure optimum light. Additionally, keep the plant away from draughts and maintain a constant temperature at a minimum of 13°C. Since this kind of fig originates in the rainforest, it likes a humid environment, so keep the surrounding air moist by lightly misting it, standing it on pebbles in a water-filled tray and keeping the compost moist but not waterlogged – and remember to allow the compost surface to dry out before re-watering with tepid water. Providing the plant is healthy, any leaves that are lost in winter will be replaced in the spring at the latest.

Ficus benjamina is part of the *Moraceae* family, a large group that is well represented in the tropics. When in fruit they attract all the local animals and birds, who feast on them. Many species of this same family can be successfully grown outdoors in milder

FACT!

When growing houseplants, aim to mimic their native habitat where possible. Then stand back and marvel at their ability to cope in variable, often less than ideal, conditions in a house thousands of miles from home!

Several varieties of Aglaonema *or 'Chinese evergreen' are grown as houseplants and are ideal for a shady position.*

NEW PLANTS IN THE HUMID TROPICS BIOME

THE NEW SAPLINGS planted at Eden are of fast-growing species. The best known, balsa wood (*Ochroma lagopus*), comes from tropical America and is used commercially as the world's lightest timber. The speed of growth of this particular tree is spectacular – it grows about 5m every year, so it's not a plant for small spaces! Other favourites that all add to the rainforest effect include cecropias – which are so common in parts of the Amazon basin that their silvery leaf undersides can be seen from the air – and twenty-one species of inga, including *Inga edulis* with its extremely long pods.

parts of Britain, including the mulberry and the edible fig which are found in temperate zones, and the creeping *Ficus pumila*, which is sometimes found growing outdoors in parts of Britain where the climate is warm enough, perhaps influenced by the Gulf Stream or the North Atlantic Drift.

Climbers are an essential part of the rainforest landscape. Most are very vigorous – in the Biome they are pruned more than any other plant in order to keep them under control. If *not* kept in check, they would smother other plants, and damage or break branches, as well as climbing into the canopy where access (for humans) is difficult – even using a cherry picker. The most vigorous are *Tetrastigma dentatum* and *Ipomoea alba* – a morning glory with lovely white flowers that grows several feet a week at Eden, reflecting the excellent growing conditions. Others are more restrained, including some of the most stylish climbers the tropics can offer such as the red jade vine or New Guinea creeper *Mucuna bennettii*; and the legendary jade vine, the exquisite, exotic *Strongylodon macrobotrys*, an endangered species from the Philippines.

When planting a climber against a tree, whether indoors or out, make sure that the tree will be able to support the mature plant without toppling over, and that the climber itself is not too vigorous. If possible, plant on a line with the edge of the tree's crown on the windward side, so that any strong winds will blow the climber's stems towards the tree.

Keeping the conditions right

Plants should be watered thoroughly all in one go, rather than a little and often, and during summer those in the garden should be watered in the evening, so that moisture soaks into the soil overnight rather than evaporating from the surface (as it does during the day). The healthiest way to water is at the base of the plant rather than over the foliage, as the latter encourages fungal problems and can damage the leaves as well as wasting water. Aim the water around the roots where it is needed. Or, if the size of your garden merits it, you could install computer-controlled water-saving irrigation systems at ground level that can be set to water containers regularly – particularly when you are away.

Hanging baskets, in particular, need checking around three times a day during the heat of summer, as they dry out more rapidly than low-level containers. Remember, too, that plants like basil should be watered before midday as they don't like going to bed with wet feet!

In today's changing climate, with water shortages and hosepipe bans a reality, do your best to conserve water. It's a precious commodity and you'll be helping the environment as well as, in many cases, your own wallet! As mentioned in Good Groundwork, it's a good idea to install water butts around the outside of your house and shed (and greenhouse, if you have one) and do make sure they are placed high enough above the ground for the watering-can to fit under the tap.

Adequate light is crucial for maintaining the health of your plants, but the quantity of light required varies depending on the species.

Begonias, aglaonemas (Chinese evergreen) and anthuriums warrant their status as ideal houseplants for shady locations. Begonias and aglaonemas are easy to grow in moderate temperatures, but anthuriums are more difficult, needing constant warmth and humidity, so they are best tried in a draught-free bathroom with some diffused light. Given time and good conditions, these plants, like those planted at Eden, will eventually flower. Others such as *Ctenanthe oppenheimiana*, the never-never plant, have purple undersides that reflect light back through the chlorophyll, making the plant twice as efficient. Shortage of light in the Biome in winter makes even these plants drop their leaves, but they rapidly recover in spring when light levels increase. Other plants needing shade include cocoa, coffee, the palm *Chamaedorea metallica* and many *Amorphophallus* species.

Most plants are allowed to develop naturally within the Humid Tropics Biome, creating a sense of realism, but if an area is cleared for replanting or a tree falls, they are often divided and planted in the gaps. Unlike in the garden, where plants are traditionally divided in autumn or spring, the growing conditions in the Biome are like those of a giant propagator, which means that herbaceous plants can be divided at any time by simply removing and replanting a rooted section.

Controlling growth

As any gardener knows, some plants present pruning hazards. Pruning plants such as rue, or even brushing your skin against their leaves on a sunny day, can cause photosensitivity and blistering from the effects of the sap; and when pruning ivy, you may need to consider wearing gloves, safety spectacles or goggles, long-sleeved protective

The jade vine (Strongylodon macrobotrys) *(top) and the New Guinea creeper* (Mucuna bennettii) *are two of Eden's most exotic climbers.*

PLANTING WITHOUT SOIL

AT EDEN, a major programme to introduce epiphytes is under way, using seeds and plants from botanic gardens. Epiphytes are plants that live on another plant, but without taking nutrients from it; they are not parasites, damaging the host only when the sheer volume of their numbers breaks the branches they are perched on.

These plants are a common feature in rainforests and are often found high up in the trees – they like some sun. Epiphytes include bromeliads such as the guzmanias, which can be found in the Humid Tropics Biome; they form pools of water at their leaf bases and collect organic matter at soil level as their own personal growing bag. Many such plants are grown commercially as houseplants, such as the Christmas cactus which originates from the rainforest of south-eastern Brazil. Air plants, or tillandsias, and exotics such as the moth orchid all need free-draining compost or, in cases such as the Spanish moss, *Tillandsia usneoides*, no compost at all!

In the Biome epiphytes are introduced by removing most of the compost from their roots, which are then wrapped in natural or synthetic wool moss before being wedged into a cleft or tied on to a branch. Nylon fishing-line is most often used for this job because it is strong and transparent; however, it also cuts into the bark and, in time, needs replacing. Natural garden twine has been used successfully – it eventually rots, leaving established plants secure in the trees; old tights are ideal, too, because they are soft and flexible.

It is difficult to make larger epiphytes look natural in a contrived situation, because the established roots don't cling to the bark as they would in the wild. New roots are most obvious with orchids, as they creep over the host's bark, holding themselves in place.

The smaller plants can be wedged into cracks and crevices of the intended host. A special water-based adhesive from America called Elmer's glue, trialled by the Dutch Canopy Foundation, is being used to attach the seeds of epiphytes directly on to the tree branches where (it is hoped) they will establish naturally with good anchorage. With a view to populating the shady areas of the Biome, the same team are also sending seeds of *Guzmania monostachia* and several other quick-growing species that tolerate low light levels.

clothing – and even a face-mask – to protect yourself from the dust and fine hairs from its leaves. In the Humid Tropics Biome pruning plants such as mangoes and figs can be an unpleasant experience: mangoes exude a sticky sap, while some tropical figs have leaves whose hairs can stick in the back of your throat, so gloves, goggles and masks have to be used.

Tree-pruning in the humid tropics is different from pruning in temperate zones because plant growth is faster, and health and safety regulations are less stringent, or even non-existent. Staff who have visited the tropics say it's not uncommon to see people shinning up trees with a small chainsaw, wearing no protective clothing, and hanging from branches without a safety rope while pruning the branch they are suspended from. Their only aim is to make a tree safe or to thin out the branches, so many trees are harshly pruned and the bark is often ripped in the process. Yet, despite this rough treatment, the trees are healthy and vigorous because the climate and the ideal growing conditions encourage rapid regrowth. By contrast, woody plants in cooler climates dislike poor pruning, which can cause the plant to die back and become diseased.

Pruning at Eden is done carefully, to maintain the shape of the tree, and the pruner is guided by another member of staff on the ground who has a better all-round view; once a branch is pruned there is no going back, so accuracy is essential. Many plants are carefully pruned when they are young; good early pruning shapes their future and saves work in the long term – with this good start, they will

always be well balanced. As mentioned earlier, at Eden there have been a few problems with pot-bound trees, their basic instability meaning that if climbed they would probably fall over! In order to carry out any pruning of such trees, a cherry-picker is used extensively. When the cherry-picker isn't high enough either, staff sometimes climb out along the framework of the Biome, attached by nothing but safety ropes, to lower themselves down into the tree and prune without standing on the branches. All healthy prunings are then recycled as compost.

Eden staff always use well-maintained equipment when pruning. Bow-saws, loppers and secateurs are all thoroughly cleaned immediately after use to avoid spreading infections from one plant to another, and blades are oiled to prevent rusting. This is important in the domestic setting, too.

LIGHT LEVELS IN THE RAINFOREST

IN THE HUMID TROPICS BIOME, the light levels mimic those found in the rainforest by decreasing dramatically towards ground level – less than 2 per cent of the light up above reaches the ground in the rainforest. Although many under-storey plants – those growing at ground level – tolerate shade in their native habitat, the small amount of available light at Eden, particularly in winter, limits the number of species that can be grown there. The canopy is dense and difficult to prune, and so some low-growing plants have suffered quite badly. But members of the *Araceae* family flourish in low light alongside other tropical ground-cover plants such as pilea, prayer plants and ferns; *Impatiens gordonii*, the endangered plant from the Seychelles, does well too. Staff are always trying to source unusual ground-cover plants from their global contacts, and are currently propagating *Cola heterophylla* from West Africa, an attractive plant with bright-red seedpods.

THE PALMS

RIGHT: *Their perfectly pleated leaves and bold shapes ensure that palms are the ultimate 'must-have' architectural plants.*

BELOW: *The oil palm is one of the most important economic crops in the world, producing oil for everything from cooking to domestic soap.*

Palms are a mainstay of tropical rainforests, and some are endangered in their native habitat. Some reach great heights, but many can be cultivated in a more restrained fashion in less tropical climes. There are over sixty palm species in the Humid Tropics Biome. They are well watered, mulched and fed monthly with a general fertilizer during the growing season (March to September), and are also foliar-fed alongside other plants in the Biome. This feeding regime is sometimes modified to include high-potash or nitrogen fertilizer, depending on each plant's individual needs.

▇ Palms as houseplants

Several of the palms featured in the Biome are important commercially and economically and are often sold as houseplants. A group of coconuts (*Cocos nucifera*) that have flourished and fruited at Eden fall into this category, but I wouldn't recommend them! Coconuts are true lovers of tropical conditions and dislike the climate in the temperate home, particularly the lack of humidity. Furthermore, they suffer badly from red spider (two-spotted) mite. If you really do want one at home, then regard it as a 'novelty' houseplant and give it VIP treatment. But think short-term, just as you would with cut flowers, and don't take it personally when it dies!

Palms that are tried and tested houseplants include the parlour palm (*Chamaedorea elegans*), which is found in the Mexican rainforest and in cloud forests – its preferred location being in low light under a canopy of foliage in damp conditions among ferns. It is one of the most popular house palms in the world, renowned for its tolerance of low light, dry air, waterlogging and general neglect. Produced commercially in its thousands, it is ironic that it is now endangered in the wild through over-collecting in the past.

Another palm that has proved to be excellent indoors is the Kentia palm (*Howea forsteriana*), which became famous in Victorian and Edwardian times for bringing a touch of exotica to tea-dances. Tough, yet elegant, it tolerates low light and is ideal for a shady corner of the house. This one, too, tolerates drought and central heating but, as with all plants, the best specimens are those that are well treated. Planting in a rich loamy compost (such as John Innes No. 3), keeping the compost moist, feeding monthly during the growing season and spraying occasionally with tepid water all encourage healthy growth. One member of staff at Eden relates this story: after a fire at their home, soot fell down the chimney and settled all over the sitting-room, covering everything including a Kentia palm standing in the corner. The plant remained like that for several weeks quite contentedly before being cleaned and carrying on, while other palms around it slowly died. You're unlikely to find anything tougher than that!

The date palm (*Phoenix dactylifera*) has one of the longest cultivation records: it was grown at least eight thousand years ago in Babylonia. In less clement conditions it can be grown as a novelty houseplant; seeds will germinate in a pot of moist multipurpose compost placed in the airing cupboard, and it will become an attractive house or conservatory plant that can be enjoyed until it becomes too large.

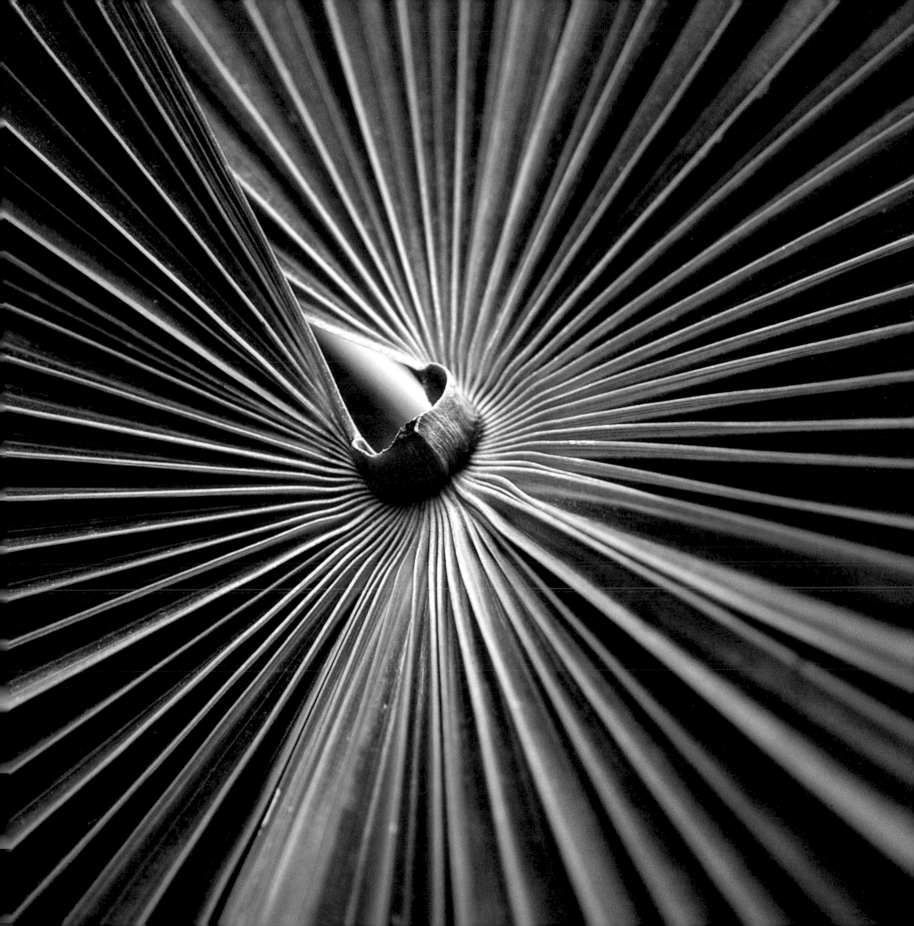

Try backlighting palms in your home or garden to emphasize the extraordinary construction of their leaves.

discovered in 1986 by Dr John Dransfield from the Royal Botanic Gardens, Kew. It is threatened by mining projects, rainforest destruction, harvesting of leaves for hats known as manarano seeds, and collection of its edible palm hearts, which causes the death of the plant. It is consequently on the verge of extinction as there are fewer than twenty mature plants left in the wild. Since its re-discovery there has been a boom in its popularity as a palm for the home or garden.

Some of the palms in the Biome can be seen in tropical gardens and would be suitable for a holiday home in Florida, but wouldn't survive a British winter. *Areca triandra* is an elegant slim-stemmed clump-forming palm, with sweetly fragrant flowers and dark-green leaves. It is commonly grown as a garden plant in moist, shady locations. This palm in particular finds the Humid Tropics Biome to its liking, as does the fast-growing *Areca vestiaria*, a small to medium-sized, slim-stemmed palm native to north Sulawesi in Indonesia and noted for its beautiful bright-orange stem and fruits. It's almost as glamorous as the sealing-wax palm (*Cyrtostachys renda*), with its bright-red stems, that you can find in the Malaysian Garden near the rice paddy. Often a feature plant in tropical gardens, its natural habitat is swampy. Sadly, it isn't suitable as a garden or houseplant – it's difficult to cultivate and hates being moved.

Beccariophoenix madagascariensis is a beautiful species that is found only in a small area of humid forest in Madagascar, as its name suggests. It was once thought to be extinct in the wild but was re-

◼ Palms for British gardens

There are a surprising number of hardy palms that are suitable for British gardens. The most popular and widely planted is the Chusan palm (*Trachycarpus fortunei*), followed by the European fan palm (*Chamaerops humilis*), which tolerates temperatures down to −12°C. The toughest of all, *Rhapidophyllum hystrix*, is a beautiful fan palm that can survive a staggering −20°C. You can buy this from specialist suppliers and it is well worth seeking out.

Butia capitata, with its glorious blue-green leaves, is a less hardy palm, but it is fine for sheltered gardens; it vies with *Brahea armarta*, the Mexican blue palm, which has pale-blue fans with a silvery-white sheen, for the title of most attractive hardy palm. You can also grow those of borderline hardiness in pots, such as the Canary Islands' date palm (*Phoenix canariensis*); bring it inside in winter if you can, or place it in a sheltered, frost-free place. Younger palms planted in borders should be covered with horticultural fleece during the winter until they become established – they generally become hardier as they mature.

PROTECTING RARE SPECIES

ONE OF THE AIMS of the Eden Project is to play a part in protecting rare and threatened plant species across the world. This involves working with governments and international conservation bodies and, on occasion, obtaining rare seeds and importing them into Britain, then carefully nurturing them into young plants.

Islands by their very nature are isolated, and are often home to unique and unusual plants and animals that are found nowhere else in the world. Their flora and fauna are therefore irreplaceable, should they become endangered. Island communities, too, are isolated and usually have few resources to support their particular global responsibility for biodiversity conservation. Climate changes, the invasion of aggressive species and human settlement pose serious threats, but many countries now have conservation programmes that offer hope.

There are around eleven hundred types of plant in the Seychelles, of which at least seventy-five are unique to the islands. One of the greatest treasures from the Seychelles in the Humid Tropics Biome is a seedling of the rare and extraordinary coco de mer (*Lodoicea maldivica*), which is very difficult to grow as the newly formed root does not like being disturbed. (Interestingly, unlike coconuts they are killed by salt water, so they have never been found growing on other islands.) Its seeds, the largest in the world, look like giant human bottoms, which has led to over-collection as trophies, and not least for their perceived aphrodisiac qualities.

With the support of the islands' government and Mahe Botanic Gardens, Eden's specimen was brought from the Seychelles by the horticultural science curator, Alistair Griffiths. A single seed had been exchanged for eight Yale locks – they are in great demand on the islands and were immediately used to secure the nursery building in the Botanic Gardens! The seed was very fresh and still covered with its natural down when it arrived at Eden. It was planted in a border, lightly covered with organic matter, and for four years it remained dormant. In fact, it was almost forgotten until one day in February 2005 when, while clearing leaves, a member of staff noticed that it had sprouted! You should never give up hope when sowing seeds!

THE STAR PLANTS

If you welcome a challenge and like to grow unusual plants, you may be pleased to know that some of Eden's stars, or their smaller relatives, can be grown at home. They need time and effort as well as special growing conditions, but they bring a thrill of success that is not experienced with more familiar plants.

■ Water lilies

One of the gems in the Humid Tropics Biome is the giant water lily (*Victoria amazonica*). It is found in still backwaters in the lakes and tributaries of the Amazon and its circular leaves with their distinctive upturned rims are huge – reaching 2.5m in diameter and growing up to half a square metre a day. But it's not just the leaf size that makes it spectacular: the flowers, which live for only about forty-eight hours, are the size of a football and at first pure white with a pineapple fragrance. The giant water lily is pollinated by one species of night-flying beetle. As the beetles feed on the mixture of starch and sugar that the flower produces, it closes, holding them captive. While they continue to feed the ripe pollen is shed over the insects who then transfer pollen from flowers they have already visited to the female parts of the flower. The following day the flower opens, allowing them to escape. By this time the petals have turned pink, the job is done, and there's no need to attract any more pollinators. The seeds ripen under water, the flower stem finally rots, and the seed capsules float away.

Eden also grows *Victoria cruziana*, which has slightly smaller leaves, as well as an *amazonica × cruziana* cross known as 'Longwood Hybrid' that comes from the USA. The latter is sown as an annual from late January to mid-February. It flowers prolifically, and self-seeds freely where silt builds up in the pond. This is a remarkable coup: although most botanic gardens have to pollinate their water lilies by hand, at Eden they are insect-pollinated, in this case, probably by cockroaches or ants that walk over the leaves.

Although they are usually grown in greenhouses, all three of these water lilies have been grown outdoors in Britain in large, shallow, heated pools, about 1m deep. If you are inspired to try them yourself, seeds are often available over the internet, but they do need a little careful preparation to encourage germination.

The key to the successful propagation of these plants is to get good-quality seeds and to keep them constantly wet; at Eden they are stored in distilled water in a fridge at 5–10°C and away from sunlight. The seedcoats of *Victoria amazonica* lilies are filed away until the white endosperm (the inner part of the seed) appears. This procedure is called scarification; but note that if the seed has a white, fuzzy appearance, then it has started to germinate already and doesn't need to be scarified. *Victoria cruziana* and 'Longwood Hybrid' are easier to propagate as they do not need this kind of special treatment.

The seeds of *Victoria amazonica* are sown in water at a temperature of 27–30°C, whereas *Victoria cruziana* and 'Longwood Hybrid' can be sown at a slightly lower temperature – between 26°C and 28°C. Sow one seed per 1.5ltr pot, 1.5cm below the compost surface, using a 50:50 mix of John Innes seed compost and peat-free seed compost, then

RIGHT: *The leaves of the giant water lily take a while to grow to their full size, but when they do, they can cover a pond with foliage.*

THE TITAN ARUM

THIS BIZARRE yet beautiful botanical curiosity belongs to a group of up to two hundred related plants found in tropical Asia, Africa and Australasia. The first European to discover it was the Italian botanist Odoardo Beccari. In 1878, he offered a large reward to anyone who would bring him a Titan arum flower. Within hours, two men appeared carrying a whole plant in full flower, lashed to a pole. Later, Beccari sent seeds back from Sumatra to his Italian patron; several germinated, and one of the plants was sent to Kew where it flowered in 1889. In 1926 it flowered again, causing such consternation that the police were called to control the excited crowds. Sadly, this highly prized plant is now endangered through over-collecting in the wild. Although renowned for odours ranging from rotting meat to dung and rancid cheese, not all *Amorphophallus* are malodorous. *A. haematospadix* smells of bananas, *A. dunnii* has the fragrance of freshly chopped carrots, and *A. manta* that of chocolate.

finish with a fine layer of grit on the surface. At Eden the pots are lowered into germination tanks as the leaf stems develop, with the top of the compost 7cm below the water's surface. The seeds usually take two to four weeks to germinate, although seedlings have been known to appear after only eight days.

When the first true leaves appear, the plants are transferred into clay-based unsterilized loam in 7.5ltr pots then transplanted to their final home in March or April, or when they have five or six true leaves. At this last stage, each will be in a 250–1,000mltr pot with the top of the pot 20–60cm below the water. The giant waterlily is transferred from the nursery to the main site in a large bucket, to be planted out. At home, remember not to plant out until there's no longer any danger of frost.

At Eden water is circulated through a pump and heated to maintain an optimal growing temperature of 26°C (a minimum of 19°C at night and a maximum of 30°C during the day). The giant water lily is fed with slow-release fertilizer mixed into lumps of loam about the size of a tennis ball – these are pushed into the compost every two weeks once the plant is mature and flowering.

■■ The history of the Titan arum

The huge water lilies are not the only stars at Eden. Staff are encouraged to follow their fancy, and the results can be astonishing! In the nursery, Tim Grigg is developing a collection of *Amorphophallus* – he's currently growing ten species including one of the most famous plants in the world, *Amorphophallus titanum*.

The Titan arum originates in the Sumatran rainforests and is an extraordinary, surreal giant – the bloom, which can reach 3m tall, dies down after flowering and is followed by a single leaf with a 3m spread, topping a 4m stem that looks more like a small tree! Its flowering is greeted with great excitement because of its magnificence and its pungent pong! In fact, this arum is one of the few plants to be fêted by the media worldwide – Eden's bloom has appeared everywhere, from the Eden Project website to national newspapers and television. The Titan arum flowered for three days, and achieved a height of 2.22m. The renowned smell, produced in pulses from the column, or spadix, rising from the centre of the bloom, was reminiscent – exactly as it has been described – of a rotting elephant corpse!

The leaf and flower of this spectacular plant grow from an underground tuber, or storage organ. The leaf grows for eight months, then dies back for another four until the tuber is large enough to flower. After each resting period a bud appears, but for several weeks there is no way of telling whether it's a leaf or a flower bud – heightening everyone's sense of expectation. From a small tuber donated by Bonn Botanic Gardens, it took seven years for Eden's Titan arum to develop into the massive 34kg tuber that produced the first flower. The emerging growth was identified as a flower bud just before Easter 2005. It arrived from Watering Lane Nursery in a van, its tip almost scraping the roof. Once settled in the Humid Tropics Biome, its growth rocketed to around 15cm – sometimes 20cm – a day. You could almost see it moving! The bud started opening at 4.30 p.m. on

Friday 8 April, and by 10 p.m. the outer layers were peeling away as it finally opened into its full, astounding glory.

Each giant bloom contains thousands of separate male and female flowers. On the first night, the pink female flowers are receptive to pollen, and once they are ready, the central column heats up and pumps out that distinctive rancid stench. The Titan arum was once thought to be pollinated by elephants, but it is now known that sweat-bees, attracted by the smell, carry the pollen from flower to flower. Plants rarely grow close to one another, so the smell attracts the bees from afar.

As there are no sweat-bees at Eden, attempts were made to pollinate the flowers by hand, thus encouraging them to set seed. Pollen from a flowering plant sent from Cambridge University Botanic Garden the previous year had been stored in a cool fridge, but there was a problem: how would those carrying out the procedure know when the optimum time for pollination was? Emails exchanged with the botanic gardens at both Cambridge and Bonn yielded the vital information: the flowers would be at their most receptive from 1.30 a.m. – but only for two hours. The key to success was to pollinate them around the central column of the plant rather than concentrating on one area; this would reduce the chance of any rot that occurred spreading from one flower to another. The receptive surface on the female is about 3mm wide – just visible to the naked eye. Two members of staff pollinated the flowers from 1.30 a.m. until 3 a.m., using an artist's paintbrush attached to a bamboo cane so as to reach 1m down into the bloom.

The next night they were back, this time to collect pollen from the male flowers. At 7 p.m. nothing was happening; by 10 p.m. it was almost too late – most pollen had already fallen. But they collected enough to pass on to the Royal Botanic Garden at Kew, who successfully pollinated their Titan arum flowers because the pollen was so fresh. Unfortunately, despite these strenuous efforts, the Eden arum did not set seed – but there's always another time!

Each specimen of the *Amorphophallus* collection in the nursery at Eden is repotted when the leaf dies down. It is put into organic-rich compost in a container several inches larger than the tuber, with its top 5cm below the compost surface. The leaf can last up to eighteen months before it dies down, depending on the species. In spring the plants are fed with slow-release fertilizer, then once a week during the growing season with a general-purpose fertilizer, and kept well watered.

HAND POLLINATION

HOME GARDENERS pollinate by hand, transferring pollen from one flower to another to ensure good crops, particularly early in the season when low temperatures mean reduced insect activity outdoors, or where plants are grown under glass making access difficult for pollinators. Like the Titan arum, apricots and peaches are pollinated with a soft artist's brush. When pollen release is at its peak – usually around noon on a dry day – the pollen is transferred from one flower to the receptive female part of the next. Courgettes, squashes and marrows too, are pollinated by hand. Pick a male flower, then dab its pollen on to a female flower – you can identify the female by the presence of a developing fruit behind the bloom and the absence of stamens and pollen.

MORE EXTRAORDINARY EXOTICS

IN MOIST SUBTROPICAL climates such as Florida, *Amorphophallus bulbifer* has escaped from the garden and become a pernicious weed, overwhelming native species. In Britain it is sold by some exotic plant nurseries for outdoor display in summer, in borders or pots, and is not a problem plant here. Arisaemas, its relatives in temperate climates, are equally extraordinary, with cowl-like flowerheads in unusual colours. There are many species in cultivation: *Arisaema consanguineum* has chocolate-striped green flowers, *Arisaema candidissimum* is sweetly scented and striped like candy-pink pyjamas; *Arisaema sikokianum* is one of the most stunning, with its flowers' dark outers and glossy white interiors. Most need moist, dappled shade and are ideal for woodland gardens or for adding a tropical touch to borders of large-leafed plants. If quirky novelty plants are more your scene, *Dracunculus vulgaris* (the dragon arum), with its sinister dark-purple flowers and putrid odour, is gleefully enjoyed by flies – and by children of all ages!

THE MALAYSIAN GARDEN

Eden's shady Malaysian Garden, with its raised beds and dirt paths, is typical of kitchen gardens found throughout the tropics.

The Humid Tropics Biome is not just home to dramatic palms and the more ornamental plants – it also demonstrates subsistence cultivation in the tropics, particularly in the rainforest. As you make your way along the winding path in the Biome's Asian rainforest you will come upon a typical Malaysian home and garden, created by the Royal Society South-East Asia Rainforest Research Programme and smallholders of Sabah in Malaysia. The garden is of a working kind typical of the humid tropics: it would feed a family with fresh food all year round and provide medicinal as well as culinary herbs. Many of the vegetables grown on the plot, such as sweet potato and yard-long beans, can also be grown in cooler climates and are available to British gardeners: they can be grown in a greenhouse or a polythene tunnel, or started off in pots indoors then planted out in a sheltered, sunny position in the garden once the danger of frost has passed. Treat them as you would treat squashes, runner beans and sweetcorn. In fact, most of the familiar plants found in a temperate vegetable plot have been gathered from around the

globe: runner beans from Mexico, potatoes from South America, spinach from south-west Asia and broad beans from the Mediterranean.

Since the Eden garden is predominantly a practical one, there are few ornamental plants apart from one or two in the surrounding hedge, plus some orchids and *Medinilla magnifica* on the balcony. The Malaysian Garden is planted in three zones: herbs nearest the house, vegetables in a secondary band, and trees for fruit and shade around the perimeter. It shares many similarities with kitchen gardens in the West: the vegetables are grown in raised beds and the soil is improved with green waste before planting.

South-East Asian varieties of beans, leaves and roots predominate. Yard-long beans, trained over bamboo frames, replace our runner beans; in both cultures the roots of legumes, with their special nitrogen-producing nodules, are left in the ground so as to provide a useful source of nitrogen for later crops. Pak choi replaces cabbage, and there are rice and taro instead of potatoes. Rainwater is used for watering. Vegetables like Malabar spinach and sweet potatoes trail freely under the trees and shrubs; herbs and vegetables are also planted randomly, as in an English cottage garden. The boundaries are the hedges, part productive and part ornamental: plants such as pink *Cordyline fruticosa* – the Ti or good-luck plant – grow alongside guavas and bananas.

In Malaysia, plants are sown successively so that there are always crops at several stages of growth, from sowing to harvest, throughout the year. In Eden's Malaysian Garden there are also repeat sowings throughout the year. Maintenance consists of keeping the crops weed-free: beds are hand-weeded rather than hoed – in such good growing conditions weeds tend to reroot after hoeing. Pruning from time to time keeps the shrubs and trees under control.

■■ The vegetable crops

Some crops, such as manioc and cubeb pepper, are distinctly tropical, whereas other plants that feature in the Humid Tropics Biome can usually be grown outdoors in temperate climates, with a little care.

Thai ball aubergines are an essential ingredient in Malaysian cooking, and so are must-have crops in a Malaysian garden. The seed pods are added to curries, soups and stews. These plants produce round fruits that don't look like the familiar garden aubergine at all. Initially at Eden there were pollination problems – the flowers kept dropping off – but with the help of hand-pollination they are now bearing fruit. Thai ball aubergines are ideal for containers in a greenhouse alongside okra, otherwise known as bhindi or ladies' fingers (*Abelmoschus esculentus*), which needs similar growing conditions. Okra is a close relative of the ornamental hibiscus. Soak the seeds for twenty-four hours before sowing them at 16°C, from early spring onwards. In cooler climates, they should be grown indoors in containers using a soil-based compost. The plants need some support, so grow them up canes, pinching out the growth tips when the main stems are around 30cm tall. All fruiting or podding vegetables should be harvested regularly to ensure a good long crop.

The aubergine plant sports gorgeous flowers followed by attractive fruits that taste fantastic.

The sweet potato (*Ipomoea batatas*) is not related to our potato, but to bindweed and morning glory. Its origins are a mystery, but it was grown by the Mayas and Incas and by the Maoris of New Zealand well before the sixteenth century. It is now grown throughout the tropics, and is a staple in Polynesia. How it travelled so far is uncertain, but it is believed to have clung to vines on logs swept out to sea, or to have been introduced to South America by visiting Polynesians. In the Humid Tropics Biome the sweet potato is harvested when it is mature, and the tubers are roasted or boiled like potatoes. The young leaves and shoots are prepared in the same way as spinach. The plant is also used as ground cover.

Like your fellow-gardeners in the tropics, you too could be eating homegrown sweet potato. There are hundreds of varieties of this vegetable available worldwide. In Britain, suppliers offer cuttings to be grown in rich free-draining soil supplemented with plenty of well-rotted compost. Pot them into 7.5cm pots of multipurpose compost and put in the greenhouse for three weeks before acclimatizing them to outdoor conditions. Ideally, plant them through black polythene to suppress weeds and warm the soil. Covering them with horticultural fleece will help them to become established. Keep them well watered, feed every two weeks with a high-potash fertilizer, and harvest as late in the autumn as possible but before the first frosts. They flourish in temperatures from 24°C, so in cooler parts of the country they should spend their entire lives in a greenhouse or in polythene tunnels. In spring, once the danger of frost has passed, plant out young specimens 37–45cm apart in a warm, sheltered spot. Use the potatoes immediately, or store at temperatures no lower than 10°C.

The yard-long bean (*Vigna unguiculata* subspecies *sesquipedalis*) is one of several varieties of a group of cowpeas that are planted in Malaysia. They are cultivated extensively in South-East Asia, China, the Philippines and the Caribbean, and are used in stir-fries, omelettes, spicy soups, salads and curries. Their stems reach several metres and they produce pencil-thin pods up to 1m long. They are grown over bamboo frames to keep the pods off the ground. Although they thrive on high rainfall and humidity, they will grow outdoors in Britain when planted in deep, rich soil in a sheltered, sunny position. Sow the seeds indoors in April and plant out after acclimatizing in May, after the last frost, or sow outdoors under cloches from April. Grow in double rows, allowing 1.5m between them, and harvest from August until the first frosts.

Taro, eddo and dasheen are three slightly different forms of *Colocasia esculenta* that feature in the Humid Tropics Biome's vegetable garden. These perennials, with their large, arrow-shaped leaves, are widely grown for their edible corms and are familiar garden and agricultural plants in the tropics. They are a staple crop in many Pacific islands and in West Africa, and have been cultivated for over two thousand years in South-East Asia.

The corms cannot be eaten raw: they require careful preparation because some forms contain calcium oxalate, which causes extreme

RIGHT: *Almost every part of the horseradish tree is edible, it has many medicinal uses and it is used to purify water – hence it is also known as the 'miracle tree'.*

inflammation of the mouth and throat. They need to be boiled first, and the water should be changed several times during this process so as to remove the toxins, just as we do when soaking red beans. Once boiled, the corms can be roasted, grilled, fried, puréed or made into soup. In Britain you can buy them from Asian grocers and, if you have a pond, you can grow them as ornamentals along the edges in containers of organic-rich compost.

Start them off indoors in mid-spring or in a warm greenhouse, then acclimatize to cooler conditions by putting them outdoors in the day and bringing them in at night for two to three weeks. Then you can plant them outdoors permanently after the last frost of spring until the first of autumn. If they are not by a pond, keep the plants well watered and fed during the growing season, and overwinter indoors. It takes up to two seasons to produce edible-sized tubers from smaller plants.

The bottle gourd, or doodhi (*Lagenaria siceraria*), is another dual-purpose plant. It is edible when young and tender, but the skin hardens as the fruits mature and, once dried, they are used in South-East Asia as essential household utensils such as bowls and pots, and as musical instruments. It was one of the few plants cultivated in the Old and New Worlds in prehistoric times. In early Peruvian civilizations bottle gourds were used in cranial surgery: a broken piece of skull would be replaced by a piece of gourd shell and the skin stitched back over it. It is a rampant scrambler that should be pruned regularly to keep it in check. It is grown over bamboo frames so that the fruits hang well away

Few flowers are grown in the Malaysian Garden; the focus is on survival: it supplies medicinal and food plants for the family.

from the soil, produce a well-formed capsule and do not rot. Its relatives the marrows and pumpkins are grown on straw or through black polythene, again to prevent rotting.

Bottle gourds can be cultivated successfully in a glasshouse, or even in a sheltered spot outdoors in milder parts of Britain. Sow the seeds in the spring in moist multipurpose compost – just as you would marrows or courgettes – then plant in rich well-drained soil and keep them well watered through the growing season using tepid water. They can be grown in full sun or partial shade, and require a minimum temperature of 18°C.

The bitter gourd, or karela (*Momordica charantia*), is another pan-tropical climber that has the most extraordinary golden-orange, ribbed, warty fruit. It is eaten as a vegetable, cooked (in stir-fries), or can be added to pickles and curries. The mature fruit with their bright-red seeds are soaked in salted water to remove the bitterness, and the young shoots can be cooked like spinach. It is also widely used medicinally for the treatment of diabetes and skin complaints – in Malaysia the seeds are used as a poultice for elephants with sore eyes! This is another gourd that can be grown under glass in Britain after sowing in early spring.

At Eden, both this gourd and the bottle gourd are started off at Watering Lane Nursery and transplanted when they are 30cm tall – they could be sown directly, but there can be problems with cockroaches nibbling the developing seedlings. One year, self-sown bitter gourd seedlings were left to develop on their own, but they were so successful – and the overcrowding was such – that the fruits on the adult plants remained underdeveloped. Rather than leave all the fallen seeds, it's better to reduce to just two to four well-spaced seedlings so as to give them a chance to prosper. Both these gourds are grown as annuals, as they die over winter when the light is too dim, and are planted again in late February. Most of the other garden plants are pruned to keep them in shape or within their allotted space, but these two rampant individuals have to be trimmed several times a week when they are in full growth.

Malabar spinach (*Basella rubra* var. *alba*) is another fast-growing climber (or scrambler), with red or green stems and thick, fleshy leaves that taste like our own spinach. Grown extensively in India and Malaysia, it is found in tropical Africa, the Caribbean and South America too. The young leaves and stems are eaten as a vegetable, in salads or in stews (beware – they become slimy when overcooked). Malabar spinach is a good source of vitamins A and C, calcium and iron. It is perennial in the tropics but grows happily as a greenhouse annual in cooler climates – it is frost-tender – and can be found in British seed catalogues. You may be able to grow it outdoors, though, in a sheltered sunny position. Soak the seeds overnight in spring, then sow indoors at 18–21°C. Malabar spinach

tolerates low light, as the plants grown at Eden prove; it needs a minimum daytime temperature of 15°C to maintain growth, and moisture-retentive, organic-rich, free-draining soil. It must be kept watered and fed with a general fertilizer to encourage healthy growth, and is easily grown from seed or cuttings.

Cubeb pepper (*Piper cubeba*), a shrub related to our black pepper, grows happily in the shade in the Malaysian Garden, adding to the lush rainforest effect. It originates in Indonesia, and most of today's commercial production takes place in Java. The berries have a ridged surface, are a little larger than peppercorns, and have a bitter-spicy taste; they are used as a pepper substitute. Sold whole, they are crushed or ground before use. Cubeb pepper is also used commercially in soaps and perfumes; it is a carminative, a diuretic, an expectorant, a stimulant and an antiseptic, and is used to treat chronic bronchitis.

■ Unusual crops

It may come as a surprise to find jute (*Corchorus olitorius*), famous as a fibre crop for making sacks and rugs, growing in a vegetable garden. However, young shoots from selected forms of this bushy perennial are widely eaten as a vegetable in Africa, India, Malaysia and Latin America, and the dried leaves are used as a thickener and can be stored after drying, for a famine crop.

Another unusual plant in the Malaysian Garden is sweetleaf (*Sauropus androgynus*), which belongs to the *Euphorbia* family, renowned for its toxic sap. However, at Eden it is grown as a hedging plant, and

Malabar spinach can be grown under glass in cooler climates or in a sheltered sunny position outside in the summer.

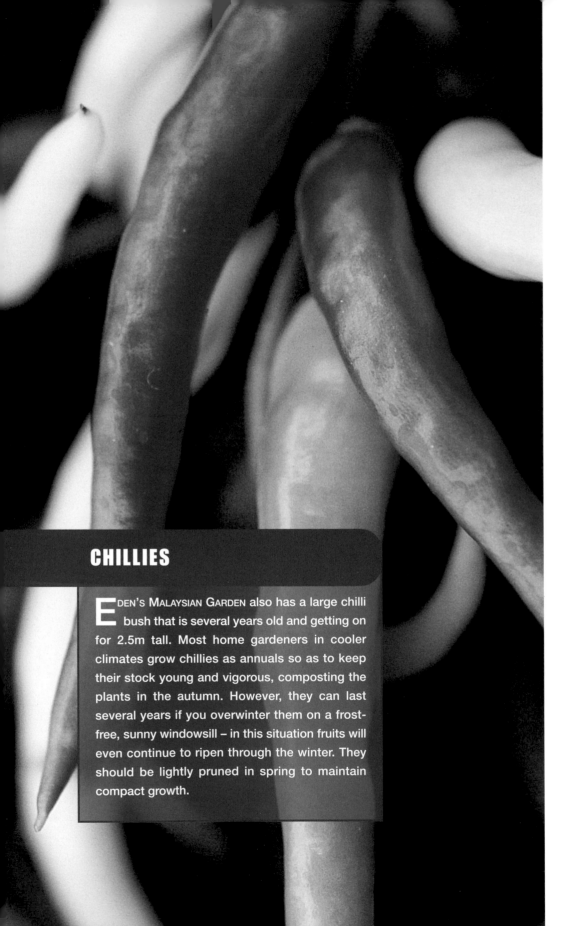

cut back to the base every few months. The top 15cm of the shoot tips are edible. The shoots taste similar to garden peas, but with a hint of nuts, and are used in many dishes including salads, stews and stir-fries; the older leaves are also edible, but less tasty. It's a popular leafy vegetable in Malaysia, where farmers force growth by stepping up the amounts of water and fertilizer used. It came to prominence in Taiwan as a dietary aid for weight control, taken with fruit juice; however, in 1995 several cases of poisoning, which caused lung congestion, were reported, particularly by people who had eaten uncooked shoots.

Spices to grow at home

Other plants in the Malaysian vegetable garden are grown as flavourings. **Ginger** (*Zingiber officinale*), regarded as a native of South-East Asia, is often called stem ginger because the underground rhizomes are actually swollen stems. It is used extensively throughout the world in sweet and savoury dishes, and also medicinally as a calmative and anti-inflammatory; it is an excellent treatment for nausea, including travel sickness, and has an antibacterial action in food. During the Middle Ages in Europe it was used in the making of gingerbread, to mask the taste of tainted wheat.

In the tropics it needs a high growing temperature – over 30°C – and takes around nine months to produce a crop – the clump at Eden is still expanding. But you can try it as a houseplant in cooler climes by planting sections, each at least 5cm long, of shop-bought rhizome in early spring.

CHILLIES

EDEN'S MALAYSIAN GARDEN also has a large chilli bush that is several years old and getting on for 2.5m tall. Most home gardeners in cooler climates grow chillies as annuals so as to keep their stock young and vigorous, composting the plants in the autumn. However, they can last several years if you overwinter them on a frost-free, sunny windowsill – in this situation fruits will even continue to ripen through the winter. They should be lightly pruned in spring to maintain compact growth.

OTHER TROPICAL CROPS OF THE HUMID TROPICS BIOME

MANY OF THE STAPLE plants that form the basis of an average diet in the humid tropics are found growing in Eden's Malaysian Garden, but not all of them. Others tropical crops, such as groundnuts, an essential foodstuff in many parts of the world, are found in displays representing Africa and the Americas.

CASSAVA, or manioc (Manihot esculenta), is a woody shrub up to 2m tall which is cultivated throughout the tropics. It is one of the most important staple crops in the world, feeding over 500 million people. It has prominently lobed leaves, and the starchy underground tubers contain a high quantity of prussic acid. Fortunately, this poison is destroyed by washing and cooking. But there are stories of starving European explorers eating raw manioc and dying at the moment they thought they had found sustenance.

Cassava is an essential element of Brazilian farinha and West African gari cuisine. It is also a staple crop of the Amazonian Native South Americans. Their preparation of it is extremely time-consuming: first, they soak it in a stream or water-filled canoe for three days to soften the skin; then they peel it, and mash it to a pulp with a mortar and pestle. They then place the pulp in a manioc press to remove the prussic acid and excess moisture (you can see this equipment in the manioc display in the Tropical South America centre at Eden), and the end result of this process is tapioca. The remains of the tubers are sieved to remove the fibres, then ground into flour, which is made into dough and rolled into large tortilla shapes, to be cooked on the griddle of a cassava oven.

At Eden, cassava is grown from hardwood cuttings of one-year-old stems cut into 15cm lengths; these are then planted at a 45° angle, with two buds above ground, and about 60cm apart. They propagate more rapidly in summer, and must be kept constantly moist. Cuttings of about a pencil thickness are taken during the dormant season from the previous season's growth. These are then planted into a shallow trench about 12cm deep, whose soil has been improved with sharp sand. They are placed vertically about 45cm apart with the top 2.5cm exposed. The technique used to take hardwood cuttings from cassava is the same as that used by domestic gardeners for gooseberries, red and white currants and ornamentals such as buddleia.

Gooseberry cuttings should normally be 15–30cm long with all the buds removed apart from those in the top 5cm, which remain above ground.

The cassava crop follows the same monthly feeding programme as the rest of the Biome; the tubers take between eighteen months and two years to mature, but considerably less in the tropics where growth is not restricted by low light in winter.

GROUNDNUTS, or peanuts (Arachis hypogaea), provide three crops a year in Africa and two at Eden. This is yet another South American plant that was cultivated long before the Spanish arrived. It is an annual, and belongs to the same legume family that provides kitchen gardeners with podded crops such as peas and runner, broad and French beans. It can be either grown as an upright, or allowed to creep over the soil. The yellow flowers bloom only for a day and are self-pollinating.

In temperate regions they make great novelty plants for growing indoors. Simply remove fresh (not roasted or salted!) nuts from their shells and plant them around 5cm deep in a pot of moist, organic-rich compost, then put the pot in a clear polythene bag in a warm place such as the airing cupboard. After germination, keep the compost moist with tepid water. Around three months later the plant will produce flowers, whose stems will then turn downwards and burrow into the ground; six weeks later reduce watering, and four weeks after that you can harvest your peanuts. Peanuts are used worldwide in curries, soups and stews, and are a staple crop in Africa.

ABOVE: *Lemon grass is found growing throughout the tropics and is essential in South-East-Asian cooking.*

RIGHT: *In temperate climates the pineapple is now a novelty crop but successful cultivation in the Victorian kitchen garden demanded skill and brought great status.*

Make sure each piece of rhizome has several leaf buds developing, and plant them with the buds facing upwards, in multipurpose compost. Keep warm and moist during the growing season, using tepid water, and transplant each into a larger pot as the rhizome grows. Mist the leaves regularly, or put the pot on a tray of pebbles containing enough water to reach just above its base. During the growing season, feed every two to three weeks with liquid general fertilizer. If you want a crop from your houseplant, reduce watering in autumn, then let the compost dry out: this encourages rhizome production, though it may take several years to build up each rhizome to a usable size. If you have the patience to wait till they are ready, lift them carefully in late autumn for use in cooking, and replant some for the next crop.

In the Malaysian Garden there's a small patch of **lemon grass** (*Cymbopogon citratus*) too. This is a common flavouring in South-East Asian and Caribbean dishes, that adds a delicate, lemony tang. It is not hardy outdoors over winter in the UK, but it can be grown in pots outdoors from late spring to late summer in a sheltered, sunny spot, in the greenhouse or on a bright windowsill. Several suppliers sell seeds – but be warned, germination can be slow and erratic, so pot on each seedling as it develops. Keep the plants well watered in the growing season, and a large clump will eventually form. Always harvest lemon grass from the outer edge. It can also be propagated from fresh stalks. Just put them in a glass of water until roots form, then transplant into pots of compost.

Fruit

The pineapple (*Ananas comosus*) is grown throughout Malaysia. Where in your garden there might be a patch of rhubarb, in Malaysia it would be pineapples. They are eaten there fresh as a snack or dessert, and used for tenderizing meat to make it more easily digestible – hence its use here with gammon. Also, in the Philippines there is a local industry making fine garments such as shirts from pineapple fibre.

There are over twenty varieties growing in the Biome. They need a year to become established before they will fruit. Pineapples are ready to harvest when they change from green to yellow from the base upwards, and start to soften, producing their distinctive fragrance. You harvest them by cutting them at their base from the stem they grow on. Offsets – short lateral shoots – are produced when the fruit is cut, and are detached from the parent once there are sufficient roots. The nursery at Eden grows on young pineapple offsets to replace older plants.

Despite being tropical fruits, pineapples have been grown as a luxury crop in country-house gardens since Victorian times. They were grown in 'stove houses', or pits, using rotting horse manure to create heat – you can see such pits at the gardens at Heligan in Cornwall.

Pineapples can also be propagated from the crown of the fruit – that is, the cluster of leaves at the top. Twist or cut off the crown and remove the excess flesh, then leave what's left to dry off. Once it's dry, slice the base of the crown until small circles are revealed – this is where the roots will develop – and remove the lower leaves. Place the base in a jar

RIGHT: *Eating mangoes can be a messy business – no wonder one tradition dictates they should be eaten in the bath!*

BELOW: *With its clusters of pink flowers, the star fruit is a beautiful ornamental fruit tree that is popular throughout the tropics.*

of water for about three weeks, then put it in a warm, bright spot until roots form. Once this happens, plant out in cactus compost, keeping it moist. Repot as the plant grows, keeping it by a sunny window or in a greenhouse protected from frost at 16°C. Water it once a week in the growing season and mist regularly; the compost must not dry out. Fertilize monthly during the growing season using high-potash fertilizer. It can go outdoors once there's no danger of frost. If you grow pineapples in the house or in a greenhouse it can take several seasons to produce fruit, although not so long if the greenhouse or polythene tunnel is humid.

Fruit trees

As in Malaysia itself, fruit trees feature extensively in Eden's self-sufficient Malaysian Garden. In one corner there's a coconut palm – others in the Biome have already fruited, and it's expected that this specimen will do the same on reaching maturity.

As mentioned earlier, many plants that flower and grow all year round in the tropics become seasonal at Eden because of the low winter light levels. The star fruit (*Averrhoa carambola*) originated in South-East Asia and is a popular Malaysian garden tree, producing tiny pink flowers and fruits all year round, except in periods of low light. Amazingly, the clusters of star-shaped fruit that start off green have ripened at Eden. You'll find them in supermarkets, but needless to say, they are much better picked from the tree when pale golden-yellow, sweetly flavoured and packed with juice. There are both sweet and acid kinds that are used in salads and drinks – and the juice can also be used for

cleaning brass! Other tropical crops that have successfully flowered and fruited include cocoa, coffee, mango, cola, cashew and coconut – and to everyone's delight Eden's mangosteen (*Garcinia mangostana*) also produced a fruit! In Britain tropical fruit trees can't be grown outside all year round, of course, but you can have a lot of fun just growing them from seed as novelty houseplants. The nearest to an outside tropical tree you will get are plants from mediterranean regions like figs, peaches and guavas. They will grow under glass, then can go outside during the summer – or all year round in milder spots, depending on the plant and cultivar.

The Malay apple (*Syzygium malaccense*) is another 'first' for UK gardens, and in 2005 it flowered and fruited at Eden for the first time. It's a signature plant in almost every Malaysian garden, as both an ornamental and a fruit tree. Its flowers, which appear mainly on the older branches, are a mass of stamens and look like bright-pink shaving brushes. When they drop, they carpet the ground with their conspicuous pink for up to two days before fading. The fruits that follow are bright red and refreshing, tasting of sweet apple. Their soft skins mean they are rarely sold in markets – they are usually eaten straight from the tree, or cooked with spices for desserts, or made into jam.

A jackfruit (*Artocarpus heterophyllus*) grows in the Malaysian Garden. This is a giant tree related to the mulberry and fig that produces the largest fruit in cultivation, weighing up to 50kg. This plant is valued as much for its shade as its fruit; in Thailand it is said to bring good luck, and its bark supplies the yellow dye used for Buddhist monks' robes. The 'jack' part of its name comes from the Malaysian word for 'round', which describes its shape. Such is the fruit's weight that the trees produce their clusters of female flowers, and thus their fruit, on the main trunk and branches, because the smaller branches (which produce the male flowers) would break under the strain! And again because of their size, the fruits are usually sold in the markets in pieces.

They can be deep-fried, pickled, salted or puréed – often served with ice as a drink. The boiled seeds taste of chestnut and the unripe fruit is eaten as a vegetable. It is sold by some grocers and supermarkets in Britain and, like any fruit or vegetable, is worth adding to your diet.

The Mango (*Mangifera indica*) – no tropical garden would be complete without it. More than two hundred different cultivars are grown in different parts of the world. They can be eaten fresh, pickled or salted, and as juices and 'smoothies', and are the main ingredient of one of Britain's favourite chutneys. Tradition recommends that they be eaten fresh, in the bath, with a glass of champagne! Although many grow to become massive trees there are now more garden-friendly varieties available for subtropical gardens, such as 'Duncan', 'Glen' and 'Cogshall' – many of them bred in Florida. They can be controlled by careful pruning, and they fruit after three years. There is an excellent collection of these and other exotic fruit at the Fairchild Tropical Botanic Garden in Florida, where an annual mango festival is held.

THE BANANA COLLECTION

RIGHT: *The fruits of the banana plant are some of the most spectacular in the business. The male flowers hide under the bold pink-purple bracts.*

The Humid Tropics Biome features several globally important crops including: coffee, which is occasionally grown in more temperate climates as a house or conservatory plant; cocoa, whose scientific name *Theobroma* derives from the Greek for 'Food of the Gods', and the banana. Over 80 per cent of the world's bananas are grown in the tropics; they are used as a sweet or savoury food and as an ingredient of beer, for making cloth and roofing material; and the leaves also make an effective temporary umbrella.

Eden has a collection of thirty-two different bananas, including *Musa acuminata* and *M. balbisiana*, which visitors from the Banana and Plantain Research Institute have described as the best they've seen in cultivation. The display is laid out like a plantation, showing the three main stages of growth from plants barely 30cm tall to mature fruiting adults.

Bananas naturally form large clumps; prune too late, when there's a mass of congested shoots growing up from the rootstock, and it is very difficult to cut older stems back to ground level. So the plants are pruned regularly with a view to directing all their energy into the three best shoots at each stage of growth. When older stems are being removed, the plants are cut back in sections from the top, often using a cherry-picker to support the weight of leaves and stems. It's a messy business – the plants are packed with gallons of sap and with each new cut more pours down the stems. Although the sap is clear, brown stains appear after your clothes have been washed, so the gardeners at Eden always wear their oldest clothes when clearing bananas. When the plants are cut back at the base the sap continues to flow, and in areas where wild bananas are found, the indigenous people fell them, hollow out the base like a bowl, then collect the sap welling up from the roots and drink it.

It takes about nine months for bananas to reach maturity and fruit. They need plenty of moisture, food and good drainage. At Eden they are mulched with a potent combination of rotted horse manure, green waste and chicken manure in a layer about 12cm deep, in winter or early spring; they are watered every day in summer and roughly every two days in winter.

Hardy ornamental bananas have become popular again as outdoor plants in our home gardens, particularly among those of us wanting to create a tropical look. As well as rich soil and plenty of water, bananas need sunshine, shelter and winter protection to flourish, but are otherwise fairly low-maintenance additions to the garden. The most

COMMON COMPLAINTS WITH BANANAS

BANANAS ARE **prone to magnesium deficiency, and will rapidly show the symptoms – a yellowing between the leaf veins and browning round the margins. It is a problem you may have come across when growing tomatoes. When supplies are low, the plant moves magnesium to the new leaves, so the old ones suffer first. It is often a problem with plants growing in very acid soil, or after a period of heavy rain or watering, as magnesium is easily washed out. Signs of deficiency can also appear after excessive use of high-potash fertilizers, which block the uptake of magnesium. Spray plants with a solution of Epsom salts (magnesium sulphate), adding a few drops of detergent so as to stop it from running off the leaves too readily; or apply the salts to the soil around the base of the plant in granular form, as they do with the bananas at Eden.**

BANANAS IN BRITAIN

MUSA CAVENDISHII is named after the Cavendish family, better known as the Dukes of Devonshire, who have lived at Chatsworth House for generations. Sir Joseph Paxton (1801–65), gardener and architect to the 6th Duke, saw an illustration of an unknown dwarf banana on some hand-painted Chinese wallpaper in the great house. In 1826, two similar plants were sent from Mauritius to Young's Nursery in Epsom by a British resident there, one Charles Telfair. Paxton spotted the likeness, bought one of them and named it *Musa cavendishii*, after his patron; the other was sent abroad. At 1.5m tall, Paxton's plant flowered for the first time in 1835, and by May the following year, over a hundred fruit were ripening, to produce a crop weighing almost 18kg.

The banana plant created a sensation when exhibited at the Royal Horticultural Society in London; Paxton won the Knightian medal and was hailed for his skill. Young's Nursery eventually bought back twenty plants from the Duke. And one of his plants was taken to Samoa by a missionary, whence it spread to Tonga, Fiji and eventually Australia and became an important commercial crop. It is now known as *Musa acuminata* 'Dwarf Cavendish'.

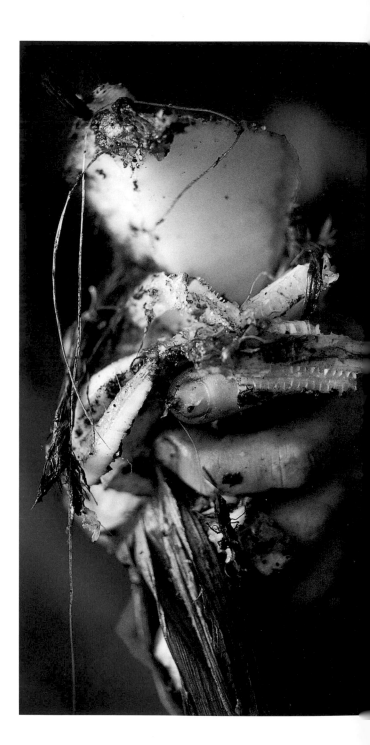

common specimen, *Musa basjoo*, the Japanese banana (used in Japan for the small-scale production of the cloth used for kimonos), was introduced to Britain in 1881 and became such a fashionable feature of Cornish estate gardens such as Heligan that the region became known as the 'banana belt'. Although the rootstock is hardy outdoors in much of Britain, it helps to have some protection over winter, so mulch its roots with a thick layer of straw or well-rotted manure, and wrap the stems in straw, held in place by chicken wire or horticultural fleece.

The cultivar 'Sakhalin', from the Russian island north of Japan, is possibly the hardiest of all banana plants and has survived temperatures down to –7°C. *Musa sikkimensis* and *M. hookerii* have the potential to be hardy too, while *Musa lasiocarpa*, only 1.5m tall, is ideal for growing in large containers.

RIGHT: *The stems and roots of banana plants are full of sap. If the plant is cut down and the base hollowed out, enough sap will collect to drink and it will continue to flow.*

THE RICE DISPLAY

One of the globe's most important foods, and one that feeds half the world – 90 per cent of the annual production is consumed in flood-prone Asia – is rice (*Oryza sativa*). It grows in a range of conditions, from damp soil to deeply flooded areas, where the plants shoot up at speed in a race to stay above the rising waters. The aim of the Eden display within the Humid Tropics Biome is to grow native valley varieties using the same cultivation techniques as they do in the East. In March or early April, the rice is soaked overnight, drained, then put in a hessian bag (in the Bario region of Indonesia, one of the world's great rice-growing areas, it would be a large sack) and covered. It takes about two days to germinate

using this method – a week, if not – and it is then scattered over a seedbed until, about three weeks later, it reaches the seedling stage. It is finally planted out when three leaves have formed, and with about 15cm between the plants.

In Britain and other cool temperate climates rice can be grown in a greenhouse, and can produce moderate yields if there is enough artificial heating to maintain a minimum temperature of 16°C. The shorter, highland varieties are better suited to a temperate climate. Sow the seeds in late spring or early summer, scattering them thinly over the potting compost, in a pot at least 15cm across. Then place the pot in shallow water so that the compost stays wet. If possible, put the pot in a propagator to

GERMINATING GRASS SEED

A TECHNIQUE SIMILAR to that used for rice (pictured) is used for germinating grass seed, a relative of rice. Moisten it and mix it with damp multipurpose compost, and put it in a plastic bag in the airing cupboard. Avoid adding too much water, as seed tends to form clumps – adding the compost, which acts as a carrier, will prevent the problem in the first place. When the seed starts to germinate, scatter it all over the lawn, or use it to repair patches. This is an ideal way to speed up germination earlier in the season and reduce seed loss to birds.

encourage germination. Rice grows rapidly, and seedheads can appear after only three months. The plants will dry out when the rice is ripe, at which time the compost should also be dried out.

To encourage rapid growth, the rice at Eden is sown directly into the damp terraces, just as it would be in many places in the tropics. The foundations of the terrace walls are made from sandbags at the lower levels, and breeze blocks were used where more height was needed. They were then covered with chicken wire, and upside-down turves were attached with metal pegs. This was then covered with 'cob' – a mixture of subsoil, clay and hemp straw. Once the cob starts to dry, cracks appear in the same way that they do in the tropics, and they are repaired every year.

The terraces in which rice is grown support a huge amount of wildlife; in places like Bangladesh, Thailand and Cambodia, rice terraces have been traditionally irrigated from rivers so that fish, shrimp and snails are washed into the paddy fields. As a result, all three have become staples, the foundations of the daily diet. In fact, people in Asia feel so strongly about their relationship with 'rice and fish' that in Vietnam they are referred to as 'mother and child'.

Rice is not the only plant that grows well in water or damp soil. Watercress, usually associated with clean, fast-flowing streams, can also be grown as a garden plant in a damp spot, and it takes less space to produce a decent yield!

If you want to grow your own watercress, take healthy shoot tips in spring from shop-bought watercress and root them in a glass of water. Then, in a damp, shady part of the garden dig a 60 × 30cm trench, line it with polythene or sheets of damp newspaper, then put a thick layer of moisture-retentive, well-rotted compost or manure in the base. Fill the trench with earth until it reaches a level slightly lower than the surrounding soil sides, then plant out the rooted cuttings about 15cm apart. Keep the plants well watered and harvest regularly to maintain bushy growth, but don't cut too much until they are well established. Never allow watercress to flower, as the leaves change and become tough to eat and the plants reduce their leafy growth. If you haven't space for a trench, watercress can also be grown in large plastic pots with or without a drainage hole, in an 80:20 mix of soil-based and multipurpose compost. Cover the plants with fleece or cloches in winter to guarantee a continuous harvest.

HARVEST TIME

HARVESTING RICE in Malaysia is usually a community effort. On a particular day, the whole village is enlisted to help one farmer in his fields. They arrive at 6 a.m. and work all morning. Often singing as they labour in the hot sun, they make their slow way through the thick, oozing mud, their feet frequently lacerated by the rice leaves. There are several harvesting techniques. Traditionally, individual stalks are harvested with a small knife, while clumps are cut at the base to make bundles, then put into baskets tied to the harvesters' bodies and delivered later to the threshing area. In the Bario region people are keen to save local rice varieties, even if they have very low yields – sometimes only a couple of sacks each season.

LEFT: *Rice planted in the Humid Tropics Biome will eventually create a dense mat of green foliage with sprays of tiny seeds.*

PLANTS FOR MEDICINAL USE

As well as flowers, fruit and vegetables, most tropical gardeners cultivate their own medicinal plants. At Eden there is a fine selection growing in the Malaysian Garden and throughout the Humid Tropics Biome.

Pawpaw (*Carica papaya*), like the banana, is a tall herbaceous plant that looks more like a tree, and is an essential component of the tropical garden. It is known as the 'medicine tree' because there is barely a part of it that is not used to treat some problem or illness, including beriberi, rheumatism, dysentery, warts, indigestion and piles, and in Western medicine it has been used for treating slipped discs. Furthermore, the fruits are edible, varying in size and shape from small pears to long melons, some tipping the scales at a whopping 4.5kg or more. The male and female flowers appear on separate plants and in Kenya it is said that you must be able to see a male tree from a female, or the female tree will be barren.

The pawpaw has been cultivated for centuries, spreading from lowland Central and South America throughout the tropics. Columbus noted that 'natives of the Caribbean were very strong and lived on a tree melon called the 'Fruit of Angels'. This tastes delicious and should be eaten fresh as a snack or dessert, or for breakfast as it is in the tropics. The juice makes an equally delicious drink. When unripe it can be stuffed with meat and baked, and it is used to tenderize meat, in the manufacture of chewing-gum, and instead of rennet to curdle milk. The seeds can be sprouted and used in the same way as mustard and cress.

The miracle tree (*Moringa oleifera*), a native of India, enjoys even greater status. Almost every part, except the outer covering of the roots, is edible and rich in vitamins and minerals. The leaves and shoot tips can be cooked like spinach, the roots are used like horseradish, the flowers are used in infusions, the young seedpods taste of asparagus, and the crushed seeds provide oil for cooking and fine watch-making. In fact, Ayurvedic medicine describes three hundred treatments for a variety of ailments including skin infections, high blood pressure and gastric ulcers. A compound found in the flowers and roots of the miracle tree has powerful antibiotic and fungicidal effects, and the powdered seeds have proved to be more effective at purifying water than most chemicals, killing 99 per cent of bacteria – a vital requirement in parts of the world where drinking water is usually contaminated.

The seeds germinate rapidly and branches root freely; the plant is fast-growing, grows back rapidly after pruning, and the timber can be used as firewood. You can see why it's called the miracle tree! Although it does not reach maturity in cooler climates, it can be grown from seed in a glasshouse or conservatory as an ornamental plant.

The Indian mulberry (*Morinda citrifolia*) is a native of Australia, Polynesia and South-East Asia and has spread throughout the tropics. It is also found in the Malaysian Garden. Its strange compound fruit, like a large white mulberry, smells dreadful, but is good for treating conditions ranging from diarrhoea to worms. Added to fruit drinks, it is known as 'noni juice'. The edible leaves contain up

The pawpaw and the Indian mulberry (bottom) are two of the most useful plants grown in the tropics. Both are unlikely to fruit in a green-house, but you could try!

to 6 per cent protein. Different parts of the plant are used for treating fever, eye and breathing problems, abscesses, burns and boils, and in Malaysia it is also used to treat colic, coughs and nausea. Western researchers are currently analyzing the Indian mulberry for its anti-cancer potential. It can be grown in a warm greenhouse in cooler climates, but is unlikely to fruit.

The neem tree (*Azadirachita indica*) is another wonder tree of the humid tropics; in India there are over twenty million of them. In parts of the world it has been valued as a medicinal plant for over four thousand years. Many parts of the tree possess antimicrobial properties and in Eastern medicine it is regarded as a cure-all; it also produces a repellent and poison that protects stored food from insect damage, which is used extensively. The active chemical, called azadirachtin, prevents insects from feeding and reproducing properly. It is one of the world's most powerful plant-based insecticides, along with pyrethrum and derris from the roots of the tropical climber *Derris elliptica*, long used by gardeners in pest control. This and other traditional functions of the tree have now been translated into commercial products and patented, causing considerable controversy over ownership rights.

Commercial neem-based insecticides have proved to be effective against over two hundred types of insect, including head lice, fleas, locusts and mosquitoes. The neem also makes an attractive foliage houseplant in cooler climates, provided you can maintain a temperature of around 18°C.

SOW YOUR OWN EXOTICS

IT IS WELL WORTH having a go at sowing seeds of exotic fruit bought from the grocer, or from specialist seed suppliers. Put them in pots of multipurpose compost, moisten with tepid water, pop them in a clear plastic bag and into the airing cupboard or other warm spot. Check them regularly and, once they have germinated, remove the polythene bag and keep them in a warm bright place – the bathroom is ideal as long as it's not too draughty. Try mango, lychee, jackfruit, date or avocado. Most will never grow large enough to fruit, but they make great novelty houseplants.

THE BAMBOO

The typical Malaysian garden is simple, highly productive and sustainable; even building materials like bamboo are commonly cultivated too – indeed, such home-produced plants are bartered at local markets. Bamboo is a vital plant for construction in the tropics, making anything from scaffolding to the actual structures themselves. Imagine growing your own house extension!

Bamboo plants with patterned canes, such as this Gigantochloa verticillata *look great in both tropical and temperate gardens.*

In the West, gardeners use cut bamboo as fencing or screens, or create living screens from running or clump-forming bamboos. There is a wide variety of species available in Britain now, ranging from tiny specimens like *Pleioblastus akebono* (barely 30cm tall), to jungle giants with canes that can be mottled, striped or beautifully coloured and with either plain or variegated leaves.

Bamboos are vigorous and are not affected by harvesting, so do research their growth habit before planting them in your garden. Removing up to a third of the shoots from a clump reduces the ornamental impact, but will control the more vigorous species. Stems can be thinned to vary the character and density of plants, and harvested canes can be used for supporting beans and other climbers – though black canes will fade after they have been cut.

Bamboos become spectacular living sculptures when lit from the base, and the sound of their leaves rustling gently in the breeze, or of the canes crashing together in a gale, is often overlooked as a potential garden feature. If you have planted an edible variety to use in salads or stir-fries, you can harvest from early- to mid-spring, using a sharp knife to cut the shoots off at ground level when they are 13mm or more in diameter and before they reach 30cm high; any taller and they become fibrous and inedible. When preparing them, cut them lengthways, removing the leafy sheaths. New shoots grow rapidly, so check clumps daily.

Bamboos need little care and attention for maximum effect – just feed and water well during the growing season and keep them moist over winter. A little mulch in spring with well-rotted organic matter ensures a constant supply of new shoots.

BAMBOOS GOOD ENOUGH TO EAT

A LL BAMBOOS are edible but some are tastier than others. The sweetest are *Phyllostachys dulcis*, which reaches up to 12m, and *P. edulis*, which is slow to establish and usually smaller; both grow well in warmer parts of Britain. Others worth trying include *Phyllostachys angusta, P. aurea, P. aureosulcata, P. edulis* 'Heterocycla', *P. nigra* 'Henonis', *P. rubromarginata, P. viridiglaucescens, Pleioblastus hindsii, Pseudosasa japonica, Yushania anceps* and *Y. maculata*. Some, like *Phyllostachys vivax* and *Semiarundinaria fastuosa*, are bitter and need boiling for up to twenty minutes to make them edible.

FARMING IN THE TROPICS

Sustainable cultivation

The people who live and grow their foodstuffs in the rainforest are part of the ecosystem: the rainforest looks after them, and they look after the rainforest. It is their habitat as well as their home. There is spiritual respect and understanding of the forest, too, and often tradition locates their gods among the plants and animals, which they perceive as interdependent with themselves.

Rainforests easily support small numbers of indigenous village people, once they have cleared the land using either traditional slash-and-burn or the shifting-cultivation technique. The farmers will plant the cleared area with sweet potato, maize, peanut or cassava, harvest their crops, then simply move on when the soil loses its fertility, leaving the rainforest to reclaim the space. In Africa, clearing the land is a community effort, and families also help one another with the subsequent sowing. Cultivating the land provides a constant supply of food, some to feed the family and the rest to be sold in the local market. It is more reliable than harvesting from the rainforest, where the best plants may have already been taken, or eaten by animals, and you can reduce your chance of contact with poisonous snakes and spiders. If plants *are* harvested from the wild, a few fruits should always be left to develop into seedlings, so as to maintain sustainable cropping.

This philosophy is the same all around the world. Cultivating on a specific patch means that you have more control over the growing environment, you can inspect your plants regularly for pests and diseases, and you can feed and water them for optimum production. In many parts of the world, horticultural knowledge is passed on orally through the generations, and even when combined with Western techniques, problems may still arise. Indigenous people may find themselves being taught to sow at a certain date, rather than in response to weather conditions around that date; then, if the rains arrive late, the crops may fail.

Sowing in response to nature is one of the most important aspects of successful gardening. So although the seed packets will always specify certain sowing dates, use them as a guideline only. Gardeners often talk of an 'early' or 'late' spring, thus acknowledging, in fact, that sowing times are variable. If the packet says 'sow in March' but there's excessive rain that month and unusually low temperatures, be flexible. Seeds sown in cold, wet soils will probably rot. Wait until the soil is warm and moist – it's amazing how rapidly crops will grow in ideal conditions – and any 'lost' weeks are soon recovered.

■ Terracing

Terracing land to create workable plots for cultivation is a practice that can be seen all over the world. It is an excellent way of cutting into steep landscapes and making a slope a more practical and usable space; and it doesn't have to be confined to agricultural usage.

In Eden's Outdoor Biome, the eco-engineering display demonstrates how the roots of willow and dogwood are used to bind and stabilize the terraced earth on the steeper parts of the pit

POPULAR TERRACE PLANTS

IN WEST AFRICA terraces are planted with trees such as *Calliandra calothyrsus*. A fast-growing individual, valued for its rapid regrowth, it has excellent potential as a source of sustainable firewood. It coppices readily, and in Indonesia it grows so rapidly that it can be harvested for fuel after one year. It is also an excellent fodder crop on poor land, a good source of nectar for bees, and the trees produce nitrogen in nodules on their roots, thus 'fixing' nitrogen in the soil. *Calliandra calothyrsus* also makes a wonderful pot-grown feature plant for warm conservatories, and looks spectacular in full bloom.

In sheltered parts of the British Isles gardeners have been successful with its relative *Albizia julibrissin*, which has similar pink powder-puff flowers and delicate leaves. Juvenile specimens grown from seed and planted in containers make an excellent feature in tropical planting schemes. In order to grow to maturity they need a sheltered, south-facing site on free-draining soil and as much sunshine as possible.

CLEARANCE SYSTEMS

The small-scale slash-and-burn and shifting-cultivation systems are both simple and productive; but on a large scale they destroy the rainforest. At a local level, an area of land is cleared of vegetation, tree roots are removed, it is dug and fertilized, then sown with crops. After a few years when the soil becomes impoverished and is left to be reclaimed, tree seedlings germinate and secondary forest takes over: this is a sustainable system. By contrast, once an area is cleared for commercial agriculture, which is unlikely to treat the forest or any other features of the environment sympathetically, the ensuing regeneration will be inadequate, and that patch of rainforest is lost for good.

(see p. 21). In the Humid Tropics Biome the same principle is demonstrated using vetiver grass (*Vetiveria zizanioides*), which can be found along the terrace edges of the alley cropping display (see Glossary). The theory behind this method of planting is that the plants' dense, thick roots, growing vertically, create a barrier rather like a thick, low underground hedge, which traps rain-washed soil. The roots' vertical structure also prevents them from impeding the growth of crops growing nearby. In their native habitat the vetiver leaves are used for making hats, baskets, mats and mulch, and the roots for handbags, blinds and screens and to provide fragrant oils for soaps.

Also on display is the agro-forestry taungya system, employed throughout the tropics to optimize land use while trees are being established. In a tiered production system, crops are planted among rows of new trees for several seasons, until there is not enough light filtering down for these secondary crops to survive, and the trees are then left to become a mature plantation. Shade-loving coffee and cocoa are grown beneath useful trees such as *Prunus africana*, used to treat prostate cancer. Eden only has space to demonstrate small terraces; in Africa they are much wider.

This system of intercropping can be applied to the domestic setting to optimize production. The spaces between slow-growing or tall crops can be used for fast-growing ones, such as lettuce, or those needing shade, such as spinach, or as seedbeds for plants such as brassicas, which can then be transplanted. Also called 'catch-cropping', it only works if there is enough moisture, nutrients and light for the secondary crops to thrive, though any moisture or nutrient problems can usually be solved by using the spaces between rows of deep-rooted crops so that the two lots of roots are at different levels; or you can space the plants a little further apart. Catch-cropping is a good method of growing fast-maturing vegetables like radish or cut-and-come-again crops that are sown and harvested before later tender crops such as tomatoes and sweetcorn are ready to be planted in their place.

The terracing exhibits at Eden were prepared in late winter; the soil was treated to a layer of green waste with added composted 'zoo poo' from herbivorous animals at Paignton Zoo – a similar recipe to that used in parts of Africa, where terraces are cleared of roots and weeds with a mattock, then fertilized with rotted animal manure which is thoroughly mixed into the soil.

A SENSE OF COMMUNITY

Until recently, every gardener on the globe was a steward of our plant heritage, saving seed for planting the following year and maintaining the world's biodiversity, a process that began in Neolithic times when crops were first domesticated. In the West, the mass-production of food and the need to transport it over long distances now dictate the direction of breeding programmes. Such programmes may be highly productive, producing crops suitable for harvesting by machine and for being flown across the world, but they lose quality and taste. Most such crops are hybrids, like the F1 (first-generation) seeds you see in the garden centre, and are bred for uniformity, vigour and high yield; new generations will not be identical to the parents if seed is saved and used the following year.

If we want to be able to enjoy crops that are as tender, tasty and disease resistant as possible, it is essential that the old varieties, that have been nurtured over many years and that, ideally, only have to travel as far as the kitchen, are conserved. The National Fruit Collection at Brogdale in Kent holds almost 4,000 different varieties of fruit that can be grown in the UK. In the case of major crops like wheat, maize and beans there are thousands of different types available across the world. It is these plants that provide the genetic material for future breeding, so it is essential they are not lost.

The main message we get from Asian gardeners is to do with the importance of understanding and learning from the forest: a respect for plants and for their environment in general is ingrained in their lifestyle, and this extends to respect for their fellow-man. In Thailand, Buddhist monks take schoolchildren out to learn about the rainforest. The community ethic is strong: young and old plant and harvest together, working as family and community units, and no one lacks for food.

Gardening together works in Bario, it works at Eden, and it can work for you. At Eden the staff draw much inspiration from the idea – at bulb-planting time, for instance, everyone lends a hand, gardeners and staff from the Foundation Building working together. Similarly, if a local charity or community gardening scheme needs help, you could be the one to volunteer. From the community Peace Gardens in Kosovo (to which Eden has contributed) to the Coriander Club for Bangladeshi women in London's East End, gardening helps and heals. It can be great therapy working alone, but working together is even better. We are all part of the global community: if we can share our passion and understanding about the importance of plants, then the world will benefit now and in the future.

A 'rondavel' is a structure used as temporary accommodation by African farmers tending their cattle and crops.

THE WARM
TEMPERATE BIOME

WELCOME TO THE MEDITERRANEAN

The pelargonium, seen here in its 'natural' South-African habitat, is also a popular garden plant in the Mediterranean.

With no blueprint or reference books to go by, and little past experience, Eden's horticulturists stepped out along the cutting edge to create the Warm Temperate Biome. Its aim was to create cameos of mediterranean plants and their habitats from around the globe. The mediterranean climate that lies within the warm temperate zones is home to myriad glorious plants as well as being beloved of holiday-makers. We are not talking, though, just about Europe's Mediterranean, but also about the world's other mediterranean regions – South Africa, western Australia, central Chile and parts of North America.

The warm temperate zones are incredibly seasonal and often experience cool wet winters and hot dry summers. The landscape suffers from poor soils and, in summer, from drought, scorching sun, even fire – but there are plants that revel even in that hostile environment. Shrubs tend to be more common than trees, and many have spines, or leaves that are waxy or evergreen, or grey so as to reflect the sunlight; others have aromatic leaves that discourage predators, or succulent ones that retain water.

Bulbs and annuals are also a major part of the natural flora; in some regions they avoid fire and drought by hiding in the sun-baked soil. When the rain eventually comes and softens the earth they spring into life again, creating nature's own flower festival in a billion brilliant blooms.

The Warm Temperate Biome is divided into distinct areas that represent the mediterranean regions'

main characteristic features. The arid displays with their low-growing shrubs, succulents, bulbs and colourful annuals contrast strikingly with the lush greenery of the Humid Tropics Biome; they also illustrate the link between the world's rainforests and the arid-tropical regions, soon to be represented at Eden by the Dry Tropics Biome, still in the early stages of construction.

Imagine the challenge of replicating natural habitats within the artificial environment of an indoor Biome! It requires meticulous attention to detail and constant care. In the Warm Temperate Biome there are cameo landscapes ranging from the Maquis – named after the hilly southern European landscape of prickly oak, juniper and broom – to California's

Sonoran Desert and the South African Fynbos, all growing within metres of vineyards and olive groves. There's a whole world of 'gardening' going on here, put together so skilfully that you just don't notice it! The extremes of the seasons and the varying availability of water affect both the farming techniques and the range of plants in the warm temperate zones, so this too is represented in the Biome. Most botanic gardens display mediterranean exhibits to reflect the natural cycle of the native habitat, with bulbs, annuals and orchard blossom flowering in the spring followed by a partial resting period in the summer and a reappearance of blooms in the autumn. For the benefit of its visitors, at Eden horticultural techniques are used to expand some of these seasons.

The challenge is to maintain healthy plants that look as they would in the wild, without their appearance being changed by overfeeding, overwatering or the low light levels that encourage spindly growth, particularly in winter. The only way to create the natural look is by using a technique that Peter Thoday, one of Eden's first horticultural directors, has described as 'covert management'. This entails much discreet trimming and pruning. Without it, plants in the Biome would grow larger than in the wild because they are not being grazed – they would also grow longer and thinner because of the lower light. Presenting nature as it is in the wild often requires a delicate compromise. Take an area like the Californian valley grassland, where the annual flowering season only lasts from March to May each year. Clearly, visitors to Eden don't want to see nothing but arid landscape for nine months of the year, so, for the benefit and education of all, the horticulturists extend the flowering season until early autumn.

■ Creating and maintaining the mediterranean garden

In the Warm Temperate Biome there is only 75cm of manufactured soil, then a layer of heavy clay. The manufactured soil suffers from 'capping' – a common problem indoors or out in soils with poor structures and a high proportion of fine sand, clay or silt with small particles that become closely packed together. When the surface dries out, it forms a solid barrier so that water runs off it rather than soaking in. This may cause additional problems at seed-sowing time: the

seeds are put into moist soil, and as the ground dries it becomes so hard that the seedlings cannot grow through it, suffer from oxygen starvation and slowly rot. Happily, there's a simple solution – already mentioned in other contexts – which is to improve the soil structure before sowing by adding well-rotted organic matter or green waste. Mediterranean plants need free-draining soil, so grit or sharp sand should be added to heavy or poorly structured soils.

One advantage that domestic gardens have over the Warm Temperate Biome is that humidity and condensation are less of a problem, unless you are gardening in a particularly cold area and bring plants into the greenhouse over the winter. Mediterranean plants particularly dislike the combination of damp and cold, so ventilation is vital to reduce the likelihood of such problems as powdery mildew (see p. 300) and grey mould (see p. 308).

One of the advantages of a Biome over an outdoor garden is that cultural conditions can be controlled. There are no problems with frost or wind damage or periods of drought, so plants automatically look greener, healthier and tidier than they would in the wild.

At Eden, many of the plants bought from nurseries were too lush when they arrived, so to make them look more natural they were put on a water-deprivation diet; but it soon became clear that this would only create poor-quality specimens, so the gardeners changed tack and watered well; then, once the plants were established, the watering was reduced. In the wild, roots penetrate considerable depths in search of water; to replicate this process, garden, house and potted plants should all be

IT'S ALL IN THE DETAIL

O NE OF THE REASONS why the 'natural' areas in the Warm Temperate Biome are so successful is that they replicate the individual habitats in minute detail, even down to the pebble sizes and the colour of the sand. In the display representing the Fynbos – areas in South Africa characterized by nutrient-poor soil and home to a range of evergreen, fire-prone trees and shrubs – bulbs such as *Amaryllis belladonna* burst through charcoal-covered ground littered with 'smouldering' twigs and 'glowing embers' – the effect produced by red glitter – to remind visitors of the impact of fire on the landscape. Also in this Biome, the use of sand, gravel, limestone, slate and granite reflects the colour and form of what is found in each region. For instance, smaller rocks, stones and particles are mixed and scattered randomly over a given area until a natural density is reached. (Stored weathered granite becomes brittle and is perfect, when ground down, for creating a sandy effect.)

This attention to detail begins with an understanding of the habitats that are being created and of what grows where. Glen Leishman, the horticultural supervisor of this Biome, visits many parts of the world with a mediterranean climate including south-western USA, the Cape region in South Africa, Sardinia, the Côte d'Azur in France, Cephalonia in Greece, Morocco and Almeria in Spain, an arid region famed for its horticulture. He takes photos, makes notes, talks to local growers and studies landscapes and terracing styles. Like all Eden investigators, he attempts to absorb every element – noting how plants are naturally grouped, the shape of stones used for terracing, how the terracing follows the landscape, and so on.

CAPPING

WHEN SOWING SEEDS in a soil that is prone to developing a thin, hard surface, keep it moist by regular watering using a can with a fine rose. This softens the 'cap' so seedlings can grow through. In certain circumstances a cap can be a minor advantage, as it prevents weed seedlings from germinating too.

watered thoroughly at the base around the roots so that the soil is soaked, encouraging them to search for water at a greater depth.

Remember that drought-tolerant plants sometimes will need watering. In outdoor gardens this can mean occasional supplementary watering during dry periods, particularly of containers in summer, and in the Warm Temperate Biome the artificial environment makes it an even more crucial job. All areas are watered with a sprinkler for about two hours once a week or once a fortnight, depending on temperature and the amount of light entering the Biome; at the height of summer, the frequency can increase to twice a week. Just as in an outdoor garden, tobacco, grains and other cultivated crops need regular watering when in growth and particularly when flowering and developing their fruit or seeds. Every other day is the norm, but sunshine and temperature may dictate up to twice a day.

Plants are pruned to keep them within their allotted space, to encourage flowers and fruit, to remove damaged, weak or diseased stems and to ensure that they develop into healthy specimens. In most cases, plants that are being pruned so as to balance their shape should be fed with general fertilizer, watered, then mulched, to help them recover from the effects of the secateurs. Crops and plants in the mediterranean courtyard garden need feeding more often than those in the natural areas that are used to growing in impoverished conditions. In general, in most parts of Britain, feeding with general fertilizer should be halted from mid-August onwards, as new growth doesn't have time to ripen sufficiently before the first autumn frosts.

THE WOODLAND

The Warm Temperate Biome covers a huge swathe of the Mediterranean, replicating many key conditions and areas and encompassing a huge variety of plantings and plants.

Within this Biome, one area replicates a Mediterranean woodland. Few examples of this, the region's natural vegetation, remain, because human activity has modified the landscape over thousands of years. Trees have been felled for timber and firewood or cleared for crops, and the landscape that we now consider to be natural was in fact artificially created.

The two main Mediterranean types of vegetation – the Maquis (French) or Macchia (Italian – or Corsican, to be precise) and the Garrigue (the name of an area of low scrubland in the South of France) – are both displayed in this Biome. Both habitats contain unique plants, insects and reptiles but their importance is underestimated, and conservationists find it difficult to generate public interest because they lack the wow! factor of the tropical landscape.

BELOW: *The Maquis is a colourful tangle of shrubs containing many herbs and ornamental garden plants.*

THE MEDITERRANEAN CISTUS

AMONG THE MOST RELIABLE plants in the Biome is the cistus, which is everything that an Eden horticulturist could want: fast-growing, pest- and disease-free, and it flowers throughout the first half of the year. Many of the original plants were imported from Spanish nurseries as rooted cuttings, then grown on in the nursery at Watering Lane. Now that they are established, they are producing seed which the gardeners collect. The combination of plants from different locations ensures genetic variation within the Eden population, so they are of all different shapes and sizes, just as they would be in the wild.

■ The Maquis

The Maquis display at Eden is a dense tangle of small evergreen trees and shrubs found particularly along south- or south-west-facing coasts, and is a landscape that is partially man-managed and can grow into woods if not grazed. The French Resistance movement during the Second World War was known as the 'Maquis', because its members hid out in this almost impenetrable habitat.

Most of the plants found in the Maquis are evergreen with thick, waxy, leathery, hairy or aromatic leaves, including many familiar garden plants such as the dwarf fan palm, the strawberry tree, bay, myrtle, rock rose, tree heather, rosemary and broom. There are also many bulbs such as *Narcissus tazetta* subspecies *lacticolor*, the bright-blue Armenian grape hyacinth (*Muscari armeniacum*) and the rock tulip (*Tulipa saxatilis*) with its pink to lilac flowers.

All of the plants in this area recover rapidly from fire, particularly *Arbutus unedo* and *Erica arborea*, which sprout from the base within weeks of the tops being destroyed. The *Arbutus unedo* is a form of strawberry tree which has an unusual distribution, being found both in the Mediterranean and in southern Ireland! It boasts a spectacular brown flaking bark and has lily-of-the-valley shaped flowers. The round red-and-yellow fruit are edible, but beware! – *unedo* can be translated as 'I only eat one', and the fruits are distilled in Portugal to make 'fire water'! Although it is acid-loving it will tolerate an alkaline soil; the cultivar 'Elfin King' is an attractive and unusual tree for smaller gardens, reaching only 2m high by 1.5m wide.

The garden snapdragon (Antirrhinum majus), a native of the Mediterranean, grows in rocky nooks and crannies on cliffs and old buildings.

■ The Garrigue

The Garrigue is a community of mainly aromatic dwarf shrubs (rarely more than 0.5m high), with colourful flowers, that is dominant on drier soils. Because it is more open than the Maquis, the ground in the Garrigue is covered with a host of smaller annuals, orchids and bulbs – particularly in spring.

The Eden display contains a selection of bulbs that would happily grow outdoors in a garden, including the giant snowdrop, *Galanthus elwesii*, with flowers up to 3cm long; the polyanthus narcissus (*Narcissus tazetta*), each stem bearing up to twenty sweetly scented flowers, white with a yellow cup; the yellow-flowered wild tulip (*Tulipa sylvestris*), and the glorious crown anemone (*Anemone coronaria*) that bears flowers from pink to red and lavender to purple. Many familiar garden plants can also be found in the Garrigue, including the cotton lavender

(*Santolina chamaecyparissus*) and the yellow-flowered Jerusalem sage (*Phlomis fruticosa*); the tree heather (*Erica arborea*), which is covered in delicious honey-scented flowers – and bees – in the summer; the clump-forming dwarf fan palm (*Chamaerops humilis*), which is hardy, low-growing and produces several stems; and the myrtle (*Myrtus communis*) – with its aromatic evergreen foliage and clouds of creamy-white flowers from mid- to late summer. The Warm Temperate Biome also houses a range of rock-rose hybrids (*Helianthemum* species) with

brightly coloured flowers from pink to orange, and broom (*Cytisus scoparius*) such as 'Cornish Cream' – another with beautiful white flowers. For gardeners creating a mediterranean look, there's a wonderful choice when it comes to selecting the most appropriate plants and garden features. For a constant supply of short-lived flowers in mid-summer, be sure to include several cistus, or sun roses, in your garden; the flowers might not hang around for very long, but they are still worth having. A particularly good variety is *Cistus ladanifer*, the gum cistus, with its wonderfully fragrant 'gum'.

Many commonly used kitchen herbs come from the Garrigue, among them basil, garlic, hyssop, lavender, oregano, rosemary, sage, savory and thyme. Rosemary and bay (*Laurus nobilis*), from the Maquis, can be trimmed into globes or pyramids. Although herb gardens are traditionally formal, they also lend themselves well to the naturalistic Mediterranean-border style – you can harvest some of the herbs, and leave the rest to flower.

Herbs are happiest in an open location on free-draining soil – a sun-baked bank is ideal – and in summer they fill the air with bewitching fragrances, so make sure your herb garden is sited near a patio or a bench. For the best flavour, grow Mediterranean herbs hard – don't feed them (unless they are in containers) or overwater them – and don't water before harvesting as it dilutes the oils. Also, always harvest herbs early in the morning before their essential oils evaporate in the sunshine; and even if you are not actually using the crops, trim the plants regularly to keep them compact and encourage the regrowth of young aroma-filled shoots.

TERRACES AND OLIVE GROVES

Fig trees flourish throughout the Mediterranean; the seeds are dispersed by birds so the trees are found in the most inhospitable of locations.

Perhaps two of the sights most reminiscent of the Mediterranean are terraces cut into the hillsides and groves of silvery olive trees. As the Warm Temperate Biome is on a sloping site, it's perfect for demonstrating the effectiveness of terracing, and the principles behind it make it a form of landscaping that can be easily adapted to a smaller, sloping garden (although the cost of construction, without a supply of free building materials, can be extremely high).

As mentioned earlier, terracing has been traditionally used for centuries to make steeply sloping land accessible and to retain soil for cultivation and block run-off water so that it soaks into the ground, thereby preventing soil erosion. Terracing is practised all over the world, from southern Europe's olive groves and the vegetable plots tended on steep Madeiran hillsides, to Incan dry-stone walls. Terraces are usually constructed from the most freely available natural material – stones. A dry-stone retaining wall allows excess water to flow horizontally through the stones and drain away. Olives are often grown on terraces in mountainous areas. Once underplanted with cereals, traditional olive groves are now more likely to be the habitat of a shrubby, species-rich flora, supporting more wildlife such as insects, reptiles, birds and bats than a pine forest. Olives can be grown successfully in the UK, but are hardy outdoors only in milder areas; one of the oldest outdoor specimens grows at the Chelsea Physic Garden in London.

As they are relatively undemanding – even in Britain – they are becoming increasingly popular as container plants (they are available at the Eden shop, under an initiative to sell plants produced in local nurseries). If you live in a frost-prone area and you do decide to try your luck with an olive, grow it in a container so that you can easily move it into the greenhouse over winter – it must be cool and frost-free – preferably at a temperature above 10°C. Water it sparingly over that period. In early spring, when plenty of roots are starting to show on the outside of the rootball, repot it into a container two sizes larger, using John Innes No. 2 compost plus 20 per cent bark chips or horticultural grit to improve drainage. Also in spring, cut back new shoots to four or five leaves, or the main shoots to an outward-growing replacement. Once you're sure there will be no more frosts, stand the plant outside in a sheltered, sunny spot throughout the summer, feeding weekly with general fertilizer. The tree will need pruning during this season, to maintain a balanced shape. Flowers will appear on the young wood; shake the whole tree to simulate wind pollination or hand-pollinate with a soft paintbrush.

The fig (*Ficus carica*) is another Mediterranean classic that has been grown for centuries for both food and shade. It can be grown in a sunny, frost-free spot in a British garden, and will fruit well in the right conditions. Gardeners often train figs into fan shapes against a hot, sunny wall, then let them become overgrown. So to get the best from them do carry on pruning! Take out around one-third of the old wood every three years in April, cutting back to young branches or removing old wood completely, then thin out the weakest new shoots the following year to create a new, vigorous framework.

Some fig cultivars can be grown successfully in pots to keep them under control. Good varieties include 'Osborne's Prolific', 'Rouge de Bordeaux' and 'White Marseilles'. Start young plants in 30cm clay pots in John Innes No. 3 compost. Plant them with the stem buried 5cm deep. Feed your figs with a high-potash fertilizer every week from April, and foliar-feed with liquid seaweed. Water when growth starts – increasing the amount as leaf growth increases. Move them into larger pots and allow them to grow to any size, as long as you are happy you can still move the pot to a frost-free environment in the winter.

UNDERPLANTING OLIVE TREES

IN ADDITION TO WOODY HERBS such as sage and thyme, the ground beneath the olive trees at Eden is dotted with bulbs. These include the golden-yellow goblets of *Sternbergia lutea*, the white to pale-pink ivy-leafed sowbread (*Cyclamen hederifolium*) and the yellow *Narcissus jonquilla*, one of the sweetest-scented of all plants, from autumn to spring. Many shrubs also grow well underneath the olive canopy, including the fragrant gum cistus (*Cistus ladanifer*). Sub-shrubs such as the intermediate periwinkle (*Vinca difformis*), with gorgeous pale-mauve flowers, like a sheltered sunny spot, as do biennials such as the woolly-stemmed spires of great mullein (*Verbascum thapsus*) and annuals including the pink-flowered corncockle (*Agrostemma githago*). Most of these can be grown in warmer parts of the UK.

ABOVE: *The orchard is spangled with wild flowers that bloom and set seed in spring before the onset of the hot, dry summer.*

FACT!

Saffron (*Crocus sativus*), which is cultivated in most countries around the Mediterranean through to Kashmir and China, used to be grown in Cornwall, the Cotswolds and Chipping Walden, later renamed Saffron Walden. It is used in liqueurs, notably Chartreuse, for colouring rice, and in paella. It is also used medicinally as a mild sedative, and is rich in vitamin B.

THE ORCHARD

Loquats (*Eriobotrya japonica*) and kiwi fruit (*Actinidia chinensis*) from China, apricots from Iran and sweet almonds from the Middle East have moved to the European Mediterranean and to California to soak up the sun – and the water from the irrigation lines. Mediterranean almonds are now one of the most important nuts in world trade. The peach 'Red Haven' (a commercial variety), apricots, and the nectarine 'Fantasy' are displayed in a Mediterranean orchard in the Warm Temperate Biome, underplanted with wild flowers and bulbs.

Not all of these fruits find conditions in the Biome to their liking. The almonds have struggled and been generally unhappy, possibly because they could not adapt to the light levels; they have produced few flowers and no fruit, despite being pollinated by hand. The apricots, now being replaced by a dwarf variety of peach, have had a hard time of it too, but the nectarines and the yellow-fleshed, self-fertile 'Red Haven' are thriving.

Even in Britain you can grow your own crop of peaches. Plant them in containers of well-drained compost in the greenhouse, or put them outside for the summer when there's no danger of frost. In the warmer parts of Britain, varieties like the white-fleshed 'Peregrine', which ripens in August, and 'Rochester', the best all-rounder, can be grown as a fan against a south-facing wall or as a free-standing tree. Try the nectarine 'Lord Napier' with its well-flavoured white flesh, or the reliable 'John Rivers', in a sheltered position outdoors. Peaches prefer to be grown in free-draining soil that is neutral to alkaline. Protect outdoor plants from peach-leaf curl by using a ventilated frame covered with polythene to keep off the rain, which may carry the spores, or spray with copper fungicide at leaf fall – around the end of January to mid-February. Water well while the fruit are developing, to prevent them splitting. Dwarf peaches and nectarines are ideal for growing in containers of soil-based compost such as John Innes No. 2. The peach 'Bonanza' ripens from early to mid-July, 'Garden Lady' is deep yellow, and the nectarine 'Nectrella' is similar to 'Bonanza', producing full-size fruits if you thin the crop.

■ Bulbs

At Eden in spring, the orchard bursts into blossom and the haze of fresh green grass at the foot of the trees is spangled with colour as *Tulipa sylvestris*, *Tulipa turkestanica* and *Tulipa saxatilis* emerge to brighten the lengthening days alongside the blue, white, red and pink of borage, camomile, poppy and corn cockle. These species of bulbs are dainty and small, unlike their bolder cousins, and most thrive in sun and free-draining soil. *Tulipa sylvestris*, a native of Britain and Europe, has bright-yellow sweetly scented flowers, *Tulipa turkestanica* boasts clusters of bright white stars with yellow centres and *Tulipa saxatilis* is a delicious pink-lilac, another *Tulipa marjoletti* (not in the display) is cream with a purple flush on the outside. They are perfect for smaller gardens, or naturalized in rough low-growing grass. Plant them in groups to be viewed from above or in pots and window boxes at eye level, to appreciate their finer points.

Across the Warm Temperate Biome, over forty species of mediterranean bulbs have been planted,

BUY CULTIVATED BULBS

COLLECTING WILD BULBS IS permitted in Turkey, though controlled by an export quota system. Every March a committee meets to decide the quotas and the number of CITES permits to be allocated for the year. To offer an alternative to this practice, village cooperatives grow hundreds of kilos of the bulbs of the snowdrop *Galanthus elwesii*, on steeply sloping terraces. They are sponsored by a non-governmental organization, the Indigenous Propagation Project of Threatened Turkish Bulbs (IPP). During the harvest, smaller bulbs are saved and replanted to provide the following year's crop. Eden wholeheartedly supports this conservation project in its effort to reduce the gathering of wild plants. It is bulbs cultivated in Turkey that are planted in the Warm Temperate Biome. Turkey is still one of the main suppliers of collected wild bulbs; over half of them die before they reach the garden centres of Europe. 'Passing off' is a common practice whereby wild bulbs are grown on for a year, then labelled 'Grown in Holland'. Check the *Good Bulb Guide* for nurseries that are committed to importing only cultivated bulbs, and buy yours from reliable sources.

At Eden, larger plants and trees are moved using a fork-lift truck – planting can be quite a challenge and takes several members of staff.

Cyclamen look great planted with snowdrops and crocus, but they have a tendency to swamp their companions with their vigour. You can extend their flowering season by planting *Cyclamen coum*, *Cyclamen repandum* and *Cyclamen pseudibericum* to flower in spring, and *Cyclamen purpurascens* for summer colour.

■ Trees

Transplanting large or mature specimens is a tremendous challenge, and the horticulturists at Eden have had more experience than most! Some of the plants in the indoor Biomes weighed several tonnes – but an instant impact was called for, so there was no alternative but to choose large ones. When considering trees for your garden, ponder carefully the cost, planting access and aftercare. As mentioned earlier, it is also important with all deep cultivation to know the location and depth of such things as electricity cables and gas pipes, to avoid any problems.

In the Warm Temperate Biome, trees imported from Europe helped to establish an 'instant' landscape – among them cork oaks, Italian cypresses and ancient olive trees, including some from Sicily that had reached the end of their productive life. Introducing mature trees, particularly ancient olives, poses several problems. For a start, they often go dormant for two or more years after planting so it's difficult to tell whether the transplant has been successful.

If your budget and access won't stretch to mature specimens, there are many smaller ones available that will establish themselves rapidly. But do remember to check the ultimate height and spread when purchasing a tree for a small garden, and be sure there is sufficient space for it to reach its full glory. And choose a variety with several seasonal features. Don't plant trees near walls, close to the house where they can cause loss of light, or directly under telephone or electric cables. If you do plant a larger species where space is limited, treat it as a temporary pleasure and fell it once it has outgrown its allotted space – and before it causes problems.

DEFRA legislation requires that imported plants that have not been grown in nurseries be 'root-washed' before planting, to prevent the introduction and possible spread of pests or diseases that may be in the soil around the roots. This is of no benefit to the plant – it's more likely to be detrimental – but it satisfies plant health legislation.

At Eden, this procedure takes place in the nursery. The trees are suspended over a collection tank from a forklift and the soil is slowly washed away for later disposal using a powerful jet of water. Once the job is done, they are rapidly repotted to prevent the remaining roots from drying out and further reducing the chances of survival. The plants have already suffered the shock of being dug from the ground, pruned, transported, then having their smaller, fibrous roots removed during the washing process. To help them recover from the trauma, they are potted into a special compost mix and given plenty of TLC. Plants that have gone through these import procedures are very vulnerable to overwatering, particularly in winter, so the aim is to establish them as soon as possible.

Some react badly. At Eden, several Italian cypresses (*Cupressus sempervirens*) survived until they were planted in the Biome, then slowly died; and some mature cork oaks have struggled too. The long-term impact on these and on the olives is still being assessed. The olives seem to be faring better than the oaks as previous experience suggests they are lying dormant and may suddenly burst into life. The solution to all of this, as in the Humid Tropics

IMPORTING PLANTS

The Department for the Environment, Food and Rural Affairs (DEFRA) imposes restrictions on gardeners relating to cultivated plants that can be brought into Britain. This legislation also encompasses plants that are controlled by the Convention on International Trade in Endangered Species (CITES) which protects plants under threat. The most common question that people tend to ask is: Which plants can I bring back from my holiday? Check the DEFRA website for current details. It is vital that potentially disastrous pests and diseases, as well as invasive plants, are not introduced into Britain. Plants imported to Eden arrive with all the necessary documentation.

Biome, is to grow most of the plants from seed and transplant smaller specimens.

Some plants will be unable to reach their full mature glory in the Biomes because of the limited space. The stone pine (*Pinus pinea*) is one example. It's a classic mediterranean tree, traditionally planted for its style and shade. It grows rapidly, creating an early sense of maturity and releasing a delightful resinous aroma. It has a beautifully patterned bark and an elegant, rounded crown (hence its name 'umbrella pine'). Because of its eventual size, it is only suitable for parks and large gardens. Eden's specimens will eventually become too large for the Biome and have to be felled, around ten years old, because they cannot be pruned without losing their shape. The gardeners at Eden always have smaller plants growing nearby to take the place of such casualties. The stone pine was introduced into Britain by the Romans for its edible seeds, which taste a bit like almonds. They are eaten raw, and used in sweets, cakes and savoury dishes – they are the 'pine nuts' that you buy for Mediterranean cooking.

THE STAR PLANTS

Near to the entrance of the Warm Temperate Biome, behind wrought-iron gates, is a display recreating a typical Mediterranean courtyard garden that is packed with plants from around the globe. There are familiar ones from South Africa such as agapanthus, pelargoniums and clivia; sweetly scented *Pittosporum tobira* from China, Japan and Korea, hibiscus from China and bougainvillea from South America. These plants flower profusely all year round, though they go through a quieter period in January and February when the light is at its lowest, during which time ornamental peppers are timed to give a temporary display of colour.

Agapanthus are ideal plants for containers, especially in cooler climates or where gardens are prone to waterlogging in winter. Tender evergreen species such as *A. africanus* can be planted singly in 20–22cm pots of John Innes No. 2 or 3 compost, then left undisturbed for a few years. Ignore the oft-received wisdom that they should be kept pot-bound to improve flowering, and repot them in spring when necessary. They will also appreciate a feed with high-potash fertilizer every one or two weeks in the growing season, just until the buds begin to colour. Over winter place them in a sheltered, frost-free part of the garden, preferably under the rain shadow of a wall, or keep them in a bright, frost-free greenhouse or conservatory. Keep them cool at this time – winter warmth can reduce flowering the following year. If you are planting them out in the garden they need an open, sunny spot in free-draining soil enriched with well-rotted organic matter. Evergreen agapanthus are more tender than the hardier deciduous varieties, surviving the British winter only in milder locations, unless given protection.

Bougainvillea is perfect for creating that exotic look in a conservatory, but won't be happy outside except on hot summer days. It needs bright light and produces more blooms after a cool winter rest, but let temperatures drop too far and it will take a long time to recover in spring. Keep the compost just moist in winter, and if the leaves fall, reduce watering further. Allow as many main stems to grow as possible – cutting them back to the chosen height encourages flowering sideshoots. Cut these back to two buds in late winter to keep the plants under control.

Pittosporum (*P. tobira*) is not frost-hardy, so it's suitable outdoors only in milder areas. Grow it in soil-based compost and reduce watering in winter for a healthy, happy plant. It can stand outdoors on the patio in summer as long as there is no danger of frost.

Clivias (*C. miniata*) are popular and easy-to-grow house or conservatory plants with bright-orange flowers and deep-green strap-like leaves. They need repotting only when they are severely pot-bound, and then into a container just one size larger, using a peat-substitute-based compost. Keep them in bright light, away from full sun, feed with liquid fertilizer monthly in summer, and water well. Look out for *Clivia miniata* var. *citrina*, with its clear, pale-yellow flowers.

Vireya rhododendrons, less familiar to today's gardeners, originate in the cloud forests of East Asia, New Guinea, parts of Indonesia and the

ABOVE: *Agapanthus make a bold statement when planted in drifts, yet individual flowers are beautiful and delicate.*

RIGHT: *Bougainvilleas viewed from an unusual angle show their brightly coloured bracts; the narrow tubular flowers are in the centre of the bloom.*

has a f

reticula

manda

limon

medic

grape

arose

The b

the of

tange

C

produ

chlor

most

Lemo

centu

conti

and

fruiti

in co

they

plac

frost

stan

nigh

sum

bak

wa

for

pre

dis

so

tra

WHEN PLANNING YOUR ROCK GARDEN, you probably don't intend to recreate the deserts of California (see p. 164) or the Little Karoo; what most gardeners have in mind is something resembling a tiny patch of the Alps. Whatever your inspiration, aim to create a natural-looking outcrop, not a pile of soil with stones sticking out. If you can, visit a mountainous habitat to see Nature's own rock gardens, and make detailed notes as they did when planning theirs at Eden. Rock gardens can include 'natural' cracks and fissures, screes, pools, streams, even miniature mountain tracks. The rocks should be buried to about one-third of their depth and follow the same line, or stratum, when they emerge from the ground as they would naturally. The planting pockets can be filled with acid or alkaline composts to suit a wide range of plants.

Choose your rocks carefully, in a range of sizes, as displayed in Eden's 'deserts'. Include a few of the largest you can possibly move (or afford), to make the garden look 'natural', but don't take rocks from the countryside or pebbles from the beach. Sandstone is cool and moisture-retentive, granite hard and dense, and shales disintegrate quickly. Don't buy weathered or river-washed limestone – it's unsustainable and comes from a threatened habitat. Take care when moving rocks: always wear gloves and safety footwear. Lift correctly by bending your knees, not your back. Work slowly, and stop for a while if you feel over-tired!

are open in the centre. They flower late in the year, in December and January, and the fruits ripen in late October and November.

◼ Drought-tolerant plants

The Little Karoo section at Eden replicates an area known as the 'succulent Karoo', a semi-desert region lying behind the southernmost coastal mountain range of South Africa that is dependent on winter rains of less than 25cm per year. Most of the plants here belong to the *Mesembryanthemum* family but there is a rich succulent and bulb flora too. A region of extremes, it bakes at 50°C in the summer, freezes in winter, and droughts are common.

In the Karoo display in the Biome, with its randomly placed boulders and rough stones, there are lots of succulents that are rarely watered (the annuals around them need more). The Little Karoo is

ROCK GARDENING

a very nutrient-poor area so the plants need very little food; those such as *Aloe ferox,* a beautiful succulent which forms a stem that eventually becomes a small 'tree', topped with a spiky crown of leaves, receive a little of the phosphate-free feed used for all of the South African plants, including the proteas.

Succulents make ideal container plants for the house and garden. At Eden you'll find several cultivated species including the penny plant (*Portulacaria afra*), which is sometimes grown as a houseplant, and *Cotyledon orbiculata* with its mealy grey-green leaves. In spring, repot plants into a pot one size larger, before they start growing, if needed. Most put on growth in summer. They should be soaked, then allowed to dry out before rewatering. When aloes such as Cape aloe need water, they turn pink and red and the leaf tips turn brown, and when they become seriously dry the leaves start to shrivel. Plants in pots will need watering more regularly, about once a week in summer.

Aloes need winter protection indoors but can go outdoors in summer. They need feeding with specialist cactus and succulent fertilizer or half-strength tomato fertilizer at every watering – about every one or two weeks in summer. Keep succulents at temperatures up to 10°C in winter, giving them just enough water to prevent dehydration; with only a little water, they will tolerate lower temperatures. Grow them in a specialist cactus and succulent compost or a 3:1 mix of John Innes No. 3 and horticultural grit. For plants younger than two years old, use John Innes No. 2. You'll also find the pink-flowered *Veltheimia capensis* in the Little Karoo – this makes an excellent pot plant for a cool windowsill.

CHRISTMAS GIFT FOR ALOES

THE DISPLAYS MAY MIMIC what is happening in the wild, but the staff are more generous with water than nature is – giving the plants enough to make them look healthy, not parched. Some, such as the Cape aloe (*Aloe ferox*), flower over Christmas, so towards this time and during flowering they are watered once or twice a week, depending on the amount of light they are receiving. They are watered carefully at the base because the flowers are prone to fungal growth; watering is decreased with the onset of summer.

THE FYNBOS

RIGHT: *The buds of* Protea cynaroides, *found in the Fynbos, demonstrate nature's Fibonacci spiral.*

The name Fynbos, from fyn bosch, the Afrikaans word for 'fine bush', refers to the evergreen, fire-prone shrubs that grow on the poor, acid, sandy soils stretching in a narrow band for 46,000sqkm either side of the Cape, at the southern tip of Africa. This plant community has been fire-managed for conservation since the 1960s. Here, one species rarely dominates: a single patch of vegetation may contain a mix of plants including reed-like restios, the bold-flowered proteas, fine-leafed ericas, pelargoniums and gladioli – the diversity in a small area can be spectacular, and over 120 species have been counted in one 10sqm plot.

Pelargoniums make excellent house, greenhouse or summer garden plants, and a huge range is available from specialist nurseries. *Pelargonium triste*, the first to arrive in Britain, in 1630, has fern-like leaves and creamy-yellow flowers with tiny purple blotches, and is night-fragrant with a rich scent of cloves. *Pelargonium echinatum* has spiny stems, silvery leaves and bright white flowers with red hearts on the upper petals; *Pelargonium panduriformew* displays massive balsam-scented leaves; *P. cordifolium* produces large, grey, lemon-scented leaves that curl up if it is too dry, and *P. grandiflorum* has large white flowers.

To get the best from pelargoniums, give them a bright, sunny position in John Innes No. 2, with added grit to improve drainage. Feed them weekly through the summer with a high-potash fertilizer like tomato fertilizer, to encourage flowering, and dead-head regularly to prolong the display. Avoid high-nitrogen products, or you'll have lots of foliage at the expense of flowers. One thing they can't tolerate is being over-watered. Water a little in spring, at the start of the growing season, increasing the amount until they are in full growth, then water only when the compost surface dries out. (See p. 175 for scented-leaf varieties.) Protect from frost.

The wiry-stemmed restios are characteristic Fynbos plants; their shallow root systems enable them to thrive in poor soils, from dry slopes to marshes. Soils in the Fynbos areas are generally moist but free-draining, poorly formed and low in phosphates. Restios have recently been touted in Britain as the latest trendy plant but they have yet to fully capture the public imagination – which may be no bad thing, if they are to survive their fashionable status to become established garden plants. These elegant architectural evergreens look spectacular grouped in borders or as container-grown specimens. Their growth habit varies. Some look like dark giant sedges; *Chondropetalum tectorum*, the thatching reed, forms attractive, fast-growing clumps of slender foliage about 1.5m tall, and produces dark, grass-like flowers in autumn. *Elegia capensis* resembles a giant horsetail and grows to about 2m high; it has short, wiry 'branches' surrounding the leaf joints, and golden-brown flowerheads in spring. It makes excellent foliage for floral displays. *Rhodocoma gigantea* has arching feathery foliage on 3m stems.

Most of these plants are fast-growing and drought-tolerant, once established; growth is increased by watering in summer, though most of their growth is formed in autumn and spring, so feed them with general slow-release fertilizer and avoid high-potash feeds. They need an open, sunny position with

DIVERSITY IN THE FYNBOS

PLANTS IN THE FYNBOS present four different growth forms: tall broad-leafed shrubs such as proteas, small heath-like shrubs including ericas, the unique restios, and bulbs, which only appear during the winter resting season. The first three, as well as pelargoniums and bulb species including nerines, gladioli and *Amaryllis belladonna*, are to be found in the wet Fynbos. Plus the popular garden calla lily (*Zantedeschia aethiopica*) and *Watsonia coccinea*, which, if you decide to try them in your garden, need a sheltered, moist, sunny position.

good air circulation. Plant in very free-draining, acidic, moisture-retentive soil, and incorporate well-rotted organic matter into the planting hole. Mulch well in spring, and again in autumn if necessary, to retain moisture and protect the plants from frost. Some survive winter temperatures down to −12°C, but will benefit from being wrapped in horticultural fleece to protect them from frost.

■ The Fynbos fires

Hot, dry summers in the Fynbos result in fires every twelve to fifteen years. Although this might sound like disaster to us, in our cool temperate zone, fire in the Fynbos heralds new life: seeds are prompted to germinate, and the earth receives new supplies of nutrients.

Fine-branched, closely packed plants that retain dead plant debris and often have inflammable oils in the leaves make ideal kindling. The fires are usually caused either by lightning or by humans. Some shrubs, particularly proteas, have fire-resistant bark, and bulbs hide underground to avoid damage. After the fire has passed, the earth is

RIGHT: *Stunning ericas are found in many of the world's mediterranean landscapes. This plant,* Erica discolor, *is a native of South Africa.*

covered with warm ash. The seeds of the fire-resistant proteas and leucadendrons are the first to show signs of life, as their seedcoats start to break open; *Leucadendron rubrum* is one of the quickest to react, its seedcoats splitting within an hour or two of the fire.

The intensity of the fire determines which species germinate: some seeds need more intense heat, while others, once the vegetation cover has gone, respond to the higher daytime and lower night-time temperatures. Some bulbs and annuals are triggered into germination by the smoke. All of them relish their new-found space and the reduced competition for light, moisture and nutrients, especially during the first rainy season when the shrubs are more or less dormant – it takes them years to grow to their former size. The ashes of the burned shrubs and leaf litter release extra nutrients into the soil.

One of the main threats after fire is colonization by non-native tree species; the newly cleared landscape is also threatened by urban development, by more fires and by agricultural expansion.

At Eden, setting fire to the display isn't an option – any more than it is in your own garden – so plants are dug up and divided or replaced instead.

■ Plants of the Fynbos

The Fynbos is home to 740 of the world's 860 species of ericas, or heaths; in Britain there are only six. Most South African ericas are absolute giants compared to the garden forms we know here, with both larger stems and larger flowers. There are several to be seen in the Biome. *Erica discolor* has striking pink flowers that are 2cm long with green tips; and *Erica verticillata,* believed to be extinct in the wild, has mauve-pink blooms 1.5cm long. All of these can be grown in a conservatory or outdoors in warmer climates and are available from specialist nurseries.

Other good heaths for the garden include *Erica ciliaris* 'David McClintock' (a Dorset heath), which has mauve-pink, white-tipped flowers backed by grey foliage; the cross-leafed heath, *Erica tetralix* 'Pink Star', which has lilac-pink flowers and grey-green foliage and flowers from June until October; and *Erica canaliculata*, which was introduced from South Africa – this one reaches up to 5.5m tall and has white or pink-tinted flowers, but is only suitable for a sheltered spot.

Perhaps the most famous plants from South Africa are the proteas, of which the Warm Temperate Biome has twelve different kinds, including the magnificent king protea (*Protea cynaroides*). There are also leucadendrons including the silver-leaced *Leucadendron argenteum* which are found in the wild only in the Cape peninsula but have been introduced elsewhere, and the leucospermum, or pincushion plant, with its extravagant flowers. All of these will grow in mild climates and can be grown under glass in containers and moved outside in the summer.

The rich bulb flora of the Fynbos emerges after fires, and includes gladiolus, nerine and amaryllis, the last two are outstanding garden plants, needing a sheltered, sunny position on free-draining soil in warmer climates. In cooler conditions they can be grown under glass.

Amaryllis belladonna looks spectacular when planted against the base of a sunny wall that replicates the hot, dry conditions of its natural habitat.

The true *Amaryllis belladonna* (rather than hippeastrum which is commonly called 'amaryllis') flowers in September and October, producing a cluster of up to ten trumpet-shaped, candy-pink flowers topping a stiff, slender stem. They thrive in full sun at the base of a sheltered south-facing wall, but warmth is more important than drought in encouraging flowers, so cover the clump with a pane of glass in dull summers to warm the soil. Plant them in well-drained soil with the bulb tips 10cm below ground in areas of hard frost. In autumn, soon after the flowers fade, bright-green strap-like leaves will appear; they will last until the summer, then die back, and can be removed in July. If you live in a frost-prone area, protect leaves with a layer of bracken, straw, leaf mould, conifer branches or cloches during winter; but if the frost cuts them back, they are usually self-replacing in spring. If the clumps become too large, divide them in late summer before flowering, but keep disturbance to a minimum.

Most Fynbos bulbs remain dormant in summer, then flower during the autumn rains. This is replicated at Eden by watering them so that they flower at the same time here as they do in their native habitat. Just a little water is given at first then the amount is increased as they start to grow. The bulbs in the Fynbos don't need fire to stimulate flowering, just plenty of light and warmth which they receive when the vegetation above has been burnt off. Some watsonias, spring-flowering in South Africa, will flower in autumn here. Some Fynbos bulbs are liquid-fed with seaweed fertilizer after flowering.

INTRODUCING NEW SPECIES

INTRODUCED SPECIES CAN CAUSE considerable problems: they are often more competitive, spreading more rapidly than the native flora, which lives within an established ecological balance. In Britain, such newcomers are the second most significant threat to our native plants – after habitat destruction – and most of them come from our gardens! In Scotland, over 60 per cent of non-native plants established in the wild are garden escapees. In Snowdonia over £45 million has been spent trying to eradicate *Rhododendron ponticum* – it is also a problem plant at Eden. Japanese knotweed, introduced in 1825 as a garden plant, chokes railway embankments and derelict land – it's difficult to stop a plant that can grow through concrete and tarmac! Oxford ragwort found the clinker beds of the railways to its liking and spread around Britain, and parrot's feather, Australian swamp stonecrop and other aquatic weeds choke British waterways and ponds.

Do not buy invasive species for your garden pond, or dispose of unwanted plants in the wild. With no natural predators and a helpful climate, some species can grow up to 20cm a day and cause ecological disasters.

SOUTH AFRICAN BULBS IN BRITAIN

SOME OF THE MOST DESIRABLE garden and greenhouse bulbs come from South Africa, and over seventy are represented in the Warm Temperate Biome. Freesia, dierama, crinum, watsonia, veltheimia, scadoxus, the nerine 'Haemanthus', gladioli and moraea are suitable for the garden or greenhouse depending on the variety and your location.

NAMAQUALAND

Namaqualand, 250 miles north of Cape Town, covers an area of some 440,000sqkm. It is known as the Red Desert because of the colour of its stones, and is at the drier end of the mediterranean climate spectrum. Divided in two by the Orange River, it is world-famous for the multicoloured carpet of annuals that spring up each year after the winter rains. Most of the components of this bright-blue, yellow, orange and white display belong to the *Compositae*, or daisy family – there are around 3,000 different species in the region, from over 100 families, which makes it at least four times richer than similar places in the rest of the world.

Namaqualand is home to a staggering 456 plant species that are so rare they are threatened with extinction. Seeds of these annuals lie dormant during the hot dry summer, then germinate, flower and produce more seed. They are temperature-specific, so different flowers germinate in different years, depending both on the temperature and the rains, thus taking it in turns to share the available water. Among the bulbs from this region are the turkey lily (*Gladiolus alatus*), only 15cm tall, with tiny bicoloured flowers of reddish-brown and an unusual lime-green 'tongue'; and the house or greenhouse bulb *Lachenalia elegans*, with its soft blue, pink or purple flowers.

The spring-flowering annuals of Namaqualand, whose vibrant colours are enhanced by blue skies and bright sunlight, come mainly from the daisy family.

Eden works in partnership with the Grootbos Private Nature Reserve – one of the leading centres for nature tourism in South Africa – who supply the seed for the Project's Namaqualand display from cultivated sources. This seed is sown annually, in late February.

At home you can grow many Namaqualand plants as half-hardy annuals in a finely raked seedbed on free-draining soil – from April onwards if the soil is warm enough and you're confident there will be no more frosts. Keep the soil moist, and thin out the seedlings as they appear, leaving the strongest behind to grow on. Plants from a hot,

ANNUALS IN THE WARM TEMPERATE BIOME

To MIMIC THE RAINFALL THAT encourages germination in the plants' natural habitat, the seedbed is watered intensively until the seedlings appear. This is essential because the soil surface dries out rapidly in the Biome, even early in the year. Once the seedlings are about 7.5cm high, watering is reduced so that they develop slowly. Flowering starts in April and lasts until early autumn, when the seed is collected and the spent plants removed. In their natural habitat the display of Namaqualand annuals lasts only a few weeks before the sun scorches them off; at Eden they are watered through the summer and last three or four times longer.

One of the problems facing the Eden horticulturists is the weed seeds from outside which are blown in through the vents, threatening to colonize both the Namaqualand and the Californian Desert display nearby. The fine sand provides perfect seedbeds for them to germinate. Staff tiptoe through the developing seedlings or reach in carefully from the perimeter, to remove the weeds by hand.

dry climate are ideal for a sunny south- or south-west-facing bank. Among the annuals you will find in the Namaqualand display are the golden-yellow *Ursinia cakilefolia*, the white-flowered *Dimorphotheca pluvialis*, *Dorotheanthus bellidiformis* (bright-pink, orange and yellow), *Felicia heterophylla* – one of the few plants in this collection with completely blue flowers – *Senecio elegans* which is bright mauve, and the bright-blue *Heliophila coronopifolia*.

Many of these – or close relatives – will be available from your local seed suppliers, so you can create a South African annual border too. For an informal display, mimic the Eden method and cover the area with stone chippings and sand. Plants such as arctotis and gazania that feature in Namaqualand can be grown as annuals outdoors, too. Either buy them as plants from the garden centre, or grow them from seed.

CALIFORNIA

As the soil dries out and flowers fade, millions of seeds are produced that remain dormant through the dry season and germinate at the onset of the next rains.

California has a range of climates, spanning desert to alpine tundra, and boasts a rich array of native plants numbering over five thousand species (almost 80 per cent of which are native). At Eden, five of California's zones are displayed, alongside the flora of the Mediterranean and of South Africa: the Chaparral, coastal sage scrub, foothill woodland, valley grassland and desert oasis.

◼ The Chaparral

The Chaparral is California's shrubby zone – similar to the Maquis and the Fynbos. It contains a dense community of evergreen oaks and mainly evergreen, drought-resistant, broad-leafed shrubs that is almost impenetrable. Many plants, as in the Fynbos, require fire for the seeds to germinate.

Two prominent plants in this zone are *Fremontodendron californicum*, or the flannel bush, and the genus ceanothus, both of which are popular and successful garden plants in Britain.

Fremontodendron californicum is a glorious plant, prized for its yellow bracts that look like flowers and are set against brown felted stems. Flowering from spring through to autumn, it is perfect for a sunny south- or south-west-facing wall on free-draining soil. When you see its spreading habit in the Warm Temperate Biome, it's hard to believe that it could ever be restrained by training; but this is done by cutting out any main stems growing away from the wall, tying in those growing parallel to the training wires, and pruning back the outward-facing shoots to two buds after the first flush of flower. In milder parts of Britain it's worth experimenting with it as a multi-stemmed, free-standing shrub; if you do grow it like this, from late spring onwards cut out any shoots damaged by winter weather. One word of caution, however: wear gloves and goggles and cover any other exposed skin when pruning, as some people have an allergic reaction to the plant's tiny hairs.

Ceanothus are a group of evergreen or deciduous, low- or tall-growing shrubs that are found from southern Canada to Guatemala, although most are found in California. They thrive in gardens in free-draining soil against a hot, sunny wall, but in milder areas they can be grown as free-standing shrubs or pruned to form small trees. They are simple to maintain: just prune the sideshoots of deciduous varieties back to within one or two buds of the previous year's growth in March, and lightly prune evergreens after flowering, if necessary. There are some wonderful evergreen cultivars well worth trying in the garden, including *Ceanothus arboreus* 'Trewithen Blue' with large clusters of deep-blue flowers, 'Autumnal Blue', renowned for its sky-blue flowers produced from late summer through autumn (and often into spring, too), and 'Puget Blue', a medium-sized hybrid that is covered in deep-blue flowers from late spring to early summer. One of the most popular deciduous cultivars is 'Gloire de Versailles', which decks itself out in large powder-blue clusters in summer and autumn.

Valley grassland

The native flora of the flat central Californian valley is grassland, but it is punctuated by several sages and many other shrubs and herbaceous plants, grasses, annuals, cacti and succulents. Like Namaqualand, the valley grassland is renowned for its display of annuals including the popular Californian poppy (*Eschscholzia californica*) and baby blue-eyes (*Nemophila menziesii*). In the Eden display, over twenty different species figure in the mix, flowering in their native habitat from mid-March until April or May, depending on the rainy season. As in the Namaqualand display, seed is broadcast evenly over the soil (around 30g to 10 square metres and covered with 5mm of sand); during germination it is watered using a hose with a fine rose, to keep the surface moist, to a depth of 5cm. The brilliant spring display fades dramatically halfway through the summer, but the flowering season is renewed by sowing the area again in July, scattering seeds among the existing plants. Some of these seeds will fall between the leaves of the old plants, and a second flush of flowers will appear later in the season. The same technique works for domestic gardens.

Many other Californian annuals are well known to gardeners and available from seed suppliers. *Clarkia amoena*, *Nemophila maculata*, *Phacelia tanacetifolia*, *Gilia tricolor* and *Layia platyglossa* all provide a brilliant show in a bright sunny position, peaking

Layia platyglossa is available in the UK and is a great plant to grow in a heatwave.

towards late summer, and are at their best in a heatwave. As with all displays of annuals, they tend to be flattened by heavy rain – though that's not a problem in the Warm Temperate Biome! – but they soon recover.

Coastal sage scrub

Coastal sage scrub is low-growing open vegetation found on rocky, gravelly coastal slopes below the Chaparral. It is characterized by drought-tolerant deciduous shrubs that are suited to the semi-arid mediterranean climate. In fact, like Mediterranean species many of the plants have aromatic foliage, such as *Artemisia californica*, the coastal sage brush, whose finely cut grey-green foliage emits a classic sage fragrance, especially when wet, and salvias such as *Salvia clevelandii*, the American blue sage, which also has grey-green leaves, plus candelabras of beautiful blue flowers and a slightly lavender-like aroma. It is said that only one plant is needed to fragrance a whole garden! This plant is slightly tender in Britain but you could try *Salvia leucophylla*, which has pale-purple flowers, blue-grey textured leaves and a strong fragrance.

There are many other tender species of salvia, both annuals and perennials. Some can be damaged by winter cold but will regrow from the base, while others are better overwintered indoors, particularly in cool, damp parts of Britain. Salvias flourish in an open sunny position on free-draining soil and dislike being waterlogged, especially in winter. All of the Californian species seen in the Biome are available from nurseries or seed companies.

Foothill woodland

The foothill woodland zone of central and northern California, surrounding the great central valley, features trees, shrubs and bulbs. The main woodland species found in this area include the blue oak (*Quercus douglasii*), *Pinus sabiniana* and *Carpenteria californica*, one of California's rarest plants. These trees are found in the oak woodlands along streams and gullies, often alongside *Mimulus aurantiacus*, within which species there is an exciting colour range featuring tones of orange, yellow and red.

Shrubs found in the foothill woodland zone at Eden, which were grown from seed from Santa Ana Botanic Gardens, near Los Angeles, include *Helianthus californicus*, the California sunflower, which sports bright-yellow daisy flowers in its native habitat from June until October, and *Helenium bigelovii*, with its short yellow petals and black 'eye'. The area also features a number of different subspecies of the low-growing shrub *Epilobium canum* (previously known as

LEFT: Salvia patens, *a native of Mexico, is a superb garden plant and a link between the Americas and Europe where numerous other salvia species are found.*

SALVIAS

SALVIAS CREATE A LINK between California and the European Mediterranean, as there is a host of species in both locations. It is one of the largest plant genera, with almost a thousand species, and belongs to the same plant family as many other mediterranean aromatic herbs such as thyme, lavender, rosemary and mint. Nearly half of the world's salvias are from America – almost one-third from Mexico; the second largest region for salvias is the Mediterranean, with India – the southern foothills of the Himalayas in particular – coming a close third.

DESERT WEEDS

OXALIS CORYMBOSA has become a problem weed in the Sonoran Desert, as it can in your garden at home. A small plant with clover-like leaves, it produces a fleshy taproot surrounded by masses of tiny bulbils that break off easily when the weed is pulled out – only to infest again. If you are careful the whole plant, complete with bulbils, can be removed with a handfork in spring, when the bulbils are still firmly attached to the parent. The plant also produces seed capsules which, if left to their own devices, explode and spread their contents over a wide area. Mulch the area so that the seeds fall in the loose layer you've just added, and the seedlings can be removed easily; or spray them with glyphosate. Like clover, Oxalis corymbosa can smother cultivated crops. At Eden it is carefully removed by hand.

Zauschneria californica), with their bright-red trumpet-like flowers that are loved by butterflies and bees. These tend to flower at slightly different times in autumn, so are planted in the Biome to extend the flowering season. Carpenteria californica is a choice garden shrub, flowering from mid-summer; it boasts clear white flowers with a central boss of golden stamens, set against luscious dark evergreen foliage. It is perfect near a sheltered, sunny wall with enough space to grow bushy; like the fremontodendron, it is drought-tolerant once established.

Lots of bulb species feature in the landscape. Most Californian bulbs are suitable for greenhouse cultivation, needing protection only from damp summers so that they can enjoy a summer rest. In milder parts of the country, it's worth trying them in an open sunny spot at the base of a south-facing wall on free-draining soil, adding grit if necessary to improve drainage. Try Brodiaea elegans with its clusters of blue-purple flowers, or the closely related Triteleia laxa 'Koningin Fabiola', a rich blue-flowered selection.

RIGHT: *Fast-growing* Washingtonia filifera *are planted widely throughout the world, with established plants showing some cold tolerance.*

Then there's Dichelostemma ida-maia, the firecracker plant, with dense clusters of cherry-red cigar-shaped flowers sporting green markings round the mouth. One of the most spectacular Californian bulbs is Calochortus luteus: its bright-yellow bowl-shaped flowers have the most exquisite markings that look as though they have been drawn with pen and ink. Plant these in autumn and protect from excessive damp with a cloche; they are not reliably hardy, but have been known to survive in British gardens.

As in the rest of the Biome, bulbs are left to form clumps and naturalize, and the Californian species tend to grow more successfully as a result.

■ The Sonoran and the desert wash

In southern California, near the Mexican border and stretching into Arizona, lies the Sonoran Desert. One of the largest in North America, the Sonoran covers 31,000 square kilometres. It demonstrates a rich diversity of plant species, brought about by its variety of soil types. It is frost-free, and receives heavy downpours in summer and prolonged lighter rain in winter – perfect conditions for summer and winter annuals and perennials that can't survive long without water. However, some low-lying areas are extremely hot and get very little rain.

Desert washes, a landscape feature throughout the area, are dry river beds that fill with water, forming temporary rivers and pools when heavy rain drains from higher areas nearby. This occasional flash-flooding prevents perennials from establishing in the bed of a wash, but some trees and shrubs survive at the margins, where water remains in the soil for a while once the flood waters have receded.

The natural bold shapes and forms of the plants in the Sonoran Desert make them ideal for a public display. *Parkinsonia aculeata*, the Mexican paloverde, arrived at Eden from a US nursery unceremoniously wrapped in newspaper – an obvious clue to its robust character – and has flourished in the Warm Temperate Biome. It is a spectacular plant, covered with yellow flowers from mid- to late summer. *Calliandra californica*, the Baja feather-duster, with its red powder-puff flowers growing from the branches, has also settled in well. (It is related to *Calliandra calothyrsus*, grown in the Humid Tropics Biome in the African alley-cropping display, so linking Africa and North America.)

Palms featuring in the desert oasis display include the rare *Washingtonia filifera*, the only native palm in California that is grown as a garden or landscaping tree. The fruit hang in massive bunches and are harvested by Native Americans; their sweet flesh (surrounding a large seed) is also enjoyed by coyotes.

Of course, a desert display would not be complete without succulents and cacti, and there are many at Eden, including opuntias, ferocactus and agaves. In Britain, most gardeners tend to grow cacti indoors, but in the right conditions many varieties can be grown outdoors all year round. They need free-draining soil, which you can create by digging in plenty of gravel and by raising your display beds to ensure they are not waterlogged in winter. Mulch them with a layer of stone chippings – and scatter Californian annuals among them in summer for an eye-catching display. The few cacti that are reliably hardy in Britain include prickly pears – the opuntias.

THE SEASONAL DISPLAYS

Bursting with flavour, chillies have been integrated into worldwide cuisines and are both edible and ornamental.

The temporary displays in containers and borders at Eden are part of a policy to provide interest and education all year round. Past features range from a Moroccan herb garden and a cactus display to pulses, and cut flowers from the Fynbos including proteas and leucospermum displayed on a bed of gravel.

In a domestic garden, the idea of temporary displays translates well to the use of containers for rotating plants so as to provide interest when parts of the garden are not at their peak. Choose seasonal plants, and replace them as their season ends. If you use containers that are not too large or too heavy, you can move them around the garden to fill gaps as required. There's a huge range of plants that are perfect for such seasonal displays, from bulbs in winter and spring to summer lilies; and climbers such as clematis and sweet peas can be trained up an ornamental obelisk or tripod of canes and placed in borders, then removed and replaced when the show is over. Pots of annuals, small shrubs at the front of borders, or several pots arranged together in a shady corner will all brighten up empty spaces.

■ Peppers

In 2005 Eden put on a summer display of thirty sweet and chilli peppers, numbered from one to ten to indicate their heat. Peppers will grow very happily in pots – some are naturally compact, others grow to large bushes – and are ideal plants for both ornamental and culinary use. Some particularly attractive varieties that are quite at home in containers in British greenhouses include *Capsicum annuum* 'Purple Tiger', which has dark stems, random creamy variegation on the leaves and hot teardrop-shaped fruits that turn green and purple to red. Then there are the long, thin, orange, yellow and red fruits of 'Medusa'; and 'Almapaprika', an early-season variety widely grown in Hungary (and commonly used for stuffing), that is also known as 'Hot Apple' because of its shape.

As peppers are technically shrubs that tend to be grown as annuals, it's possible to keep a chilli plant over winter. Put it on a bright, sunny windowsill, rotating the pot every few days so that the whole plant receives adequate light; alternatively, put it in a frost-free greenhouse, and keep the compost moist using tepid water, allowing the surface to dry out before watering again. The fruits will ripen slowly, and can be harvested as required. Prune back the main stems after harvesting to encourage regrowth in spring, or grow new plants if you want a collection that is young, compact and vigorous.

At Eden, the peppers were germinated in the nursery at Watering Lane, potted on into 7.5cm square pots, then transplanted into display containers in peat-free compost mixed with slow-release fertilizer that releases more nutrients as the temperature rises. Then they were liquid-fed weekly with high-potash fertilizer to give them a boost. Those peppers growing on the edge of the orchard were planted in holes 40cm square filled with green waste and topped with Biome soil mixed with slow-release fertilizer. They were drip-irrigated, then topped up by hand watering. They do best when grown as container plants in the greenhouse and fed with high-potash fertilizer when the first flowers have formed.

PEPPERS AND CHILLIES

SWEET PEPPERS and hot chillies came originally from South America. It is believed that the hot ones were the first to be cultivated. They were introduced to Europe by Columbus, who thought he'd discovered the highly prized black pepper. Years of selection have produced regional variants – fruits of different shapes, sizes, colours and heat. The fruit of the chilli plant contains a compound, capsaicin, in its inner wall and it's this that provides the heat. The heat is measured in Scoville units, a method developed by Wilbur Scoville in 1912 to rate the amount of sugar-water it took to neutralize the chilli heat once an individual had ingested it.

Mild chillies come in at around 600 units, really hot ones score up to 350,000; beware the variety 'Dorset Naga' that pumps up the pain (or pleasure!) to 900,000 units! As well as spicing up our food, chilli extracts have been added to sprays, paints and rubber coatings as a deterrent to ward off anything from insects to elephants, aquatic molluscs and rats. Capsaicin is also used in medicine as pain relief for neuralgia, to promote healing and treat bronchial disorders. Furthermore, it helps the body to metabolize alcohol, nicely demonstrating the wisdom of having a curry after a night out!

Sorghum bicolor var. *saccharatum* is a close relative and is known as the 'northern sugar cane'; it produces canes up to 5cm in diameter and 3m long, which are at their sweetest when the flower forms in autumn. It can be grown as a half-hardy annual in the garden in Britain, with seeds sown in pots in spring (once there's no danger of frost) and planted out in a sunny position on rich, well-drained soil.

Teff (*Eragrostis tef*) – arguably the smallest-seeded grain and one of the oldest crops in the world. It provides a quarter of Ethiopia's cereal and is used to make *injera* – a large fermented pancake-like bread. The grain is rich in iron, calcium and potassium and provides over 60 per cent of Ethiopia's protein requirement. Teff is very drought-resistant, but it has to be kept weed-free until established.

Pearl millet (*Pennisetum glaucum*) – the ultimate tough crop, it reaches over 3.5m in its native hot, dry climate where the soil is too poor for sorghum, maize or even weeds to grow. Almost unheard of in the developed world, it is the only crop that can be cultivated in parts of Africa, and 12 million tonnes of it are produced each year. It needs just 300mm of rain per season to produce a crop – half that needed by maize. It is more nutritious than maize or rice and is a good source of animal feed too. In the developing world the success or failure of this crop can mean life or death; in the developed world it is used as bird seed!

Finger millet (*Eleusine coracana*) – needs more favourable conditions than the other grains described here. Its tasty seeds are rich in methionine, which

ORNAMENTAL PEARL MILLET

PENNISETUM GLAUCUM 'Purple Majesty' is an ornamental pearl millet selection that forms a clump up to 90cm in diameter and 1.5m tall with purple leaves, a red midrib and an elegant, narrow seedhead up to 35cm long. It is an annual so needs resowing every year. Germinate in moist compost in a greenhouse or on a sunny windowsill, acclimatize to outdoor temperatures and plant out permanently in a sheltered sunny position when there is no danger of frost. Although it tolerates drought, regular watering and feeding will produce larger, healthier specimens. The purple pigmentation does not appear until three weeks after germination.

breaks down fats and stops their build-up in the arteries, and it is a potential treatment for liver disease, arthritis pain and depression. Methionine is absent in the diets of millions. The grain can be stored for years. Malted finger millet makes nutritious weaning food, as does malted sorghum, because malted grains contain a chemical that turns starch into sugar. In the display put on at Eden foxtail millet (*Setaria italica*) and proso millet (*Panicum miliaceum*) also featured. The protein- and oil-rich seeds of these millets are eaten like rice, used as a fodder crop and were known to the Romans as *milum*.

A walk through the Warm Temperate Biome allows the visitor to appreciate the diversity of the world's mediterranean vegetation. It may lack the mystique of the rainforest and is not as species-rich, but there's more to the 'mediterranean' than beaches! It supplies those of us who live in more northerly regions with desirable garden plants both edible and ornamental. Far more important, from the olive terraces of southern Europe to South Africa's Fynbos, it furnishes a priceless natural habitat that is home to some of the most beautiful – and endangered – plants in the world.

LEFT: *Foxtail millet (*Setaria italica*) is a member of the grass family – one of the most influential plant groups in the world.*

THE OUTDOOR
BIOME

Fascicularia bicolor is just one of the many wonderful Chilean plants that would be happy growing in your garden.

Plants have influenced politics and economics, are the subject of some of the most important conservation projects of our time, have provided food during famine, and been the cause of it too!

A visit to the Outdoor Biome will transform your attitude to the garden plants that you grow at home. The phormiums (bush flax) that you use as architectural garden features are actually grown for their fibre; the globe artichoke produces a gourmet delicacy as well as providing sustainable biomass; pot marigolds are used industrially – in paint thinners! – as well as in salads; the sunflowers that win prizes at the village show supply the oil used in some racing-car engines; while the humble potato has had its own social and political impact on the history of the world. Whatever is growing in your plot, it's almost certainly not common or garden!

With over twenty-five different displays, the Outdoor Biome is gardened in a series of elegantly shaped terraces and borders packed with familiar plants both useful and ornamental that are found in the natural landscapes of the cool temperate world. Choosing the plants to be grown in the Biome each year involves the whole Eden gardening team, who put together their ideas for approval by the curator. The team aim to ring the changes: one year the theme may be pastel pinks; the next, the most brilliant colours they can come up with. Global gardening involves experimenting, modifying techniques and challenging established practice, and it's no different at Eden. The bedding plants chosen won't be just the tender annuals – anything is up for discussion. In summer there are traditional plants such as heliotropes, *Pelargonium* 'Cherry Red' and the beautiful ruby-red (but hideously named) *Verbena* 'Usbena 5122' (in the 'Superbena' series), alongside herbaceous plants like the red-leafed and deeper-red-veined *Heuchera* 'Amethyst Myst', creeping *Thymus serpyllum* 'Russetings', and the bushy lilac-pink *Salvia* 'Trenance'. Spring schemes may include dog-tooth violets (*Erythronium* species) bedded out with ferns, flowers, fruit, vegetables or bulbs.

GETTING OFF TO THE RIGHT START

Almost all of Eden's soil has been manufactured, as noted earlier, because it would have been impossible to grow any type of plant in the original china clay. The experience was similar to developing a garden from a building site, and the introduced soil, a mix of green waste, bark chippings and china clay, has to be treated differently from most garden soils (see p. 40).

When ground is rotavated in the ongoing process of improving soil, fine particles come to the surface which compact readily when walked on, and any nutrients are easily washed away. To ensure that there are plenty of nutrients available to the plants, the intensively cultivated shallow soil is top-dressed with a rich, manure-based compost, composted green waste and seaweed granules (for trace elements), as well as a pelleted organic general fertilizer which is dug in each year in spring.

The soil is now developing a better structure and an ever-increasing population of microbes and invertebrates. Crops are particularly hungry, so more composted green waste is dug into the vegetable beds at every opportunity. There's much debate about the soil structure in the cropping exhibits. Some of the gardeners believe it contains too many tiny particles: fine sand washes down from the topsoil and blocks the drainage spaces lower down, making some areas prone to waterlogging. After really heavy rain, the water lies in the top 30cm of soil for a long while, filtering through very slowly. It seems to be causing a certain amount of root rot – discovered in the root systems of lifted plants. This is due to the roots being shallow and spreading laterally rather than down so as to avoid the stagnant, anaerobic conditions below. Others consider that the green waste is *too* green, and needs further rotting to release the nutrients. It takes time and patience and a certain amount of trial and error to develop soils, and after five years at Eden the soil is beginning to improve.

If you are using organic matter, always ensure that it is well rotted before incorporating it into the soil. Nitrogen is needed for rotting, so it is first removed from the soil to help the decaying process then released back into it. To compensate for any nitrogen lost, and if the compost is not completely rotted, scatter high-nitrogen fertilizer over the soil before mulching.

GREEN MANURE

GROUND IS rarely left bare at Eden and plants are often grown as 'green manures' – crops that are sown, usually over winter, purely to be dug into the soil to improve its structure and fertility in spring. Because they grow densely, these crops also serve the dual purpose of suppressing weeds and preventing nutrients being washed through the soil during winter rains. Members of the pea family (*Leguminosae*) are particularly suitable for green manure because of the nitrogen-producing nodules on their roots. At Eden they sow grazing rye too, a fibrous-rooted plant that increases the organic content of the soil; alfalfa, which is deep-rooted and breaks up the soil at the lower levels; and bitter lupin, which fulfils a similar role. Most are dug in just before flowering, although some are dug in a few months after: one such is *Phacelia tanacetifolia*, a fast-growing, leafy crop that releases nitrogen rapidly (it also produces eye-catching blue flowers which are a rich nectar source for useful insects and can also be grown as an ornamental or companion plant).

PLANT NUTRIENTS

NITROGEN IS NECESSARY to help develop leaves and shoots, but don't overdo it because the soft growth it encourages breaks easily and is vulnerable to diseases and sap-sucking pests such as aphids. Phosphorus helps seed germination and fruit ripening, and potassium ensures there are plenty of flowers and fruit. The many types of fertilizer available are geared to serve specific functions: 'general' fertilizers promote a balanced diet and are suitable for a large range of plants; others are high in certain nutrients and are useful for certain plants or groups of plants, such as flower-inducing tomato fertilizer which has extra potassium.

BULBMANIA

Spring is a time when visitors flock to Cornwall's gardens. At first at Eden, there were few floral attractions outdoors. Here, clearly, was an opportunity missed, so in 2002 the team decided to do something about it. They wanted to brighten the site with early blooms, but there was not much enthusiasm for creating a traditional garden with magnolias and camellias – there are plenty of those already – so they decided to add to the Cornish garden experience.

It was in spring 2003 that 'Bulbmania' broke out. It offered an opportunity to be adventurous, ignore convention and break down barriers. Now there are bulbs in the Warm Temperate Biome, in outdoor beds, among permanent plantings, around the perimeter of the pit and along the edge of the ice rink. They also appeared in less likely places: in March a stream of blue grape hyacinths flows over the Link Building roof, anemones burst from containers, and hyacinths and dog-tooth violets peep out from among tiny ferns. Tradition is challenged in many ways – here, by juxtaposing delicate dabs of colour against bold brush strokes. One year, tulips with different flowering times started at the bottom of the grand staircase by the stage and bloomed seamlessly in sequence from orange to red, through pink to purple, till they reached the top in a triumphant technicolour crescendo. Over fifty different cultivars were planted in 2006. Every year the site is transformed into a work of living art.

Like all passionate gardeners, the team are constantly searching for inspiration – nothing escapes their notice, from the bulb fields of Holland, to the Chelsea Flower Show, to tiny front gardens.

The landscape architect and project manager works with the art director and the Green Team to create designs that combine new plant varieties with those that have been successful over the years. Conservative designs are usually rejected in favour of unorthodox combinations of vibrant colours, like purple and orange, red and pink. One way they work out what they want for the annual bulb project is to cut out pictures from catalogues, arrange them over the floor in colour and flowering sequence, then list their names on a spreadsheet.

It can be argued that the tones created by Nature always mix. Her juxtapositions may not reflect your personal taste – indeed, may not even be deemed 'good' taste – but take a look at some of Nature's more bizarre combinations in the Humid Tropics Biome and you'll see that they always work. Light and backdrop have an impact too; at the Dutch bulb industry's display garden in Keukenhof, in Liffe, Holland, the bulbs are viewed against unnaturally bright-green grass, thereby

THE BULB RUSH AT EDEN

PLANTING takes around eight weeks, from mid-October to mid-December, and it takes another four to lift them in late spring. Most are planted by three teams of six people each, with occasional help from others within the Green Team – some hardy souls from the Science Team and the offices have been known to venture out too! On average, between 750,000 and 1 million bulbs are planted annually, all by hand. By the time they have finished everyone in the team is exhausted but exhilarated, with an aching back, blisters and what feels like the permanent imprint of a trowel on their hands!

adding to the overall vibrancy, whereas soil and mulch inevitably neutralize colours.

At Eden, the season starts with a splash of yellow daffodils, which begin in mid-December and peak in mid-March. The choices for 2006 included 'Rijnveld's Early Sensation', a bulb grown in Cornwall for decades, and the classics 'February Gold' and 'Tamara'. The multicoloured magnificence of the tulips follows. The earliest tulip display takes place in the Warm Temperate Biome: the bulbs used here have been refrigerated in Holland to simulate winter dormancy, then are well watered after planting to keep them cool so the flowers are not aborted. Ground temperatures are kept at around 10°C at night, and 17°C during the day, making them flower two weeks earlier than those planted outside. The whole glorious show reaches its peak in the third week of March, when the widest range is in flower, and continues into May.

Planting bulbs

There's more than one way to plant bulbs, as will soon be revealed. But this is the way it's traditionally done wherever displays are planted.

Place them in the ground or container with the tip at three times the depth of the bulb. This is especially important for those planted permanently. If they are too near the soil surface, they may dry out and struggle to find the food and water needed to form flower buds for the following year; too deep, and they take longer to establish and may not flower; too close, and they might not flower as long as they otherwise would.

One of the hazards of planting tulips on a large scale year after year is that a virulent fungal disease called tulip fire (see p. 308) can be a serious problem if they are always planted in the same beds. So to prevent this disease taking hold, it's recommended that you change their accommodation regularly. Clearly, if you have a favoured bed for your tulips, or only have limited space, this is not as easy as it sounds. One way to deal with the problem is to plant other bulbs in alternate years, such as hyacinths. At Eden, tulip fire has appeared in some beds but, thankfully, it has not yet spread.

The gardeners at Eden have discovered how surprisingly adaptable bulbs can be – in fact they will grow in the most difficult locations. On the steep sides of the pit, where the soil is very shallow and dries out quickly, the team has successfully treated bulbs as annuals. The flower bud and food supply are already held within the bulb, so depth and spacing are not critical, and this allows for exciting short cuts. With temporary display in mind, they have ignored all traditional ideas of spacing and depth, packed the bulbs together all over the surface, covered them with a mulch of composted green waste using a digger bucket (for speed), then raked level.

This method was also successful with 7,000 tulips on the higher slopes of the pit. Here, rather than resting on soil, the grass was strimmed almost to ground level and the tulip bulbs were packed close together on top, then covered in green waste. They flowered magnificently and created the perfect display. The final confirmation of the success of the surface-planting technique came when 300,000 grape hyacinths

TULIPMANIA

TULIPS HAVE long been desirable plants. Tulipmania swept through Holland in the seventeenth century in the wake of a bubonic plague epidemic, when bulb speculation was seen by many as a possible way of escaping from their circumstances. Whole fortunes were made and lost on tulip bulbs. Merchants earned the equivalent of £30,000 a month by trading in bulb 'futures'; bulbs were sold while still in the ground, or were bartered for land, livestock or houses. A single specimen could fetch £400 – a large amount of money even by today's standards. One of the most highly prized was the variety 'Semper Augustus', which was offered for sale at 13,000 florins for one bulb – more expensive than the most costly house and garden with coach-house on a central Amsterdam canal, which would have cost a mere 10,000. Many people speculated in the hope of getting rich quickly, much as we use the lottery today. But when the market crashed, they were left destitute.

bloomed profusely on the Link Building roof. It was also certainly a much simpler procedure than stripping off turf or making 300,000 planting holes. There is no doubt about it – bulbs make perfect annuals!

This temporary planting technique – though, admittedly, calling for a radical change of attitude! – is ideal for the home gardener too. It means that, ignoring time-honoured methods, bulbs can be crammed into pots and beds, and you can look forward to a riotous display of full-on flower power. It may seem extravagant to use bulbs as annuals, but when you compare the pros and cons of replacing plantings with vigorous, healthy bulbs in a new colour scheme each year, it actually works out as good value for money.

LEFT: *Plant your bulbs in early autumn to ensure they become established over winter and are ready to flower in early spring.*

■ Bulb care at Eden

As a selection of early-, mid- and late-season tulips are planted around the Biomes, the flowering season peaks from the middle of March to early May, when the bulbs are finally lifted and composted. Tulips are composted with other green waste, but daffodils are lifted as late as possible after flowering, then spread in batches in the long grass around the car parks where they will naturalize. During the summer they die down and dry out, before being covered in composted green waste which encourages them to root the following year. This saves composting the bulbs, a difficult process as when lifted they are juicy and wet; and it also avoids the problem of stray daffodils passing whole through the composting machine, then popping up randomly all over the site.

Those bulbs that remain in the ground throughout the year as permanent plantings are fed in January and February with organic or inorganic high-potash feed to encourage flowering. At Eden they have found that organic fertilizers work more effectively on the manufactured soil in the pit: over-use of artificial fertilizers causes a build-up of phosphates, making the soil very acidic. In the long term, a change to seaweed and other organic-based fertilizers will certainly be more beneficial.

As the Bulbmania display fades in late spring and the bulbs are lifted, tubers and other crops are immediately planted – this is one of the busiest times of the year. In spring and autumn the ground is prepared for the new vegetable and other crops by rotavating the soil and incorporating a mix of chicken manure, seaweed and the same green-waste mulch that was used as a weed-suppressant over the winter. This combination creates a fine crumbly structure ideal for sowing and planting. Towards the centre of the Outdoor Biome where the soil is deeper the ground is rotavated to a depth of 25cm, but most of the higher, steeper slopes are dug by hand.

THE VEGETABLE GARDEN

Visitors tucking into fresh salads outside the Eden restaurant, Zzub Zzub, can't help being reminded of the origins of their food – the restaurant overlooks the dazzling vegetable garden planted on a slope close by. Featuring vegetables of all shapes, sizes and colours, it has been there since Eden opened, and it has proved to even the most sceptical visitor that vegetables can be ornamental as well as edible.

The way vegetables are planted in most parts of the world reminds us of their role and of our attitude to them – marching in rows, often as far as the eye can see, in their regimentation they show us vegetable gardening as the epitome of no-nonsense functionality. However, as the plot at Eden proves, with a little imagination the vegetable garden can be transformed from production line into living landscape – and still be practical.

Planting a potager, or ornamental vegetable garden, is a compromise: the plants with the finest flavour are not always the most colourful, yet even if not all are top gourmet varieties, there's always the benefit of eating fresh vegetables that certainly taste

better than those from a shop. At Eden, ornamental containers are dotted around the outdoor eating area – a perfect way to grow vegetables if you don't have a lot of space to spare, and ideal for a city gardener. Try them with a Mediterranean, Thai or other oriental theme, so you'll have a head start when it comes to more exotic cooking.

The canopy over part of the garden here provides extra protection for the plants, so conditions are hotter and drier than for those that are completely exposed to the outdoors. Also, the process of 'hardening off' is unnecessary here. Such protection makes it a perfect spot for the more tender vegetables, which are started off in Watering Lane Nursery and transplanted once the soil is warm enough. Among them are the pepper 'Volcano', a compact Hungarian variety ideal for containers, whose fruits can be lime green, bright orange or red, according to the stage of growth. A white aubergine called 'Mohican' always catches the visitor's eye, while 'Baby Bel', which is loaded, in season, with golf-ball-sized aubergines, is suitable for the small

Watering the ornamental vegetables in the 'Plants for Taste' display – one of the first daily tasks of the Eden gardeners.

ABOVE: *You don't need acres of space to produce salad crops – lettuces will grow happily in containers.*

RIGHT: *Carefully placed canes and twine provide planting guides for the gardeners; within weeks they will be covered with beautiful foliage.*

garden. You may also see the bright-yellow, heavy-cropping patty-pan squash called 'Sunburst'; its unusual shape – as much like tiny space ships or planets as patty-pans, depending on your imaginative bent – regularly draws comment.

■ Creating a vegetable plot

As the Outdoor Biome clearly shows, growing your own is not exclusively for those who have acres of space, a kitchen garden or even an allotment. There are types of vegetables and fruit that are suitable for even the smallest areas. However, in order to achieve the best yield from the space available, there are a few factors you should take into account.

First, when planting an ornamental vegetable garden it is essential to prepare the soil thoroughly – these crops are going to be hungry. Plan the design carefully, bearing in mind such things as spacing, timing, continuity and the height and spread of your chosen plants; keep the design simple – you can make it more elaborate when you've had more experience. Use a combination of direct sowings and pot- or 'plug'-grown plants (ideal for achieving continuity). Keep sowing and planting, and try to be one step ahead of the display at all times.

From the aesthetic point of view, don't be afraid to bring in extra colour by incorporating flowering companion plants – especially those that are edible or attract helpful insects. These can add special interest and brilliance, while also encouraging bees and other pollinating insects. Make sure your design is three-dimensional – you can add height by using 'wigwams' and taller specimens for 'dot' plants.

The importance of soil

The best soil for growing vegetables should act like a sponge, holding moisture but allowing any excess to drain away, and leaving air spaces so that the roots can breathe. In poor soils, food and water drain away so quickly that they cannot be used, leaving fast-growing vegetables both hungry and thirsty – add well-rotted organic matter. Sharp sand and horticultural grit will open up heavier soils, allowing more water to be retained but at the same time preventing it from becoming waterlogged. If you give it a chance, a healthy, highly productive soil will gradually develop, though it may take some time!

A good soil structure can also be created by using raised beds, so that the soil surface is never walked on and the centre of the bed can be easily reached from the margins. Raised beds, developed centuries ago in China, are still found throughout Asia and can be seen at Eden in the Malaysian Garden (see p. 102). They were standard practice in the West, too, until the invention of the horse-drawn hoe led to crops being spaced further apart and in long lines for ease of cultivation. The practice was then adopted by home gardeners, and vegetables have been planted in straight lines ever since! There is nothing stopping you from growing crops at a diagonal or in a chequer pattern or even in waves; if you have the time and the patience, you can mark out the shape on a piece of old plywood and cut out a template with a jig-saw.

At Eden, every time a row of vegetables is lifted, even if it is only 15cm wide, more of the mix of chicken manure, seaweed and the green-waste mulch is forked into the soil, in preparation for the

With their mottled, 'hand-painted' patterns, ornamental gourds grown at Watering Lane are a major feature in the Eden displays.

next occupants. Plants are also foliar-fed, as required, with comfrey and liquid seaweed. There are other advantages to adding organic matter: it creates a fine seedbed and a light soil which warms up quickly for early sowing in spring. Chicken manure is high in nitrogen which encourages lush leafy growth, so the volumes needed by different crops will vary: it can be up to 8 litres per square metre for leafy crops like brassicas, but is much lower for tubers like potatoes that flourish on a diet of 2 litres per square metre, plus 50g each of seaweed and slow-release fertilizer, raked into the soil surface before it is levelled.

Rotating crops, as we all know, gives you a good and healthy yield. The system is advocated by gardeners throughout the world because it prevents the soil from becoming impoverished and minimizes the build-up of pests and diseases. Rotation is

achieved simply by sowing each crop in a different section of the plot each year. Typically, a gardener divides the plot into four sections – legumes (such as peas and beans), brassicas (cabbage and broccoli), roots (parsnips, carrots and so on), and finally anything that doesn't belong in the previous groups, such as garlic and onions. The groups stay permanently in this order, moving one step to the next bit of plot each year. (There's also a three-step rotation – brassicas, roots and other crops.)

But when you're creating an ornamental vegetable garden it's impossible to practise the strict regime required by crop rotation. All the same, you can still overcome the problems this technique addresses, because with only a few rows – or swirls or circles! – of each vegetable, the previous year's planting plan can be tweaked to ensure that, for example, brassicas are not planted in the same spot year after year.

Choosing your crops

If you're like most keen gardeners, you'll start planning your vegetable beds for the following year in December, with a trawl through the seed catalogues for new and old varieties. It is possible to have a productive plot that will lie fallow only from January to March, but to achieve this you must know exactly where each plant is going, how long it will take to mature, how long it will contribute to the display, and what will replace it. It also helps if you're familiar with each plant, its habits and culinary uses!

If you are not new to vegetable gardening, you will select some crops on their past performance; others on their ornamental features or on the length of their seasonal interest; others will attract you for being pest- and disease-free or quick to mature. Whatever your requirements, planning and organization are essential for success.

When choosing which crops you would like to grow, remember that some seeds can be sown directly into the soil, while others may need to be sown under glass, then transplanted into the gaps left when the previous crop is harvested. During the summer, growth is rapid, so in order to maintain productivity, lifting and replanting will be your constant task. The key is to have seedlings in waiting at the correct state of maturity so that when transplanted they fill the gap left by the previous crop. At Eden, in March, an early display of lettuce will last until semi-mature plants of the following crop, usually coloured-stemmed chard, are ready to take its place.

The aim at Eden, as you will know by now, and as it is in the domestic garden to some degree, is to create a seamless transition between the seasons.

This in itself requires a lot of planning and a careful choice of vegetables in order to keep the plot productive through autumn and into winter, when fewer crops are in their prime. For example, a late sowing of red mustard and mizuna greens provides useful colour alongside late summer/autumn-maturing cauliflowers such as the lime green 'Trevi' and the bright-pink 'Graffiti': both last for a long time and look good well into November. Good varieties of winter kale that can be transplanted from a seedbed include the curly kale 'Winterbor' and 'Redbor', and 'Black Tuscany' with its elegant arching leaves. The chard 'Bright Lights' is a mainstay crop in a mix sporting red, pink, orange, purple, yellow and white stems. As well as its long-term good looks, it provides excellent quality throughout the growing season and on into the following winter. Summer squashes, courgettes and pumpkins, planted towards the end of May, are valued for their large circular leaves and bold-yellow flowers and fruits. If crops mature early, flower buds from globe artichokes or small chunks of chard stem can be scattered along the rows in a cheerful vegetable mosaic, filling in gaps where crops are due to be planted.

Designing the plot

Clearly, you will have chosen the plants you wish to grow before you draw up the layout of your vegetable bed, so that you leave sufficient space for each variety and can allow for crop rotation, or successional planting, whichever suits you better.

So start by making a list of the varieties you'd like to grow, and note the height and spread of each so that when mature they will just overlap and create

Vegetables need constant weeding and attention as they grow – not an easy task for those with bad backs!

a continuous carpet of colour. Make sure you also note their light requirements, so that sun-lovers are not overshadowed by an adjoining crop. It is helpful to sketch out the plot on graph paper, noting sowing and harvesting times next to each row (or whatever shapes you are planning). Use clothes pegs to group seed packets together in chronological order of sowing for each month, or put them together in order in a shoe box with the months divided by labelled cards. Keep records of the performance of each variety in a diary, noting their disease-resistance and overall effect, along with sowing and maturing dates. Whatever you do, don't rely on your memory!

The vegetable bed at Eden is planted in broad and narrow curving bands, some of them tapering, laid out like a rainbow; this curving shape has a practical as well as an aesthetic purpose, as it takes advantage of the slope and of the natural undulations of the land.

The rows are laid out using a technique familiar to the domestic gardener – it involves the use of string! The central line, which is the most important, is first laid by eye; this can take a long time, but it must be absolutely correct as the spacing of all the other lines is dependent on the position of this one. The other lines are then measured from it, and marked with closely spaced canes linked with string to form the curves. (These are 1m apart at Eden, but something like 30cm would probably be appropriate in a smaller space.) 'Backbone' plants that last most of the season, such as chard and perpetual spinach, are planted along these lines, then half- and quarter-metre lines are measured off for other sowings. At

VEGETABLE GARDENING PAR EXCELLENCE

MANY ENTHUSIASTS argue that there is nothing more attractive than a vegetable plot, even in straight rows, but it was French gardeners who pioneered the ornamental vegetable garden and turned kitchen gardening into an art form. The classic example is to be found at the early-seventeenth-century Château de Villandry near Tours in western France, with its formal vegetable beds; the *potager du roi* at Versailles is also outstanding. The technique of growing fruit ornamentally as cordons and espaliers that was developed in the French royal garden is used in the orchard on the Eden estate, and it is ideal for domestic gardens, too.

Eden the gardeners use string made from biodegradable natural products such as sisal or coir, and the canes are cut at exactly the same height; the string lines remain in place for the whole season so that replacement crops too will be correctly spaced. The finished plot looks like a work of art and there is often some reluctance to plant it up! But the work must go on! Now the seed drills are plotted by measuring the distance above or below the string line with a calibrated stick, marking a section of the drill, then moving half a metre along the line, measuring again and marking the next section and so on, until the end of the row is reached. The rule is 'Check by eye as you go, and then before you sow.'

Maintenance

If you give your vegetables the best start you can, you should be able to minimize some aspects of maintenance. Make sure that the soil is prepared correctly to suit the needs of the various plants to begin with – for example, avoid having to fork in manure where root crops are already in occupation. Also, plants are better able to maintain their quality

LEFT: *Globe artichokes are highly ornamental. If they are not picked and eaten, the buds burst open to reveal huge, thistle-like flower heads beloved by bees.*

FACT!

At Eden, no footprints are allowed on the beds! Gillian Cartwright, who designed and also maintains the vegetable garden, uses one access track then steps out among the rows. With a well-developed sense of balance, great care and no alcohol at lunchtime, she has become skilled at tiptoeing among the vegetables!

throughout the season if they are grown from fresh seed obtained from a reliable supplier. Choose long-standing vegetable varieties with good colours and interesting shapes and with some disease-resistance. Organic seed tends to be more robust, particularly when coping with organic conditions.

Follow your string-and-cane guidelines carefully, double-checking them just before sowing and planting – for the proud gardener there's no worse sight than a row of seedlings that have strayed off line – and it will make hoeing and weeding easier if you can see where the true plant seedlings are. Weeding and hoeing should be a daily task – removing weeds before they flower and set seed ensures they are kept under control. Bitter-cress, willowherb and chickweed are among the most common unwanted visitors at Eden, but worst of all is cress, which seems to escape from the children's packed lunches in the Zzub Zzub café into the vegetable and herb gardens!

Don't be afraid to add extra sowings in between more advanced plants. As long as you are aware of the spacing required for the mature plants and know when they are likely to be removed, you will ensure continuity. This kind of thing comes with practice.

As with any other part of the garden, vegetable plots should be watered first thing in the morning when it is cool, in order to reduce evaporation, and at the end of the day in summer, so the water soaks in rather than evaporating. At Eden the new canopy means that the plants need watering more often, and particular attention is paid to newly planted vegetables that are vulnerable to wilting until their root systems are established. Keep a constant lookout for pests and diseases and control them immediately; aim for organic controls on edible crops, including barriers and traps (see p. 281). Remember – healthy, well-grown plants are more resistant to pests and diseases.

Companion planting

It's always a good idea to consider allocating a little space to a few specific plants that will combat pests and diseases and help others to grow healthily. This is known as companion planting. For example, basil is often planted to keep whitefly off tomatoes; and if you plant four rows of onions to one of carrots the smell of the onions will stop carrot-fly ravaging your crop – at least while the onions are in leaf. Another option is to plant alternate rows of cabbages and French beans so as to reduce cabbage root fly and root aphid, as this mix of plants confuses the pests. You can lessen the risk of pest- and disease-infestation by planting 'mixed' vegetables rather than growing in

GETTING THE BEST FROM YOUR VEG PLANTS

Top Tips for growing healthy crops: if you want vegetables that look and taste good, never expect them to grow in less than optimum conditions. Soil preparation is extremely important. Get to know your plants and their needs, whether they like heat, cold, damp or shade, or something in between; find out what's early, mid-season and late – then plant accordingly. Keep them well fed and watered, and don't let them get stressed. Check daily for pests and diseases, and control problems immediately. Timing is crucial. Missing sowing times can be disastrous, so stay one step ahead and stick to your planting and sowing plan.

VEGETABLES FOR COLOUR

EDEN'S VEGETABLE garden proves that a practical space needn't look dull. Each year is a new opportunity for bold experimentation. Remarkably, Nature's colours rarely clash; there's something about them that makes even the most outrageous contrasts work. In 2005 one bit of the plot became the 'pink corner': vivid cerise and purple-pink sweet william (called 'Purple Novarna') set among orange and yellow tagetes would challenge most people's idea of how colour can be used, but it worked!

Any gardener can succeed with the aesthetic approach to sowing – it just takes a little artistic inclination, some careful research, and a massive dose of courage. Rules are there to be broken, so including crops such as 'Purple Norvana' for artistic rather than culinary reasons is perfectly acceptable. Exhibits in the pink corner also included the fabulous purple-flowered and -podded mangetout pea 'Ezetha's Krombek Blaauwschok'; an exceptionally tall mangetout, 'Carouby de Mausanne' which reaches 1.8m, with purple flowers; and the borlotto bean 'Lingua di Fuoco' with its cream- and pink-blotched pods jostling with the aubergine 'Red Egg', 'Giant Red Mustard' and red cabbage 'Early Red Marner'.

Lettuces always give a lush display, and offer a wonderful range of colour depending on the varieties you choose. At Eden the vegetable beds include such tasty and vibrant individuals as 'Tom Thumb', 'Little Gem', 'Funly' (hedgehog-shaped), 'Revolution' (deep red), 'Lollo Bionda', 'Freckles' ('freckles' appear as it matures and the plant lasts well into the late spring), 'Concorde' (a massive oak-leaf type), lollo rossa 'Ravita' (deep red, 'cut and come again'), and 'Solsun' (a lollo rossa type, very deep red).

Colour schemes in the Eden vegetable patch tend towards oranges, reds and mauves. Orange is prominent because tagetes – types of marigold – which are edible, appear in every scheme; nasturtiums with their distinctive leaf shapes feature strongly too, including the nineteenth-century classic 'Empress of India' – a non-trailing variety with dark bluish-green foliage, edible leaves and scarlet flowers (also edible).

If you plant your nasturtium crops early in spring, by mid-summer the self-seeded specimens will be pushing up in the surrounding soil just as the mature plants are probably infested with blackfly, so now is the time to remove the old plants (with accompanying pests), and the younger self-seeded plants will take their place. Aphids find nasturtiums irresistible, so they are often used as a 'sacrificial crop' for aphid control. However, they are vigorous plants and if they self-seed too freely, the weaklings will disappear leaving only strong, robust specimens. (Be warned, they do tend to reappear annually, but they can easily be trimmed back if they outgrow their allotted space.)

At Eden the nasturtiums are followed in late summer by beetroot such as the long-rooted 'Cylindra' and 'Bolthardy', which are densely sown in rows then thinned to about 3cm apart. (In ornamental displays especially, it's better to sow densely and thin the seedlings out than to sow sparsely and have gaps where seeds have not germinated.) Although tried and tested varieties are preferred, 'Bull's Blood', one of the most ornamental with its dark-red leaves, and the flat-rooted 'Mr Crosby's Egyptian', are certain to be tried in the future.

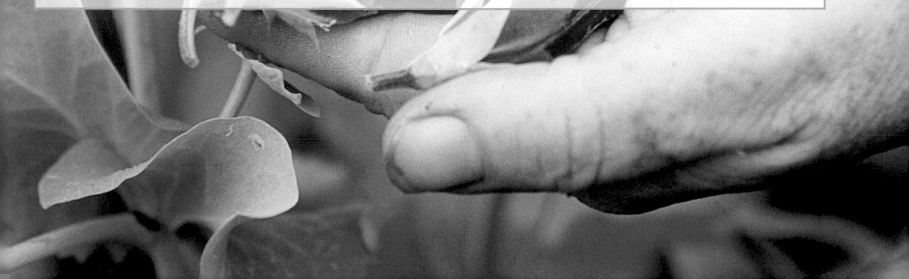

TAGETES

THERE ARE THREE MAIN types of marigold: the tall, large-flowered African marigold, the shorter, smaller-flowered French marigold and *Tagetes minuta*, which is grown at Eden and is often used by vegetable gardeners to deter whitefly and eelworms. Tagetes flower for five months or more: their masses of dainty flowers sit on cushions of lacy foliage until they are cut down by the first frosts. They prefer a warm, sunny position in free-draining soil and make the perfect edging plant, needing little maintenance except the removal of faded blooms by lightly trimming to prolong the flowering season. Tagetes are also believed to discourage the spread of several weeds including couch grass, ground elder and convolvulus. Slugs and snails can't resist young plants, so use biological controls or 'slug traps' to keep them in check.

lines or blocks – this is one of the advantages of an ornamental vegetable garden. This way, when pest or disease strikes, only one area will be affected.

As these examples suggest, companion plants have a dual purpose, and one that demonstrates this admirably is *Tagetes minuta*. It's an edible marigold with brightly coloured blooms: the petals of some varieties have a tangy citrus flavour and can be used in sorbets and salads. The leaves have an apple-like flavour are used as a seasoning for soups. Their smell discourages flies and moths. The cultivars 'Lemon Gem' and 'Orange Gem' are considered to be the best, and always perform well at Eden. Easy

to grow and manage, tagetes needs trimming three times a year, and respond each time with a new flush of flowers.

Cornish crops

The Cornish crop exhibit looks magnificent in spring, when daffodils bloom among the brassicas. Calabrese is now a standard high-value early crop, and purple-sprouting broccoli fills the 'hungry gap' – the period between late winter and late spring when very few vegetables mature. This gap can be easily bridged with a little careful planning. A far from exhaustive list of possible crops includes winter cabbage, Brussels sprouts, corn salad, land cress, kale, leeks, spring cauliflower, turnip tops and overwintering lettuce; plus stored vegetables such as beetroot and carrots.

A double-cropping technique is used in many of Eden's cropping areas. Daffodils are grown as they are commercially, on ridges. Using this system, a crop of daffodils can be grown above or in between beds of courgettes, which then crop all summer, while young squashes such as 'Crown Prince' scramble over the daffodil ridges.

There's a collection of crops telling the Cornish pasty story, featuring swedes, potatoes (the main ingredient) and onions, but minus the meat – there's nowhere to tether cows in the Cornish section! Swedes can be sown in early summer about 2cm deep, in drills that have been watered before sowing; or they can be sown in modules at three seeds per module, then thinned later so as to leave the strongest seedling.

Swedes prefer an open site in cool, moist conditions – parts of south-west England and Scotland have long grown them as agricultural crops. If you decide to try them, and if your soil is of the lighter type, dig in plenty of well-rotted organic matter; if your soil is on the heavy side, improve it with grit, and water before it dries out. With swedes, the old roots can be 'forced' in spring: cover their shoots with an old box, and blanch them (see Glossary) as you would seakale. Or you can sow seed in late summer for a crop of greens in early spring. The only major problem that swedes encounter is flea beetle (see p. 291), which you can prevent by growing them under horticultural fleece.

The onions at Eden are grown singly from seed in pots in the nursery, before planting out in spring. In fact, the easiest way to grow them is by buying 'sets' (young bulbs), thereby avoiding the slow and tricky process of germination. Early growth is important because onions mature by mid-summer, whatever size they have reached, and a late start means smaller bulbs. Of course, smaller bulbs can be tastier . . . Onions are more likely to 'bolt', or put their energy into producing flowers, when grown from sets, but they can be bought heat-treated, which helps to avoid this problem. It's essential to keep them weed-free and watered in dry spells. In mid- to late summer they start to ripen, the leaves turn yellow and bend over, and then you can lift them. At Eden, if the weather is fine, they are left to dry naturally on the ground and turned regularly so as to dry them thoroughly and avoid the attentions of slugs and centipedes. In wet weather, the onions are dried on a wire rack to improve the air circulation around them.

Broccoli – one of the vegetables that can be used to fill the 'hungry gap' between late winter and early spring.

THE HERB GARDEN

The bay tree – feeding container-grown plants with a solution of Epsom salts stops the leaves from turning yellow.

Opposite Eden's vegetable garden is one showing yet more culinary temptations, all of which will grow very happily in a British garden. Around twenty different herbs, mostly from the European Mediterranean, are laid out in blocks divided by clipped box (*Buxus sempervirens*) in the elegantly sweeping curve of a south-facing raised bed. Most are low-growing, although fennel, dill, mint and rosemary provide some height, and there's a selection of herbs such as lovage, hyssop and winter savory that were once popular but are now almost forgotten. Herbs can be grown successfully in beds, borders or containers.

The canopy over the eating area has reduced the amount of light coming through and created its own microclimate. However, few of the herbs seem to have been affected by this – only the mint seems to grow increasingly early in the season. But it does mean that all the plants need watering more often: every two or three days, depending on the weather, and at least daily during the heat of summer.

The growing season usually begins in early March and the herbs are at their best from May to September. Some herbs are grown in pots with a layer of recycled broken polystyrene in the base (for drainage), topped with the same mix of chicken manure, seaweed and green-waste mulch that is used in the raised vegetable bed. The herbs are fed with moderate doses of organic general-fertilizer pellets and seaweed tonic twice a year, in autumn and spring. Avoiding excessive feeding and watering that prevents soft, tasteless growth: as mentioned earlier, plants that are grown 'hard' possess a higher concentration of essential oils, so watering is avoided just before harvesting because it dilutes the flavour. Occasional feeding with liquid comfrey and mulching the crowns of perennial herbs such as fennel with composted green waste over winter also improves flavour.

The main harvesting season is from June until September. Stems are cut early in the morning with secateurs, before the sun evaporates the oils. Regular harvesting also keeps the plants tidy, guarantees plenty of fresh, flavour-filled young growth and stops the herbs from becoming 'woody' and running to seed.

Herbs divide easily and root freely, and at Eden they are replaced regularly to keep the supply young and vigorous. Woody herbs are replaced every three or four years with plants that are bought in, or propagated from existing plants via soft-tip or semi-ripe cuttings (see p. 66); perennials are grown from seed or divided every two or three years in spring. Some of the compost is removed and replaced before replanting, to improve the soil.

THE SCENTS OF MOROCCO

THERE ARE PLANS to revamp the Moroccan restaurant at Eden to include a pizzeria where visitors can watch their pizzas being made. Olive trees (*Olea europaea*) in containers will be dotted about under the canopy along one side of the seating area, and there will be a low trough running from inside the restaurant filled with bay (*Laurus nobilis*) underplanted with oregano (*Origanum vulgare*), golden oregano (*Origanum vulgare* 'Aureum') and thyme (*Thymus* × *citriodorus* 'Golden Lemon'), as well as containers of herbs such as dill, parsley (*Petroselinum crispum*) and around six varieties of basil (*Ocimum basilicum*).

Herbs to grow at home

Basil (*Ocimum basilicum*) – a classic Mediterranean herb that is almost synonymous with Italian food. There are many flavoursome varieties, including 'Cinnamon', very good with pasta or spicy food; 'Dark Opal', which has strongly flavoured purple leaves; 'Genovese', the traditional variety; low growing Bush Basil (*Ocimum minimum*); and 'Siam Queen' (*Ocimum × citriodorum*), which has an intense liquorice flavour and extra-large leaves. Basil likes full sun and should always be watered early in the day so the foliage dries before nightfall.

Bay (*Laurus nobilis*) – this reliable, noble herb adds substance and floral notes to casseroles and roast meats. It is a classic taste of the Mediterranean, a mainstay of the 'bouquet garni' and perfect for slow cooking. Bay needs a sheltered position, as the leaves are prone to scorching by cold winds. It also benefits from a winter mulch to help protect its shallow roots from frost damage.

Vietnamese coriander (*Persicaria odorata*) – the lime-flavoured leaves of this tropical herb pack a punch. Although it's a perennial, it's not frost-hardy, so it needs to be overwintered under cover. It flourishes in light soil and sheltered areas and roots easily from cuttings.

Fennel (*Foeniculum vulgare*) – widely used in Mediterranean dishes, both seeds and leaves are eaten, and their distinctive aniseed taste and fragrance are redolent of warm summer evenings. It

is often laid on the flesh of white fish before grilling or baking – a perfect combination. Fennel needs well-drained, moisture-retentive soil; don't grow it near coriander or dill, as cross-pollination reduces the amount of seed that fennel will produce.

Hyssop (*Hyssopus officinalis*) – a minty, bitter herb, hyssop was once widely used to flavour stews, soups and salads. It adds a distinctive touch to fruit desserts, and it's hyssop that imparts the bitter taste to Chartreuse. It grows well in containers and is aromatic, so plant it where it can be brushed

Vietnamese coriander has recently come to the attention of UK herb growers and is widely used in Vietnamese, Malaysian and Singaporean cuisine.

HIDDEN CROPS OF THE ANDES

RIGHT: *Colourful oca and mashua are among several Andean crops growing in the Eden display.*

The Incas were growing a wide range of crops long before they established their empire in the fifteenth century. By the time of the Spanish conquest, they had cultivated almost seventy plant species, including roots, legumes, nuts and fruit – as many as all the farmers in the whole of Europe and Asia at that time! The Incas were highly skilled landscapers and gardeners, turning mountainsides up to 4,000m high into productive land in climates ranging from tropical to polar. They knew how to keep up to seven years' supply of grains and tubers in storage in their towns and villages. Even now the Incan heritage is an important part of local culture and diet, and in many parts of the Andes villagers give thanks to Pachamama, or Mother Earth, at harvesting time.

On arrival in South America in 1523, in a fit of 'botanical colonialism', the conquering Spaniards set about suppressing the Incas and their horticultural traditions, forcing them to grow wheat, barley, carrots and broad beans. As a result, traditional vegetable production retreated higher into the Andes, where it has remained for five hundred years in the form of small-scale, high-altitude crops cultivated by the local people. Many of these crops are adaptable, tasty and extremely nutritious, and rediscovery of these treasures is reaping rewards locally and globally.

It took time for familiar Andean crops such as tomatoes and potatoes to be accepted worldwide, and it may take time for those grown in the display at Eden to be appreciated too. They are all suitable for domestic gardens; some, such as amaranthus (Inca wheat) and mashua, are both ornamental and edible, while other crops that feature in this display, such as

oca have already begun to find their way into seed catalogues. There is no doubt that their conservation is vital – they are all potential future foods.

■ Potatoes

It's believed that the potato was domesticated over six thousand years ago around Lake Titicaca, where the greatest diversity of wild species is still found. The Spaniards introduced it to Europe in the 1500s, where it adapted well to the climate and was highly productive; it has now spread throughout the world, to over 150 countries from Nepal to Burundi. This South American plant with its extraordinary history has been blamed for everything from excessive lust to leprosy, and is the basis of the million-dollar crisp industry. And you can grow these amazing plants in your garden!

The potato was the ideal crop for Ireland, with its high rainfall, and was introduced there in the late sixteenth century. People began to propagate in particular the variety 'Lumper', and to exchange the seed potatoes. This variety became the staple food, creating a vast monocrop that was susceptible to potato blight – a fungus that produces spores on the foliage that are washed down into the soil, causing the tubers to rot (see p. 304). The crop failure of 1845–6 caused the deaths of almost 1.5 million people, and prompted a million others to migrate to North America.

Several varieties of potato are grown at Eden, including 'Inca Sun' and 'Mayan Gold', which are direct descendants of the *phureja* potatoes that were among the first to be introduced into Europe and are

FACT!

Potatoes arrived in North America when the British governor of the Bahamas sent a gift box of *Solanum tuberosum* to the governor of the colony of Virginia. When Sir Walter Raleigh presented potatoes to Queen Elizabeth I, her cook is said to have discarded the tubers and cooked the leaves, which did little to promote their popularity in Britain. At one time the Scots refused to eat them because they were not mentioned in the Bible.

still grown in Peru. For more than forty years, these two have been used to breed disease-resistance into new varieties. 'Mayan Gold' has a unique creamy but dry texture that is not found in other European potatoes, and is excellent for baking, chipping and roasting, as the outside cooks to a rich gold while the inside remains light and fluffy.

Apart from their proneness to blight, potatoes are very easy to grow and you don't need an awful lot of space to produce a decent crop. You can plant them in a standard vegetable bed, or in a large, deep bin or special potato bin on your patio. The key to a continuous crop that could even take you into winter is to sow the seed potatoes successionally. They are categorized as first and second earlies and early and late maincrops according to their harvesting times.

First or second early potatoes are allowed to develop several shoots before planting (the process known as 'chitting' – see p. 63), which encourages faster growth and heavier crops. About six weeks before the last frost, put a layer of seed potatoes in a shallow tray or egg tray with the 'rose end' (the end where most of the 'eyes', or dormant buds, are concentrated) facing upwards, in a light, cool, frost-free place to encourage growth. At a temperature of 7°C this process takes about six weeks, until the shoots that have developed from the buds reach about 2.5cm long. If weather conditions aren't favourable at this point, plant the potatoes when the shoots are longer, but take care not to break them off when planting.

If you want a small crop of large potatoes, remove all but the three most vigorous shoots; for a higher yield of smaller tubers, leave all the shoots on. Plant them out in moisture-retentive soil when the

CONSERVING POTATO VARIETIES

CIP (*Centro Internacional de la Papa* or 'International Potato Centre') maintains the world's largest 'potato bank' including a hundred wild species from eight Latin American countries and almost four thousand heritage varieties. The CIP provides disease-resistant varieties to farmers and is a resource for breeding new ones with improved qualities such as disease- and drought-resistance. The CIP and local farmers in South America are working together to make a range of coloured crisps, raising local incomes and conserving varieties.

ground temperature is at least 7°C and have horticultural fleece or sheets of newspaper ready to throw over them in case of unexpected frosts. Using a hoe, make 7.5–10cm furrows, breaking up the earth with a spring-tine cultivator to improve drainage. Plant the tubers with the shoots pointing upwards and cover them with 7.5cm of soil. During the growing season, to ensure a good crop, the potatoes will need to be 'earthed up' three or four times (you do this by mounding a ridge of soil over the developing stems when they are about 12.5cm tall.) First earlies can be harvested ten weeks after planting; maincrops, fifteen to twenty weeks after.

Oca

Another tuberous plant like the potato, oca (*Oxalis tuberosa)* is a tough, pest- and disease-tolerant crop and is common at altitudes up to 4,000m – too high for most other food crops. Oca grows happily in poor, light soils, in low temperatures and where rainfall is variable. In some areas it is the second most valuable crop at altitude, producing twice the yield of the potato. Most varieties taste like sweet potato with a touch of sour cream – the flavour is sweeter when they are exposed to the sun after harvest. This potential-packed tuber from the Andes was once grown as a garden ornamental and used in southern France as pig food. Today it is eaten roasted, steamed, boiled, baked or fried, and you can use the young shoots in salads.

At Eden oca is chitted like potatoes, planted in furrows 7.5cm deep in double rows and earthed up. It flourishes in the light, free-draining soils that remind it of home. The tubers form late in the season when the day length is less than twelve hours, so it stays in the ground for as long as possible. In less favourable climates than the one at Eden, protect the foliage from frost with horticultural fleece and harvest at the end of November.

Mashua

A relative of the ornamental nasturtium, mashua (*Tropaeolum tuberosum*) is one of the top root crops in the Andes, with edible young shoots and flowers. It is easy to grow, high-yielding and cold-resistant, so it's ideal at altitude. An additional benefit is that it repels insects, soil nematodes and diseases, and is often planted alongside other crops as natural protection. When this was tried at Eden, it worked very successfully: planted next to potatoes, the mashua with its dense foliage provided weed-suppressing ground cover and kept the potatoes pest- and disease-free.

Mashua tubers look like small potatoes and are rich in vitamin C. Unlike potatoes, though, they can be eaten raw; some varieties taste peppery like radishes but become milder when boiled, and they are popular in soups and stews. Mashua is also baked or fried with eggs and onions. In some parts of South America it's topped with molasses and frozen as a dessert, or topped with honey, left outside overnight and eaten the following day.

The yields of mashua are excellent, even in poor soils and without fertilizer, but for a bumper harvest all three crops – potatoes and oca too – benefit from reasonably good soil. They are often found interplanted with each other. At Eden, oca and mashua are planted in zig-zag rows – one plant, then the other, alternately at an angle to each other in the same row – to increase productivity. Like many crops that are still close to their wild origins, both are vigorous and resistant to pests and diseases. At harvest time in the Outdoor Biome, when potato, oca and mashua are lifted, the best tubers are kept for planting the following year – just as they still are in the Andes.

Maca

A relative of the radish, this ground-hugging root crop is cultivated in Peru at altitudes up to 4,400m – probably higher than any other crop in the world! It flourishes in intense sunlight, poor, stony soils and cutting winds said to be strong enough to lift a horseman from his mount and throw him to the ground. It's even unfazed by temperatures ranging from 18°C during the day to –10°C at night – thus making some of the world's most inhospitable land productive. The starch-, protein- and mineral-rich roots can be stored for years, and have a tangy taste with the aroma of butterscotch. Maca (*Lepidium meyenii*) is believed to possess fertility-enhancing properties of benefit to both animals and humans. Soon after the conquest, when the Spanish found their livestock were reproducing poorly, local Native Americans recommended maca and the Spanish were astonished by the results. Maca is also used medicinally to stimulate the immune system and to improve vitality and mental capacity, and is often traded with communities living lower down the

mountains for other staples, such as potatoes. Considered a delicacy, it is sweet and spicy when dried, and it can be boiled, baked or roasted or the leaves eaten like watercress. Kevin Austin, the crops supervisor at Eden, reports that when roasted it tastes quite spicy, rather like horseradish.

The seeds for Eden are sown in modules at Watering Lane Nursery, about 0.5–1cm deep, in early March and are then planted out 10cm apart in early April. The root, which looks like a large radish, is harvested in mid-autumn. Unfortunately it's one crop that is not happy at Eden – the horticulturists suspect that it's because life is too easy there, so they plan to make it feel at home in future by subjecting it to a tougher growing regime. They will plant it in free-draining but poor soil, and they won't feed it. The growing location will be changed too: at present, fertilizer, washed down from higher up the slope, seeps into the border. Maca is also prone to damage by slugs, centipedes and other underground pests that attack root crops but which are less of a problem on poor, gritty soils. Because of its Viagra-like properties, it is kept away from the public – but not from the Eden staff, who reported the effects to be impressive when they tried it (all done in the name of science, of course!).

Yacon

The fast-growing yacon (*Smallanthus sonchifolius*), related to the sunflower, also flourishes in poor soil. It is grown for its roots and young stems, which are boiled, baked or used raw in salads. In South America it is grown in warm valleys, from sea level

Yacon, a potential sugar substitute for slimmers and diabetics, thrives in Eden's rich soil.

up to 3,200m. The large tubers, about 30cm long and as thick as your forearm, have a sweet taste and a crunchy texture and store well. Children in the Andes love them – they dig the root from the ground and eat it like an apple, which explains its common name, 'apple of the earth'. At Eden, the brittle tubers are harvested when the tops die back in autumn, and care is taken when lifting not to damage them. Yacon has been served in the restaurant at Eden, diced up raw in salads, as a replacement for water chestnut.

Countries outside of South America are now showing an interest in the plant as a commercial crop. It contains a sugar that cannot be absorbed by the human body so has a potential use as a sweetener for slimmers and diabetics. In South America local people have developed a simple method of extracting the syrup from the tubers, which benefits rural employment. Eden is one of the first places in Britain where yacon is being grown, but you can obtain tubers over the internet. The plant dislikes compaction and needs a deep, rich soil at least 37.5cm deep to encourage good tuber formation. Seaweed and chicken manure are added so as to raise the nitrogen level to the 75g per square metre needed to feed the huge leaves. There are legends of giant tubers being produced at Eden, reaching 2.4m long (but, knowing the depth of the soil, that may just be the size of the one that got away!).

Before planting yacon root cuttings at the end of April, the ground is raised slightly into small mounds to improve the drainage. If Eden's Bulbmania left any room for it, it would be planted much earlier in the year to increase tuber production. Although it thrives in a cold climate, the soft foliage is not frost-tolerant, so where frost is a possibility it must be protected with horticultural fleece. Little aftercare is needed, apart from constant watering, which is essential because its masses of large leaves make it susceptible to drying out. The tubers are lifted in early autumn when the leaves die down, and some are planted in pots and kept in the nursery for the following year.

Cannas are popular garden plants, valued in the UK for their spectacular flowers. A close relative, Canna edulis, is grown in the Andes for its edible tubers.

■ Cannas

The more familair cannas (*Canna indica*) are known to most gardeners for their stunning, often hot-coloured flowers that are frequently used to add a touch of the tropics to a planting scheme. They are generally half-hardy and should be overwintered indoors in all but the mildest climates. Their other attraction as garden plants is their large leaves, which are often multicoloured in a wide range of eye-catching tones.

In the Andes, *Canna edulis* is traditionally grown for its large, starchy edible tubers. Cannas are also grown in Asia, particularly Vietnam, where they are used to make the traditional transparent, or 'glass', noodles. In fact, cannas have been so successful that they have completely replaced mung beans as a main food crop. They need the same growing conditions as yacon, and even though tubers left in the ground over winter have survived quite happily, the Eden gardeners replicate the methods used in most gardens. As they are not frost-hardy cannas are lifted and overwintered in the nursery. They like rich soil and plenty of water.

The tubers are harvested when the plant starts to flower and its growth slows down. Slugs occasionally have a nibble, but the damage is not sufficient to weaken them; predatory nematodes (see p. 284) are used in the very early stages of growth to control them until the plants are well established.

At Eden, cannas and yacon are interplanted with nasturtiums, just as they would be in the Andes; as well as adding extra colour, the nasturtiums perform as a control against aphids (see page 287). After careful observation, the gardeners at Eden feel that both yacon and canna plants would benefit from being set further apart; giving them more space to develop would mean fewer plants, but they would produce larger yields.

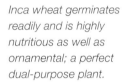

Inca wheat germinates readily and is highly nutritious as well as ornamental; a perfect dual-purpose plant.

▬ Inca wheat, or amaranthus

Amaranthus caudatus seeds last for centuries – when archaeologists sowed seeds found in an Aztec ruin, they germinated and grew. This staple grain of the Incas and Aztecs was almost forgotten after the conquest, but it is one of the most nutritious crops grown.

Amaranthus, also known as love-lies-bleeding, are tall plants with upright flowerheads which were prized by the Victorians for their bedding schemes and are excellent garden ornamentals. Their seeds can be sown in modules under glass in April at 20°C and planted after the last frosts about 60cm apart in light, well-drained soil like that found on the southern

slopes of Eden's Outdoor Biome. The seeds, barely larger than poppy seeds and produced at more than 100,000 per plant, are ripe once they begin to fall when the seedhead is rubbed between the fingers, usually from September. The easiest way to harvest is to strip the grains with your fingers, then riddle them into a bucket before drying the seeds on a tray.

▰ Quinoa

Pronounced 'keen-wa' and otherwise known as 'mother grain', *Chenopodium quinoa* is a cereal crop with a beautiful crimson seedhead, an impressive relative of the common garden weed fat hen (*Chenopodium album*) and also related to beetroot and chard. It was revered as sacred by the Incas, and at the start of each sowing season the Incan emperor would break the soil with a golden spade and plant the first seed. Quinoa was, and still is, widely grown throughout the area; the German naturalist and explorer Alexander von Humboldt (1769–1859) wrote that quinoa was to the region what 'wine was to the Greeks, what wheat was to the Romans and cotton to the Arabs'. Now, after four hundred years, it's being championed by dietitians and enjoying a resurgence as a nutritious crop for millions worldwide, often taking the place of meat in the diet. Traditionally quinoa was toasted or ground into flour, but it can also be added to soups, made into pasta or fermented to make a kind of beer.

Quinoa needs light, rich, free-draining soil. The seed is scattered over the soil and raked in, or sown in rows. It will grow happily in the British climate as a garden ornamental or vegetable. Sow it in shallow drills 1cm deep in late spring in an open sunny site, thinning to 40cm apart once there's no likelihood of frost. At Eden, the seeds are sown in modules in early spring and planted out 25cm apart in April. Quinoa plants must be watered regularly during dry periods. One of the problems with Eden's manufactured soil, as noted earlier, is that the surface 'caps' quickly, forming a hard crust. Staff aim to sow the quinoa seeds when the soil is damp; failing that they water the drills beforehand.

The whole area needs to be irrigated with care: too much water on the steep slope could cause landslips and create a huge ravine, as sometimes happened in Eden's early days. A fine spray is used to water the seedlings; potential problems are reduced as the plants grow, their root systems gradually binding the soil together like green glue. Planting in rows along the contours of the plot helps to reduce erosion; clearly, planting vertically would be impractical: channels would form and the soil would be washed down the slope. Weeding is a regular job in the early stages of growth, but once the quinoa starts to create its weed-suppressing canopy, this usually needs to be done less frequently. Unfortunately, though, the crop at Eden did become infested with its weedy relative fat hen; the seedlings of the two plants look very similar and fat hen is almost impossible to control – in the end, the weed won.

The seedbed runs out of nutrients after about five or six weeks, so the developing crops are treated with a seaweed liquid feed. Because some of the display areas at Eden get waterlogged below the

Quinoa was domesticated between three and five thousand years ago.

FACT!

Most of the crops in the Andean exhibit demand very few nutrients. At Eden, since artificial fertilizers are avoided, the staff rely on seaweed, chicken manure and organic general fertilizer made from waste products. They have tried using fertilizers made from human sewage, but it's smelly and the thought of using it is rather off-putting!

surface, the roots can be shallow and thus unable to support the soft, top-heavy growth. To counteract the consequent increased susceptibility to pests and diseases, the ideal is to feed a little and often, to encourage constant growth.

When harvested in late autumn, usually in October, the quinoa seedheads are stripped by hand or several stems are bound together and then threshed. As with many crops at Eden, there's a conflict of interest between trying to display them for as long as possible to the public and harvesting at the optimum time. The seeds are so tightly packed in the seedheads that rain before harvest can cause them to rot on the plant, or even germinate. Cultivars with open flowerheads are less prone to this. If rain

threatens before harvest, remove the seedheads and hang them upside down indoors. The seeds contain bitter-tasting chemicals called saponins, which you need to remove by soaking for at least ten hours before boiling them. Quinoa is gluten-free, can be ground into flour, made into burgers, eaten in casseroles and used for stuffing peppers.

▬ Ulluco

Like mashua, this Andean crop has a clambering, scrambling habit. The tubers are like very small, brightly coloured potatoes, coming in yellow, pink, purple or striped. The skin is thin and soft and the tubers do not need peeling before eating; the flesh is smooth, with a nutty taste. Ulluco (*Ullucus tuberosus*) is frost-resistant, produces good yields in moderately fertile soil, and is one of the few crops that are now more widely grown in the Andes than was the case a hundred years ago.

Ulluco is usually boiled, then eaten whole, mashed or sliced. Given the type of subsistence farming carried out in the Andes, every little bit of land is productive and every tuber is harvested. At Eden, ulluco has been interplanted with the cannas, though ideally it needs more light and space. The tubers are planted in April and are sometimes grown under fleece to encourage rapid early growth. Spacing when planting is fairly relaxed, as the plants scramble and root, producing tubers wherever the stem touches the ground. Ulluco is a very productive plant, growing 6–9m in a season. And despite its vigour, it doesn't seem to overrun nearby crops.

SEED CROPS

QUINOA and other crops like tarwi (*Lupinus mutabilis*) and Inca wheat play a vital role in reducing problems associated with childhood nutrition in rural Andean communities. Tarwi seeds contain more than 40 per cent protein – as much as or more than major protein crops such as soya beans and peanuts. Mixing the tarwi seed with other cereals makes a food that is almost perfect for humans. Like other lupins, tarwi also makes an excellent ornamental: its purple-blue flowers, tinged with a delicious honey smell, are among the most beautiful of all food crops. Traditionally, the seeds, like those of quinoa, would be soaked in water to remove bitterness before cooking and eating, but seed selection has now produced sweet varieties. When cooked, the seeds are used by the Andeans in soups, stews and salads or eaten as a snack. Tarwi is also a valuable 'green manure', producing nitrogen in its root nodules that can be left in the ground for following crops.

A LITTLE LIGHT REFRESHMENT?

Of course, liquid refreshment is as important as food, particularly amongst Eden's parched visitors! And the Green Team are growing plants that provide two drinks much loved by the Brits.

■ Tea

The tea plantation at Eden is developing well – there are now enough plants for one decent picking per season. One day, it will yield sufficient tea to be served in the Project's cafés.

Tea is produced from the leaves of a compact, slow-growing shrub called *Camellia sinensis*, which, with its fragrant white flowers that appear from early spring onwards, also makes a fine ornamental. Treat *Camellia sinensis* as you would any other camellia and plant it in well-drained, acidic soil in full sun or partial shade. But unless you live in a particularly mild part of the country, you'll probably do best if you grow your tea plants in containers of ericaceous compost that can be moved into a cool greenhouse over winter. This will encourage plenty of new shoots in the spring, and you can return the plants outdoors once there is no danger of frost. Unfortunately, many young plants in the middle section of the plantation at Eden have been lost through frost damage: on the south-facing bank where these are grown, any frost thaws quickly, which tends to split the bark towards the base of the main stems. Established plants survive because they have enough foliage to stop the frost getting underneath, although the leaf tips often get burned.

Water your tea plants regularly in summer, particularly from July to September when the flower

Tea – imagine brewing your own home-grown cuppa!

FACT!

Britain is the world's biggest tea-drinking country – over 70 billion cups of it are brewed each year. If you want to grow your own, pick the leaves off the shrub when small; take from each little branch the two tenderest leaves and an unopened bud (hence the name Premium Growth Tips), then air-dry them on trays before shredding and infusing.

FACT!

Hops and barley from Eden's display have been harvested by the St Austell Brewery and used to create a brew called 'Larrups' that features annually at the St Austell beer festival.

BELOW: *St Austell Brewery staff follow an ancient tradition and harvest hops (right) by hand to make the special 'Larrups' brew.*

buds for the following year are being formed, and keep a close eye on any plants in containers – they are particularly vulnerable to drying out. Camellia leaves should be dark green, and if they are not the plants need feeding, so give them a balanced ericaceous fertilizer in April, June and July, every ten days to two weeks, according to the manufacturer's instructions.

Wherever tea is grown, high humidity is essential. At Eden they are trying to achieve this by shading the tea terraces with *Robinia pseudoacacia*. Unfortunately, like many of the plants at Eden, given the shallow soil, their roots have spread laterally rather than downwards, which has affected their stability, so the trees have been pruned back in an effort to balance root production with top growth.

■ Beer and brewing

It is extraordinary to think that an anonymous British native that spent its early life quietly scrambling through the hedgerows should end up as the main ingredient of a staple drink and the basis of an international industry.

As everyone knows, beer is made from hops, and there are five varieties in the display at Eden, four of them growing up traditional hop poles. 'Phoenix' produces large 'hops' along the bine (or stem); 'Fuggles' was propagated in Kent in 1875 by Richard Fuggle and is used in traditional English ales; 'Whitbread Goldings Variety' was also bred in Kent, in 1911, and imparts a citric aroma; and 'Early Bird' is another of the group known as the

'Goldings varieties', which have long been cultivated and are most commonly grown in Herefordshire and Worcestershire. Dwarf 'Mill Primadonna' also makes a good hedge – there's one running along the back of the exhibit.

Hops (*Humulus lupulus*), of which there are ornamental forms, grow happily in British gardens. Together with other plants they make a perfect informal hedge, and if you let them scramble through plum trees, for instance, you can provide the local wildlife, and yourself, with a veritable feast! Excellent companion plants include hawthorn (*Crataegus monogyna*) from whose berries syrup can be made; elder (*Sambucus nigra*) such as the variety 'Nova' used to make 'champagne' and wine; purple hazel (*Corylus avellana* 'Purpurea') for its nuts; autumn-fruiting sloes (*Prunus spinosa*) for gin; and a good plum, the mirabelle, *Prunus cerasifera*, is for jam-making.

Alternatively, for a more ornamental style, you can grow the golden hop (*Humulus lupulus* 'Aurea') as a twining garden plant, allowing it to climb up trellis or over old tree stumps – it looks fabulous when combined with a purple clematis. When growing hops on wires for beer production, train one or two strong stems up each of the three main 'strings', and remove the remainder of the stems. It's important to keep the strings taut – otherwise, the weight of the hops drags them down. Train the stems over the top wires and tie them in occasionally to ensure they stay secure. As they are herbaceous, each autumn the stems can be cut back to the base to make room for next year's growth.

FIBROUS PLANTS

As well as the crops from which drinks are produced, there are others with equally practical, if very different, uses: the fibrous plants.

Among these, flax (*Linum usitatissimum*) is worth growing as an ornamental annual for its beautiful sky-blue flowers, as is hemp (cannabis sativa) – but we won't be giving you cultivation details for that one! Grown for its ornamental leaves, hemp was a very popular bedding plant in Victorian times. And for centuries, the law required that it be grown in people's gardens to provide fibre for rope for the British Navy. The fibres have also been used to make artists' canvas, paper, suits, bags and perfume. It has great potential as a medicinal plant for easing the symptoms of multiple sclerosis; it prevents vomiting, and researchers have also found that it improves night vision. The seeds produce oil that is used in a range of products from varnish to soap, and they are also used as birdseed – the flocks of finches feeding in the hemp display at Eden indicate its popularity! At the end of the growing season, the cut stems are laid on the slope and then bundled up for display, and the guides use them in their tours and demonstrations.

At Eden there are two New Zealand flaxes: *Phormium tenax*, and *Phormium cookianum* which has a softer leaf. The Maoris use flax for mats, hats, clothing (such as dresses) and baskets; there were once many flax mills in New Zealand, when it was first colonized by the Europeans, but most are now redundant. The leaves can be cut into strips, woven together and used as a lining for hanging baskets. Kevin Austin, from New Zealand, the crops supervisor at Eden, has a useful gardening tip: 'If you're out working in the garden and need to tie something up, cut a dead leaf from your New Zealand flax, remove a section from it the length you require, then tear it from top to bottom, following the leaf fibres, and there's your piece of string.' The plants thrive in open, sunny locations, on soil that is moisture-retentive but free-draining.

PHORMIUMS

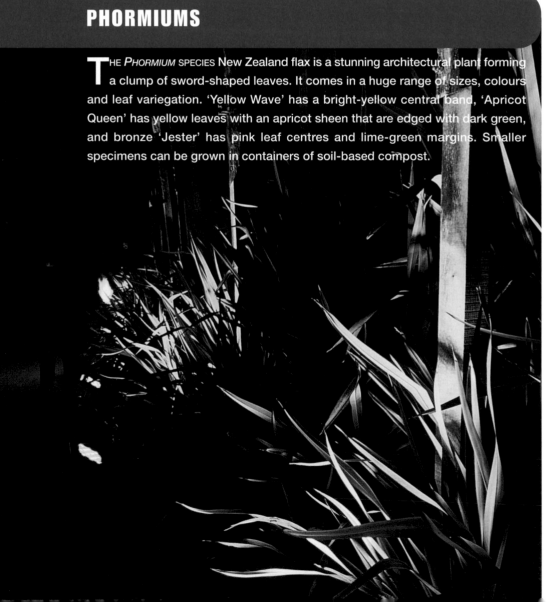

THE *PHORMIUM* SPECIES New Zealand flax is a stunning architectural plant forming a clump of sword-shaped leaves. It comes in a huge range of sizes, colours and leaf variegation. 'Yellow Wave' has a bright-yellow central band, 'Apricot Queen' has yellow leaves with an apricot sheen that are edged with dark green, and bronze 'Jester' has pink leaf centres and lime-green margins. Smaller specimens can be grown in containers of soil-based compost.

TOMORROW'S INDUSTRIES

The 'Tomorrow's Industries' exhibit at Eden contains plants which could replace synthetic materials in the future.

Two closely related plants, the globe artichoke and the cardoon, have great potential for bio-fuel production because of their rapid growth. With high yields and productivity in dry conditions, their wonderful sculptural form and grey-green leaves, they make impressive architectural perennials in the flower garden. Cardoons (*Cynara cardunculus*), popular in Victorian times, are also grown for their edible leaves, which are customarily blanched from late summer to early autumn: in order to tenderize them the leaves are gathered into a bunch and the whole surrounded with 'collars' of newspaper or cardboard or black polythene, then tied with string to exclude the light.

The smaller globe artichokes (*Cynara scolymus*), with their edible flower buds, can be grown in a flower border; you can harvest some of the buds and leave others to produce their massive thistle-like mauve flowers that are beloved of bees and, when dried, of flower arrangers! Both plants dislike winter waterlogging and summer drought, and thrive in an open site on free-draining soil improved with well-rotted organic matter the autumn or spring before planting. Apply high-potash liquid fertilizer every two weeks during the growing season.

Starch extracted from maize is used in the manufacture of bio-plastics, for such items as disposable plates and forks and other household utensils. Bio-plastics are, of course, biodegradable. Bin and garden bags made from maize starch vary in thickness, which governs the time it takes them to degrade. As mentioned earlier, biodegradable flower pots, also made from maize, are used successfully at Watering Lane Nursery.

Another popular garden plant, the pot marigold (*Calendula officinalis*), has several uses – it is used as a carrying agent in environmentally friendly paint, and its seed oil is used as a skin conditioner. Pot marigold is more familiar as the jolly orange daisy that is grown for its ornamental value and its edible petals. The Egyptians were the first to eat it, then the Greeks and Romans followed suit. It brightens up salads, cheese dishes and omelettes, and is a useful food dye when chopped or pulverized and added to any dish to which you want to add a golden colour. The sap from the plants has also been traditionally used to cure warts.

Pot marigold seed can be sown in autumn or early spring, under glass, at 18–20°C, and should be covered with its own depth of compost. When they are large enough to handle transplant the seedlings into 7.5cm pots and acclimatize them to outdoor conditions before planting out, once the danger of frost has passed, into a sunny, well-drained spot at intervals of 30cm. The seeds can also be sown directly into the soil in groups or rows from mid-spring onwards when the soil is warm, or into containers. Once they are in bloom, dead-head constantly to encourage continuous flowering until autumn – but beware, they do self-seed freely.

Soya

Soya (*Glycine max*) is one of the most nutritious of all vegetables and is rich in potassium, protein, fibre, vitamins and iron. It is used in soy and Worcestershire sauce and as a milk substitute.

Cardoons may one day fuel power stations and provide your electricity.

FACT!

Henry Ford was interested in the potential of soya for manufactured goods. He is said to have eaten it at every meal, to have had a suit made from soy fabric, and to have sponsored a sixteen-course soya dinner at the 1934 Century of Progress show in Chicago.

SPECIALIST SOWING AT EDEN

AT EDEN THE POT marigold is sown using a special tool invented by Kevin Austin. It's a kind of rake, about 60cm wide, cut from a plywood offcut and with large tines. First, the gardener pulls it through the light soil so that it leaves drills. He then broadcasts the seed over the surface, inverts the rake then draws it back at an angle so that most of the seed falls into the drills. The advantage of this method is that the seed coverage is wider and a greater depth of soil covers the seeds. The usual method of scattering the seed, then raking it over the surface, may give 75 per cent coverage of the designated area, but the seed is covered by only about 0.5cm of soil. Kevin's rake ensures a greater sowing depth of 1–2cm, thereby reducing the amount of seed lost to birds and improving the rate of germination.

Sunflowers are both prized as cheerful garden plants and grown commercially for their oil.

At Eden, soya seeds are sown in a prepared seedbed from mid- to late April, when there is no risk of frost – sow too early and low temperatures will check growth and the resulting plants will be poor. One year, two crops were sown two weeks apart for the 'Crops that Feed the World' exhibit. Cold conditions stunted the growth of the early sowing, so that the second crop overtook it and in the end matured into healthier, more productive plants. Sow the seeds 2.5–3cm deep in an open, sunny site on rich, free-draining soil. Keep the plants well watered until established, and also during drought.

Like the broad bean, soya produces pods very low down on the plant and only about 5cm from the main stem, not at the tips as many other plants do. In fact, the pods are sometimes difficult to see, so that it may appear that the crop is poor when it is really just hidden from view. Good autumn weather is critical for a decent soya harvest – an Indian summer creates the best conditions for seeds to ripen and harden; if the weather turns wet, the beans tend to rot in the pod. The soya should be harvested when the pods are just about to split.

Like beans, the roots of soya have their own nitrogen-producing nodules, which are left in the soil to provide nitrogen for following crops. (If you pull the plant over at an angle, give the stem a quick twist and a tug, then it should break, leaving the beneficial roots in the ground.) At Eden, the gardeners plant leafy crops to follow but planting plans for the annual Bulbmania always have to be taken into consideration too!

▆ Sunflowers

Sunflowers are believed to be the only major domesticated food crop to have originated in North America, although they are often associated with the Mediterranean – particularly the South of France, where Van Gogh did his famous painting in the 1880s. Today, sunflowers are grown on the largest scale in Argentina, the Ukraine and Russia, where their oil was first commercially exploited. The seeds provide protein-rich food, margarine, oil for racing-car engines and paint manufacture, as well as showing potential for fuel, medicines, cosmetics and plastics. The remaining seed meal feeds livestock, and the husks and stems can be used to fuel the oil extraction.

Sunflowers also have their place in many gardens as popular ornamental plants, particularly as they come in a range of sizes – some are less than 60cm tall. If you haven't got much space and want a dwarf form, 'Little Leo' is perfect for pots: it reaches 45cm and has bright-yellow flowerheads on single stems. 'Teddy Bear' is another more petite variety,

This special tool, invented by Kevin Austin, allows a greater sowing depth and increases germination.

Flowering vegetables encourage a wide range of insects into the garden to help with pollination.

FACT!

The tallest recorded sunflower (*Helianthus annuus*) measured just over 7.5m and was grown in the Netherlands in 1986; and the widest flowerhead was just over 80cm. The most flowerheads recorded on a single plant is 837.

with double blooms on 60cm stems, and looks great in containers or in the front of a border. Many of these smaller varieties are pollen-free because they were originally bred for flower arranging, so they are perfect for gardeners with a pollen allergy! 'Starburst Lemon Aura' is a fabulous double yellow that is planted at Eden, and it lasts over two weeks when cut and put in water.

Sunflowers are easy to grow if you have the right conditions – they need a fertile soil and a sheltered, sunny site and will grow taller against a sunny wall. Start your plants in pots, or sow seeds directly into a border, digging in plenty of well-rotted compost if necessary. From March onwards, sow each seed 5cm deep in a 7.5cm pot of seed or multipurpose compost, water thoroughly and cover the pot with

clingfilm or a polythene bag before placing it on a warm windowsill or in a propagator at 12°C. Remove the cover when the first leaves appear, and harden the seedlings off in a sheltered position before transplanting outside after the final frost. Alternatively, sow seed 5cm deep and 45cm apart in borders when the soil is warm. Water the plants regularly and use a general fertilizer every two weeks until established, then change their diet and feed with a tomato fertilizer.

For huge stems, try 'Giant Single', which can grow to 4.5m. Sow as you would any other sunflower, then water the plants thoroughly once a week during the first month to establish the root system. After that, water shallowly and frequently (at least once a day) until they flower – a 2m plant needs

about 8 gallons a week, and a 3m plant, 10. Feed weekly with a general fertilizer for the first three weeks, then switch to a high-nitrogen fertilizer, also weekly. Alternatively, you can go straight to high-nitrogen fertilizer – and stand well back! Taller varieties will need staking if positioned on a windy site.

There's nothing quite like growing plants to demonstrate the benefits of learning from experience. In 2005 the gardeners at Eden were left in no doubt about this when they planted the sunflower display the wrong way round! The blooms of sunflowers always follow the sun, but the path around the Outdoor Biome runs to the north side of the display, so the public were always viewing the flowers from behind. If you want to enjoy your sunflowers' faces always bear this in mind!

POLLINATION

ALTHOUGH IT MAY BE the flowers that attract us, it is for the most part the subsequent fruits and seeds (along with foliage and roots) that feed us. In Britain the crucial task of pollination – and thereby the creation of fruit and seeds – is usually performed by insects. A vital, yet often overlooked, aspect of gardening, pollination is showcased at Eden in a display demonstrating a range of plants and their pollinators.

Many different insects act as pollinators, including moths, bees, flies and butterflies. And some plants are wind-assisted: these include grasses, hazel, alder and birch (those with catkins) and conifers such as the yew.

Calla lilies are pollinated by several fly species, and buddleia by butterflies, which can identify only one or two colours, seeing yellow to blue as one colour and blue to purple as another. Night-fragrant evening primrose, honeysuckle and many white-flowered plants are pollinated by moths. Members of the daisy family, such as asters, have easily accessible landing pads for bees; foxgloves, their hairy petals providing a foothold, make them scramble up a tube for their reward, while others such as *Sedum spectabile* allow insects to forage on their flat flowerheads. The shapes of some flowers, such as salvia and runner beans, stop some bee species from entering the flower to enjoy the nectar, so the bees give them their come-uppance by biting a hole in the side, sticking their tongues through and stealing the nectar without helping with pollination!

Both wild bees and honey-bees help with pollination. There are around 250 species of bee in Britain and 25 per cent of them are endangered, so planting nectar-rich flowers gives you an opportunity to help in their conservation. Plants in a sheltered sunny site are more likely to be pollinated by insects than those in windswept or shady locations, particularly in spring when sunshine and shelter encourage early insects out to work and closely packed blossom obviates the need for them to fly far to the next source of nectar.

It's not worth growing one apple tree in the garden and leaving pollination to chance. Apples and pears need pollen from another tree to ensure fruit production. Some varieties like the 'Blenheim Orange' (an apple that is traditionally included in a Cornish orchard), only flower well every two years. Fruit nurseries indicate the pollination groups that the different cultivars belong to on their websites and in their catalogues: 1 is the earliest-flowering, 5 the latest. If you want to grow acid cherries such as the Morello you need only one plant, as they are self-pollinating; blueberries fruit better with two. To attract pollinators, plant sweet peas among runner beans.

ORNAMENTAL PLANTING

▪ The 'Blue' border

Among the many ornamental displays in the Outdoor Biome, set alongside the Warm Temperate Biome, is a large and predominantly herbaceous border (one or two shrubs have found their way into the display!). It was designed by Dominic Cole, who did the overall design of the Eden landscape. The border was originally intended to be blue – to incorporate as many blue-flowered plants as possible, plus silver, purple and 'black' foliage too. But other colours have now been added and the border has been extended as far as the Core, while at the same time screening the Bog Garden so as to provide visitors with an element of surprise.

There are plenty of plants in related shades of purple and mauve, but true-blue-flowering plants are quite unusual. Several were tried and rejected because they were not blue enough, while others such as salvias, delphiniums, nepetas and herbaceous geraniums fitted the bill, and are well represented. But the aim with this border, rather than just being blue-themed, is now more subtle. A long border like this one at Eden allows you to graduate colours, starting at one end with a few bold blocks of blue, and ending up with interspersed drifts of 'hot'-coloured flowers – splashes of red and orange, by way of contrast with the core.

When designing a mixed border, you have to follow a few basic principles. Begin by placing the structural plants that will provide interest all year round, using evergreens or other tall, architectural specimens, plus plants such as globe artichokes that also have seed heads later in the season. Because of the large scale of planting at Eden, the structural plants are often set in bold groups, creating considerable impact. One of the main structural elements of the mixed border is the use of topiary in the form of clipped elaeagnus and pittosporum balls, which mimic the shapes of the Biomes in the background. Once this structural planting was in place, the herbaceous plants were able to fill the gaps. Such a design will constantly evolve, like a living painting; sometimes colours clash, or plants simply don't perform. It's all trial and error – but that's the fun of gardening!

There is much interest and excitement as the first young leaves of the season appear. Flowering starts in spring with the striking sky-blue Himalayan poppy (*Meconopsis betonicifolia*) and the dainty 'forget-me-not' flowers of *Brunnera macrophylla*. Then there's a lull before other plants begin to perform, and flowering reaches its peak from the end of June onwards – the traditional time for herbaceous borders. There's another peak, from August, when the salvias and asters flower. The most stunning displays are put on by the stately blue spires of delphiniums, by *Melianthus major*, fêted for its grey-blue architectural foliage, and by unusual salvias such as *Salvia corrugata* with its wrinkled leaves and blue flowers, and the long-flowering *Salvia cacaliifolia* from Central America which is a deep mid-blue.

One plant that always catches the visitor's eye is *Acacia baileyana* 'Purpurea' because of its extraordinary-coloured cloud of deep-purple young foliage and its blue-green older leaves. This small Australian tree is tender in all but the mildest parts of the country, though the cold winter winds actually

RIGHT: *The Himalayan blue poppy – one of the most beautiful garden plants you can grow – is at its best in cool, moist parts of Britain.*

FACT!

In the 'Making of Garden Flowers' display, the day lilies, or hemerocallis, are a magnificent sight. The eighty-six cultivars growing at Eden tell a complex breeding story about the key characters involved.

The purple flowers of Verbena bonariensis *almost rival the buddlea as a nectar source for butterflies.*

help the gardener by nipping back the growth tips, which encourages shoots to appear further down the stem. Plants that don't match the original design of the Eden border, like *Hydrangea aspera*, a shrub with large heads of pale porcelain-blue flowers, will be removed. One plant that has had a massive impact, lasting all season, is *Tithonia rotundifolia* 'The Torch', a Mexican annual reaching 1.2m with bright orange-scarlet flowers rather like large single dahlias. This border proves that there's no room for plant snobbery – garden-centre plants, most of them tried, tested and thoroughly reliable, can be used to great effect. It isn't what you've got, it's the way that you use it!

■ Creating a flower border

People love to visit Eden and see all the weird and wonderful tropical plants, but they also enjoy recognizing things that they grow in their own gardens, and feel comfortable among the bedding and herbaceous plants. There are certainly plenty of areas from which they can take inspiration, particularly in the Outdoor Biome, where you can be assured that most plants are appropriate for a British climate.

As with any other border, the ground should be prepared before planting, and needs a little compost to give new plants a head start. The blue border at Eden is planted on a layer of compost 10–15cm

deep and, as with every other part of the pit, is constantly improved with green waste and boosted with flaked seaweed, which is forked into the surface. The latter is applied according to the old gardener's measure of 'a good handful per square yard' – it adds nutrients and conditions the soil because the agar flakes that it contains swell up, thus retaining moisture and opening up the soil.

Once in place, the plants are fed initially with general fertilizer and from then on individually, according to their needs. Dahlias and other hungry plants will need additional liquid feed and some mulching with chicken manure, while other, more rampant ones such as the mid-blue-flowered bog sage (*Salvia uliginosa*) get a more frugal diet and need constant cutting back to keep them under control.

How much maintenance your border needs will depend on what you choose to plant there, but if you are using tall flowering plants they may need staking to get the best effect. To maintain the natural look you could, as they do at Eden, stake them with hazel twigs when growth starts in spring. Plants such as geraniums will reward you with a second flush of flowers if you cut back the flower stems to ground level and feed them with general fertilizer as the first blooms start to fade about mid-summer.

■ Spectacular border plants

Of course, when it comes to choosing plants for your border, it's entirely up to you and your personal taste and style. At Eden the Outdoor Biome borders

The dahlia display in the 'Making of Garden Flowers' section shows the high-impact beauty of their fabulously flamboyant flowers.

ABOVE: *Always be on the lookout for the unusual – the back of this 'Juul's Allstar' dahlia flower makes an interesting study in geometry.*

RIGHT: *Never be afraid to carry a magnifying glass – it's amazing what a close-up, like this one of dahlia 'Ludwig Helfert' can reveal.*

hummingbirds. One of its parents, *Crocosmia paniculata*, is believed to have been introduced into Britain at the time of the Boer War at the turn of the last century. Crocosmias thrive in sun or part shade and in any moist soil – but not heavy clay. They should be divided in spring, once the clumps become too large.

Camellia

For historical reasons the camellia is inextricably linked with Cornwall, and is a major attraction in its early spring gardens. It was named after the botanist George Joseph Kamel (1661–1706), a native of Moravia, who Latinized his name to Camellius and wrote an account of the flora of Luzon in the Philippines.

The earliest *Camellia x williamsii*, the largest group, were hybrids created from different varieties of *Camellia saluensis*, which produces masses of flowers over a long period even in poor soil and heavy shade, and *Camellia japonica*, a robust, free-flowering plant (the oil from its seeds has long been used by Japanese women in hairdressing). In 1925, soon after *Camellia saluensis* first flowered in Britain, these hybrids were developed by J. C. Williams at Caerhays Castle, near Eden, and Colonel Stephenson Clarke at Borde Hill Gardens in Sussex. *Camellia x williamsii* hybrids flower in lower light and cooler conditions than most other camellias, and are particularly successful in the south-west.

Unfortunately, we can only guess at the parentage of some of them, because Williams lost all his botanical notes when on a memorable occasion he left his briefcase on the night sleeper to Paddington.

Some, such as rose-pink 'St Ewe', were named after local Cornish places. Stephenson created another famous cross, 'Donation', in 1941 – with its large, orchid-pink semi-double flowers, arguably one of the most beautiful of all. Many recent gardenworthy varieties have been bred in New Zealand by the Jury family at their nursery in North Island. They have been breeding camellias for over fifty years, producing many *x williamsii* hybrids such as 'Jury's Yellow' that has a mass of petal-like stamens, and the mid-pink double 'Water Lily'. And there's a Cornish connection here too: the family of Thomas Jury emigrated from Cornwall in 1842 and sailed into New Plymouth on one of the first immigrant ships.

Camellias thrive in acidic, moisture-retentive, free-draining soil and dappled shade. There are some wonderful garden specimens available, including *Camellia japonica* 'Desire' in white, with blush-pink tones and darker tips to the petals, the pale-pink semi-double 'Berenice Boddy', and 'Bob Hope' with its red flowers and bold bosses of bright golden stamens.

Dahlias

Dahlias, the queens of flamboyance, have flounced in and out of fashion for decades. There's a cast of thousands, and in ten different forms, so there's bound to be one to appeal to every taste. Each year Eden gardeners seek out different ones, including newcomers, to improve the display – there are usually around fifty varieties on view.

Towards the end of May, when Bulbmania is over, the ground is thoroughly dug over and vast amounts of chicken manure are added to it because

TOP DAHLIAS

'BISHOP OF LLANDAFF' – a classic with peony-red flowers offset by delicious dark-bronze foliage.

'TWYNING'S SMARTIE' – a single-flowered dahlia with individual petals of cerise or white – sometimes both!

'JUUL'S ALLSTAR' (pictured) – a single flower with petals that are yellow on the top and dark pink below and roll inwards.

'ARABIAN NIGHT'– notable for its burgundy flowers.

'PINK GIRAFFE' – unusual white and pink bands across the petals.

French lavender will thrive as a garden plant in a sunny spot on free-draining soil.

dahlias are hungry, thirsty plants. If you can provide a plentiful supply of food and are prepared to water them constantly, you can be certain of success; at Eden they are so vigorous that the slugs can't keep up with them and the earwigs are overwhelmed!

But dahlias do require a bit of TLC in order to give of their very best. Plant out the tubers in a sheltered, sunny spot in rich, moisture-retentive soil after the last frosts – you'll have dug in plenty of well-rotted compost the autumn before, if necessary. Dahlias need some support for their succulent stems, so insert supporting canes before planting. Make the hole slightly larger than the cluster of tubers, and plant them 15cm deep; tie soft new shoots into the cane as they develop, and keep the plot weed-free. Pinching out the growing tips encourages bushy plants and more flowers, but if you prefer fewer, larger flowers (especially on 'giant' varieties), then leave four sideshoots, and up to eight on medium-sized forms.

When the first buds start to develop, feed the plants with high-potash fertilizer. Water copiously through the growing season and never let them dry out, because dahlias are over 95 per cent water! Depending on their size, the plants can be supported with twine strung between three to five canes. Without support, large dahlias can suffer from the weather; heavy rainfall increases the weight of the bloom, and if strong winds follow, the whole display can collapse.

Dahlia tubers are not completely frost-hardy, so you can either lift them in late autumn and store them until planting out again in spring when there are no more frosts or, if the winters are relatively warm

where you are, overwinter them in the ground, as long as you cover them with a good layer of mulch. However, it's usually safer to lift immediately after the first frost. Lift them carefully, label them and allow them to dry on a greenhouse bench or other dry, warm, flat surface. Remove any pieces that are diseased or damaged, dusting the cuts with sulphur afterwards, then store them over winter in trays of multipurpose compost or boxes of anything from perlite to newspaper in a cool, frost-free place. Check the tubers regularly throughout the winter and remove any that show signs of rotting.

The imposing *Dahlia imperialis* from Mexico reaches around 4.5m tall and is often known as the tree dahlia. It produces lovely pendulous, lilac-pink flowers from the end of November to early December, if it's not cut back by frost. This stunning plant, like a giant lush-leafed bamboo, only flowers in milder climates and is grown elsewhere in Britain as a foliage plant. It sometimes flowers at Eden and is used as a foil to enhance the colours of surrounding plants.

Lavender

One of the popular spots at Eden, particularly when in bloom, is the lavender field with its neat rows of plants reminding visitors of trips to such diverse locations as Norfolk, Jersey and Provence. But lavenders are much more versatile than Eden's rows might suggest, and look fantastic in containers, as hedges, spilling over path edges or just nestling amongst other plants in the herbaceous border.

Lavandula x intermedia 'Grosso' with blue-purple flowers has long been grown for oil production, loves the free-draining soil and receives no special attention

LAVENDER CARE

ONE OF THE QUESTIONS asked most often by visitors is 'Why has my lavender gone woody?' And the answer is 'You are not cutting it back enough.' Regular pruning increases their lifespan. Be brave! Hardy lavenders with one main flowering period, particularly *L. × intermedia,* should be cut back very hard to 22cm immediately after flowering, or lightly trimmed in April, going back 2.5cm into the previous year's wood. The latter is better in cooler climates.

With an artistic eye and careful pruning, lavender can be shaped into globes that look both contemporary and architectural. Old plants can be renovated by cutting back any growth to within about 10cm of the bare wood to encourage regrowth from the older wood. If the plant breaks into growth the following year, repeat the process until it is back to ground level. In the wild, lavenders bask in hot sunshine on poor, parched neutral to alkaline soils, so add a handful of lime per square metre in spring to make the soil more alkaline, and add grit when planting in heavier soil. Plant in a raised bed if necessary – waterlogging in winter is a killer!

Each plant in Eden's lavender fields is harvested carefully by hand and the guides use bunches to tell its fascinating story.

at all at Eden. As the flowers fade, it is harvested one row at a time through August and into September to prolong the display. Each bush is trimmed over with secateurs; holding one small bunch at a time then cutting off the flowers is time-consuming, but it does prevent the heads from falling all over the plant, soil and surrounding plants as they do when harvested with shears. Annual trimming ensures plants are productive for at least ten years.

There are plenty of varieties to choose from. They are categorized as English lavender, *Lavandula*

angustifolia, and French lavender, *Lavandula stoechas* but there are also other tender treasures and handsome hybrids. Amongst all of these there is a wide range of cultivars, whose colours range from dark purple to white, pink and even red. The darker delights include 'Peter Pan', which attains a height of about 45cm and is perfect for low hedges and edging borders, and 'Gorgeous', which sports deep-purple flowers and more than lives up to its name. The perennially popular 'Richard Gray' is a wonderful hybrid that also reaches about 45cm high, and has deep-

purple flowers topping a mound of silvery-grey foliage. Among the mid-purples, the magnificent 'Melissa Lilac' creates neat globes topped with fluffy flowers, while a rich purple haze hovers over the sumptuous, silvery cushions of 'Beechwood Blue', and small but spectacular little 'Miss Muffet' is a tiny tuffet, barely 30cm tall, that is perfect for placing by a narrow path or in a container. The pick of the pale blues is 'Blue Ice', whose soft ethereal shades shimmer against silvery buds, and 'Fragrant Memories' which has delicate grey foliage offsetting serene pale-purple flowers. If you prefer your lavenders pink, then 'Miss Katherine' offers tones that are deep, soft and sensual, while the pale-pink flowers of 'Rosea' twinkle against its vivid green foliage. White selections include 'Nana Alba', a compact creation with dazzling white flowers and grey-green foliage, and 'Blue Mountain White', which is purity in perfection. And if you prefer your lavender leaves variegated, 'Walberton's Silver Edge' is outstanding for its creamy margins and pale-purple flowers.

French lavenders – *Lavandula stoechas* and its hybrids – have spectacular papery topknots of bracts

and fat flowerheads. There are the plump clusters of 'Fathead'; flighty 'Aphrodite', whose slender stems and delicate flowers are rather overwhelmed by its bold bracts, and the beautiful 'Ballerina', resplendent in a white tutu that ages to pink and purple. For something completely different, try low-growing 'Kew Red', a southern Spanish sensation with unusual cerise-coloured flowers, or sample the pale-green flowers of the form *L. viridis* with its foliage smelling of lemons. The fabulous-flowered woolly lavenders are fine for foliage too, but despite their self-made sheepskins they need protection from frost. *L. lanata* is a woolly wonder, while *L. dentata* has finely-toothed leaves and violet flowers.

Most visitors to the Canary Islands forget that they're surrounded by some of the rarest plants in the world. And among these treasures are tender lavenders that can be grown in pots (they need to be protected from frost). Unlike their single-spiked colleagues they produce clusters of slim, elegant flowers hovering daintily above the finest foliage. Look out for the super-special *Lavandula buchii* var. *buchii*, found exclusively in Tenerife, which forms a gleaming globe of silvery foliage with delicate clusters of blue-purple flowers. The foliage of *L. canariensis* is a filigree of pale green topped with dense, slender, blue spikes – they make fabulous specimen plants.

Pinks

Another old favourite featured in 'The Making of Garden Flowers' at Eden is the pinks (*Dianthus plumarius* cultivars). They have long been popular with gardeners, having been cultivated since Roman times, and were especially so in the seventeenth century. Many forms have been bred over the centuries, and perfume has always been a priority.

Often seen in borders or planted in rockeries, at Eden pinks form a summer display featuring more than twenty-five cultivars, and the fragrance is phenomenal. Some of the gardeners' particular favourites include the new super-fragrant Scent First series, such as sugar-pink 'Candy Floss', and 'Raspberry Sundae' which is blush-pink with a raspberry eye. Other good choices are 'Moulin Rouge', a new variety with old attributes including a strong clove fragrance, and double flowers – white petals flushed pale crimson; the legendary 'Mrs Sinkins', raised by John Sinkins and named after his wife: it has double white flowers, is richly fragrant, and has been a cottage-garden classic since 1868; and 'Hereford Butter Market' with its dainty double flowers, the burgundy petals lightly marked with pink.

Pinks need an open, sunny position in free-draining soil, so add plenty of grit or pea shingle to heavier soils and slightly raise the planting bed. Feed with bonemeal in spring and dress the soil with chalk or ground limestone before planting. Pinks can withstand drought, but water them well immediately after planting until they are established.

As noted earlier, plants grown on the same soil over several years can cause a build-up of disease, and with pinks there can be a problem with fusarium wilt (see p. 303). At Eden the display has suffered from this disease, and after two years of treating with various fungicides it is still not under control; the only solution appears to be to move the display elsewhere.

FACT!

The genus name *Dianthus* means 'divine flower', but the origin of the name 'pinks' is uncertain. It may have come from the 'pinks', or ornamental openings, in Elizabethan dresses that showed splashes and streaks of contrasting colours below.

LEFT: *The flowers of the pinks in the Eden display seem to float like confetti over the blue-grey foliage beneath.*

An annual poppy bows its head under the weight of glistening rain-drops – the Outdoor Biome is beautiful in any weather!

▨ Annuals

At several locations around the Eden site there are displays of annuals that combine native with non-native – these extend the flowering season from late June to late autumn, resulting in a shimmering meadow of colour. The non-native mixes have been developed after several years of trials by Dr Nigel Dunnett at the University of Sheffield; they have the advantage that they flower in the first season and so provide a quick and inexpensive way to create a display. (If you fall for them when you see them, they are available over the internet!)

As always with planting up, soil preparation is key. At Eden, once all the tulips have been lifted the borders are dug over, more green waste, manure and flaked seaweed are added, and the soil is finely raked and allowed to settle. Just before sowing the area is raked again, then the seed is lightly scattered on the surface and raked once more. Watering is the key to success in sowing annuals, as drought affects the length of the display, so water yours regularly.

Each seed mix is colour-themed, from pastels to the 'volcano' mix with blooms of red, purple and gold. Earlier in the year at Eden you may find a mix of early poppies, cornflowers, and several varieties of flax and toadflaxes such as *Linaria maroccana*, in a rainbow of yellow, pink, purple and blue. Sometimes the gardeners mix in other plants like dahlias, lilies, gladioli and alstroemeria (Peruvian lily) so as to add more structure to the display.

However, be warned that there is always a danger that more vigorous species will stifle other plants; poppies can overwhelm flax and gypsophila, and corn marigolds can have a similar impact. To avoid such problems, scatter the seed thinly over the seedbed. The only difficulty that arises at Eden occurs when annuals shed their seeds: a pastel mix may be sown the year after an orange-blue-and-red mix, whose seeds end up growing with the new ones. The only option is to remove the unwanted plants, doing as little damage as possible.

When sowing seeds in a rural areas, always select and sow carefully. If you choose a seed mix combining native and introduced annuals, as at Eden, you must avoid locating them too close to your perimeters or wherever they might be able to seed in the surrounding countryside or escape into the wild.

Sweet peas

Fragrant, charming and colourful, sweet peas are an essential component of the English summer garden – and are easy to grow: just soak the seeds or put them between two layers of damp kitchen towel for twenty-four hours, then sow the ones that swell. If any don't swell, rub the seedcoat gently with sandpaper opposite the scar, or 'eye', and then sow. Sow from November to January, or from February to March, in an unheated glasshouse or cold-frame in multipurpose compost. Keep the temperature at 18–20°C to help them germinate, although lower temperatures will still give good results. Move them into a cooler spot in good light soon after germination.

Keep the seedlings watered during warm spells and the surrounding temperature cool. Use 7.5cm pots of John Innes No. 1, or 'Roottrainers' (see Glossary), which will accommodate their long roots.

Pinch out the growth tips when three pairs of leaves have formed for more than one stem per plant. From mid-March onwards, partly depending on when they were sown, harden the seedlings off by putting them outside during the day and indoors at night when frosts are forecast. Plant them out permanently once the weather and soil have warmed up (from late March, hopefully). From March to April, depending on the weather, the seeds can also be sown directly in the ground where they are to flower. Sow them 5–7cm deep and the same distance apart. Seeds sown outside, though, are vulnerable to hungry mice, slugs and snails; and any cold weather will affect germination.

TOP ANNUALS

Limnanthes douglasii, the poached-eggplant, is low-growing with bright-yellow and white flowers and is useful for attracting beneficial insects.

Nigella damascena, or love-in-a-mist, has fabulous pale-blue flowers and delicate foliage, but can become a weed if allowed to set seed.

Centaurea cyanus is better known as the beautiful blue cornflower. There are several selections, such as the compact 'Florence Blue', mixes in shades of pink and blue, and the dark-flowered 'Black Ball'.

Papaver rhoeas is the fabulous field poppy, with rich red flowers. There are some stunning selections such as 'Fairy Wings' and 'Mother of Pearl' with its pale-pink, salmon and smoky-grey flowers.

Briza maxima, the greater quaking grass, forms dense clumps of upright leaves and wiry stems with locket-shaped flowers that dance in the wind; *Briza minor* is similar but shorter, as you might expect, and very dainty.

TOP FRAGRANT SWEET PEAS

'MATACUNA' (pictured) – introduced from Peru, it has bicoloured flowers of deep blue and purple on each stem.

'PAINTED LADY' – a bicoloured flower of deep pink and white with pink veins.

'BLACK KNIGHT' – a large, maroon-flowered beauty introduced by Henry Eckford in 1898.

'CHARLIE'S ANGEL' – one of the best blues, this one has frilly pale-blue flowers on long stems.

'JILLY' – one of the best creams, with young flowers that are almost yellow.

Sweet peas need a sunny, sheltered spot in rich, slightly acid soil – dig in plenty of well-rotted garden compost the autumn before planting, but don't overdo it on richer soils. Before planting, lightly fork in a general fertilizer. Tall varieties should be set 10–15cm apart at the base of a support, and dwarf varieties 1cm deep in large pots of compost. Alternatively, sow them in pots in March and transplant in late-spring. Water the plants regularly, early in the day; don't let them dry out, as sweet peas are prone to powdery mildew. Feed with liquid tomato fertilizer once every two weeks, when the first flowers appear. Cut or dead-head flowers regularly – if seedpods form, they stop flowering.

A HISTORY OF THE SWEET PEA

A COTTAGE-GARDEN AND contemporary classic, the sweet pea has a long, distinguished history. It was cultivated by the Moors in Spain from 1450, then in 1699 Father Francis Cupani sent seeds of a mauve and maroon flower from Sicily to Britain, where it was transformed into one of the nation's favourite flowers. In 1800 there were only five different colours including the cultivar 'Painted Lady' with deep-pink and white blooms, which is still available; now there are almost six hundred varieties.

In 1876 Henry Eckford of Wem in Shropshire began selecting and crossing sweet peas; by the early twentieth century he'd raised almost half the varieties that are now commercially available, all with large showy flowers and a fabulous fragrance. In 1907, 'Dorothy Eckford' was voted the best white sweet pea by the National Sweet Pea Society, and 'Lady Grisel Hamilton' the finest lavender-coloured variety. Later, Silas Cole, gardener to Countess Spencer at Althorp House in Northamptonshire, produced the wavy-edged 'Spencer' varieties with bolder flowers in single and contrasting colours and a range of scents. The first, 'Countess Spencer', was exhibited in 1901, the same year that one of the greatest sweet-pea seedsmen, Mr William Unwin, produced the pink, frilly-flowered 'Gladys Unwin'. Most modern varieties came from these original selections.

GARDEN THEMES

You may have in mind a specific theme for your garden, or simply want to plant individual borders in specific styles. For instance, it could be full of lush growth and very tropical, or you might follow recent trends and go for the 'prairie' style. Steppe or Mediterranean plantings may be appealing if climate change brings drier summers, or you could try a grove of hardy palms or even tree ferns to create a 'prehistoric' landscape – if you win the lottery. Eden's Bulbmania proves that mass plantings can have a huge impact – just dare to be different!

■ A tree-fern border

One particularly imposing border at Eden is packed with low-growing ferns and around forty tree ferns (*Dicksonia antarctica*) of different sizes, ranging from seedlings to over 2m. Once a mysterious feature of tropical gardens, tree ferns have become popular for their dramatic appearance and adaptability to the British climate, and are now widely available (though still very expensive). Most of the tree ferns at Eden were donated by HM Customs, who confiscated a

large shipment that arrived in Britain without the correct documentation! If you are thinking about planting some tree ferns in your garden, make sure that they come complete with all the necessary paperwork and a tag on the trunks to prove they have been sustainably harvested from a wild source – this usually means from an area being cleared for development, or from forestry plantations in Australia or Tasmania.

It's something of a myth that tree ferns need cool shelter and shade. With adequate humidity they will grow happily in the open, as they do in their native habitat, although the fronds can be damaged by winter storms. At Eden the tree ferns that are planted in the open (2–3m apart) are growing well, in part because to keep the humidity high they are sprayed from above up to four times a day in summer by a battery of four pop-up sprinklers at the edge of the bed. On hot days and during dry conditions, water yours regularly by pouring tepid water into the centre of each plant so that it drains down the inside of the trunk, and mist them as often as possible. If there's a

Despite the lack of flowers, this tree-fern border is always a hit with Eden's visitors and would be easy, if expensive, to replicate at home.

hosepipe ban, buy a chemical sprayer (a larger version of a mister), fill it with water and mist.

Tree ferns are happiest in rich, moist, slightly acid soil. Mulch them heavily with bark chippings and apply a general fertilizer annually, in spring, around the roots. Beyond this, little maintenance is required – just remove old fronds when they break or become brown and untidy. In most parts of Britain tree ferns need some frost-protection over winter, but a handful of straw packed around the crown in early November and secured in place, plus some hessian or horticultural fleece wrapped around the trunk, should keep damaging frosts at bay. The fronds can be left, folded down or removed, as they will be replaced the following year. Tree ferns grown in pots can be moved to a sheltered, frost-free part of the garden or kept in a shed, but it's vital that they don't dry out completely when in store, or your treasures will die.

Few gardeners illuminate their gardens, but they might change their minds after visiting Eden at night for one of the summer concerts – 'the Sessions' – or at the 'Time of Gifts', when the tree ferns look spectacular! Another way to highlight these magnificent plants is to underplant them with a mass of other ferns.

During the Victorian 'fern craze', enthusiasts scoured the highways and byways of Britain in search of unusual kinds, and there are almost forty species and cultivated forms in the Eden collection including many unusual ones, some with 'crested' fronds. The leaves of *Athyrium filix-femina* 'Frizelliae' take the form of tiny rounded structures along the midrib so that the fronds look like necklaces, and

'Grandiceps' has a large crest at the end of each frond. *Dryopteris affinis* 'Cristata' has large crests on the 'leaflets' and at the end of each frond, and *Dryopteris filix-mas* 'Linearis Polydactyla' has slender leaflets with long, spreading crests. All of them are hardy and perfect for damp, shady positions in organic-rich soil. Just keep the compost moist and spray during dry weather if needed.

■ Prairie planting

The original prairies, a habitat of colourful herbaceous perennials and tall, summer-growing grasses, once covered more than one million square miles of mid-western North America. Although it is thought of as a 'natural' habitat, it was in fact formed as a result of

ten thousand years of landscape management by Native Americans, who created their wildflower-rich grassland by the controlled burning of woodland so as to make travelling and hunting easier. By the start of the twentieth century, nearly all of the landscape had been ploughed up and replaced with agricultural crops. Now all that remains of the true prairie are small areas on reserves and along railway lines. These contain a range of species, some quite localized and found in particular soil types, others more widespread. The plants themselves, many now stalwarts of the British herbaceous border and cottage garden, are remarkable survivors that deserve the gardener's attention.

Very little preparation or management is required for a prairie-style garden. However, as the soil is so poor at Eden, green waste was mixed with the existing spoil before planting. Plants will show signs of nutrient deficiencies and their growth will be stunted if they are not fed twice a year, in May and June, with a balanced fertilizer such as Growmore. Enrich the ground, improve the drainage by adding grit if necessary, and remove weeds before planting. Don't plant too deeply, and make sure that the top of the rootball is just below the surface of the soil. Water the plants well before and immediately after planting.

At Eden the prairie needs strimming only once, in late January or early February, when the debris is raked off and composted; then in March the gardeners go over the area with a flame-gun to remove unwanted weeds and mimic the action of

The combination of flowers, foliage and seed heads give the prairie display the appearance of an intricately woven tapestry.

the fires that created and managed the original prairies. (This is not necessary in the domestic garden, unless you have a large space devoted to prairie and particularly want to achieve this look!) Finally, any perennial grasses and clover are treated with glyphosate systemic weedkiller, and the 'prairie' is then all set to create another magical display.

The landscape changes constantly as plants set seed and naturalize, so a different species dominates each year. With plenty of self-seeding,

minimal feeding and even less intervention, the little bit of prairie in your garden will be a constantly changing patchwork of some of Nature's richest colours. Most prairie plants bloom from mid-summer onwards, and the most common flower colour is yellow; the grasses are often at their most attractive in autumn. Rather than stay strictly with prairie species, it's better to simply plant in a prairie style, as this increases the range of plants that you can use.

■ Steppe

Once covering the vast plains of eastern Europe and Russia, this type of grassland is divided into three categories, according to how it came about. Very dry summers and poor, free-draining soils dictated that there could not be enough moisture to support trees, and so drought-tolerant grassland developed in their place. This habitat supports an abundance of early-flowering herbaceous perennials and grasses that bloom while there is moisture in the soil and then become dormant during the summer months. Then, secondary steppe was created by human activity: it is found where controlled burning and grazing prevented trees and shrubs from taking over the grassland. Third, woodland steppe is a transitional landscape scattered with trees, a terrain somewhere between forest and grassland.

Today, little original steppe exists, as most of it has been ploughed for cereal production – although, just as with the prairies, fragments still survive along railway lines or on dry hills where agricultural production wasn't possible. The tradition of land management by grazing and occasional burning in spring is still practised by some farmers: burning clears the land of trees and weedy species, maintaining a range of characteristic species such as needle-grasses (*Stipa* sp.) and herbaceous perennials such as salvia. The decline in uncommon dry-grasslands species such as the pasque flower (*Pulsatilla vulgaris*) is partly due to the phasing-out of these management practices.

A steppe planting scheme can easily be created in your garden, using a combination of pot-grown

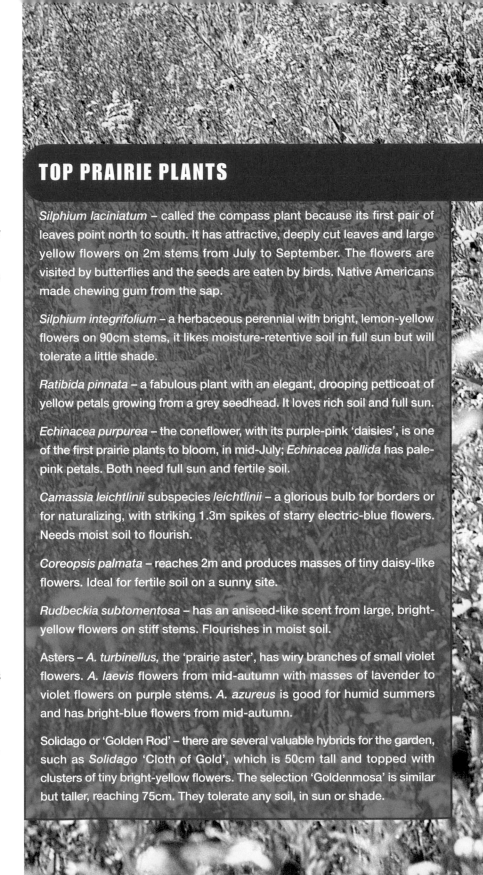

TOP PRAIRIE PLANTS

Silphium laciniatum – called the compass plant because its first pair of leaves point north to south. It has attractive, deeply cut leaves and large yellow flowers on 2m stems from July to September. The flowers are visited by butterflies and the seeds are eaten by birds. Native Americans made chewing gum from the sap.

Silphium integrifolium – a herbaceous perennial with bright, lemon-yellow flowers on 90cm stems, it likes moisture-retentive soil in full sun but will tolerate a little shade.

Ratibida pinnata – a fabulous plant with an elegant, drooping petticoat of yellow petals growing from a grey seedhead. It loves rich soil and full sun.

Echinacea purpurea – the coneflower, with its purple-pink 'daisies', is one of the first prairie plants to bloom, in mid-July; *Echinacea pallida* has pale-pink petals. Both need full sun and fertile soil.

Camassia leichtlinii subspecies *leichtlinii* – a glorious bulb for borders or for naturalizing, with striking 1.3m spikes of starry electric-blue flowers. Needs moist soil to flourish.

Coreopsis palmata – reaches 2m and produces masses of tiny daisy-like flowers. Ideal for fertile soil on a sunny site.

Rudbeckia subtomentosa – has an aniseed-like scent from large, bright-yellow flowers on stiff stems. Flourishes in moist soil.

Asters – *A. turbinellus*, the 'prairie aster', has wiry branches of small violet flowers. *A. laevis* flowers from mid-autumn with masses of lavender to violet flowers on purple stems. *A. azureus* is good for humid summers and has bright-blue flowers from mid-autumn.

Solidago or 'Golden Rod' – there are several valuable hybrids for the garden, such as *Solidago* 'Cloth of Gold', which is 50cm tall and topped with clusters of tiny bright-yellow flowers. The selection 'Goldenmosa' is similar but taller, reaching 75cm. They tolerate any soil, in sun or shade.

plants – to give an instant display – and seed sown in spring. Rake out a rough seedbed first, then scatter the seed over the area and rake it in. The plants will quickly self-seed, filling gaps and creating an even more naturalistic appearance.

In spring at Eden the steppe slope is covered with the deep-lavender bells of pasque flowers and yellow cowslip (*Primula veris*), followed in early summer by a host of euphorbias, salvias, origanums, herbaceous geraniums and bulbs such as asphodelines. The display also includes some cultivars that are close to the wild specimens in appearance, and all are good garden plants. Take, for instance, the eye-catching architectural sea hollies *Eryngium alpinum* 'Blue Star', with its metallic-blue, thistle-like flowers and imposing basal 'ruff', and *Eryngium planum* 'Blaukappe', with similar, smaller, intense-blue flowers. Also worthy of note are *Buphthalmum salicifolium* 'Alpengold', which has large leaves and clusters of bright-yellow 'daisy' flowers, plus *Iris iberica* and tulips such as *Tulipa praestans*, the white starry-flowered *Tulipa biflora*, and the fabulous water-lily tulip *Tulipa kaufmanniana*, which displays bright red flowers. All of these plants flourish on poor, free-draining soils.

The steppe being a naturally low-nutrient habitat, you need to do little soil preparation before planting beyond what you would do when planting seedlings and so on. Certainly at Eden, for this reason plants are fed sparingly, and only once a year, with Growmore. The ongoing management of the land is similar to that required by the prairie grassland – the vegetation is strimmed after flowering, once the seeds have been shed, in August, and any debris is then removed. Remove any intruding plants that shouldn't be there by hand (at Eden, buddleia, willow, gorse seedlings and escapees from the prairie infiltrate the area!), and spray glyphosate to remove any unwanted broad-leafed grasses. At Eden, as in the prairie patch, the steppe area is burned with a flame-gun in March to replicate the old tradition.

The steppe is never watered at Eden, so it develops a dynamic equilibrium – just as the prairie display does – whereby natural seeding changes the dominant species annually. Prairie planting has been fashionable with gardeners for several years – with rainfall levels falling, drought-tolerant steppe could be set to usurp its starring role!

▬ The mediterranean outdoors

The west side of the Outdoor Biome, where the slopes are at their steepest, is home to the outdoor mediterranean garden. Here is a chance to experiment, growing outdoors and all year round plants that are not normally regarded as 'hardy', even in Cornwall, while testing their drought-tolerance too.

Tradition maintains that certain 'tender' plants will not grow north of an imaginary line between Exeter and the Wash, but times are changing as human activities increase the pressure on our fragile planet. Climate change may well be increasing temperatures. Also, wherever you garden, don't forget the impact of microclimates. The base of a south-facing wall in a sheltered courtyard provides protection and radiated heat; a west-facing spot ensures that plants are protected from early-morning sun that could cause frost damage as well as being perfectly located for

RIGHT: *Puyas have foliage full of menace like barbed, exploding fireworks. If you plant these in your garden, site them with care.*

basking in the heat of a summer afternoon; a five-degree slope is roughly the equivalent of moving thirty miles south; and living in a city will also mean increased temperatures.

The key to success with plants of borderline hardiness is drainage and keeping them away from frost. Most will not survive waterlogging in winter and will simply rot off, but plants can be protected from freezing temperatures by being wrapped in fleece or straw or surrounded by hardy plants. It's the combination of damp and cold that kills. Establishing plants can be a problem on a dry site such as the mediterranean one at Eden – even drought-tolerant plants need water when they are young – so water in new plants until they are established.

The display at Eden includes four species of puya, a spiny South American genus from Chile, Peru and Bolivia – many inhabit the dry slopes of the Andes alongside other survivors like cacti, so they are used to cold, harsh conditions. *Puya alpestris* has already produced a spike of green-yellow flowers, and there are several *Puya berteroniana* with their arching spiny leaves that have survived for four years. The great hope is that they will flower en masse – another first for Eden! Encouraged by what has been achieved so far, there are plans to plant *Puya raimondii* which, when in flower, reaches up to 2m. These plants share space with the closely related *Fascicularia bicolor*, with its pale-blue flowers and bright-red leaf bases that are already starting to form clumps.

There are also echiums such as *Echium pininana* – a huge viper's bugloss from the laurel forests of Las

Echium pininana, *a native of the Canary Islands, stands like a giant exclamation mark and has naturalized along the Cornish coastline.*

Palmas in the Canary Islands. Rare in the wild but often seen in gardens in warmer parts of the UK, it has spikes of blue flowers up to 4m tall and seeds that germinate so freely that the seedlings need frequent weeding out; alternatively, as long as it's done before the rosette of leaves is 30cm tall, the plants can be moved and used to fill gaps in the display. Echiums are generally very successful in milder climates. In cooler parts of Britain you can grow them in free-draining soil and cover with cloches to prevent waterlogging.

Another rare Canary Islands endemic is *Lotus berthelotii* which has grey-green foliage and bright-red flowers. It's virtually extinct in the wild, but not in garden centres, and is often used in containers or hanging baskets! It has yet to survive a winter at Eden, but try it in your garden, planting it out in May and overwintering under glass, always remembering to bring the plant indoors before the first frost. In what may seem a strange reversal, at Eden most of the common garden plants from the mediterranean regions, such as cistus, sage, bay and bulbs like cyclamen, are growing under glass – well, under ethylene tetrafluoroethylenecopolymer, anyway – as part of the Warm Temperate Biome display.

■ The Cornish fruit collection

Fruit has long been grown in Britain, and in Cornwall the main crop was traditionally apples, with some plums and pear orchards and cherries in the Tamar Valley, often underplanted with crops of strawberries or daffodils. Traditionally, Cornish farms and homesteads included an orchard of up to three

EDEN SUCCESSES

Proteas, usually more at home in the Warm Temperate Biome, have been one of the great outdoor success stories: over ten flowers were produced in 2005 on plants only three years old that are not fed and are left to survive on their own. Six leucadendron cultivars have settled in well too, doubling in size, among them 'Mrs Stanley' with soft-pink flowers and 'Safari Sunset' which matures from claret to pink. There's a mass of spiky grevilleas, banksias and hakeas from Australia, and several species of agave, all planted together to form a natural scrub. It's hoped that the grey-blue-leafed succulent echeverias will survive there too.

In Cornwall, planting often takes place in autumn; with longer summers than most other parts of Britain, the ground stays warm for longer and there's a whole growing season for the plants to establish themselves. In addition to *Puya alpestris*, *Yucca glauca* too has flowered, so the next great hope is *Telopea speciosissima*, the New South Wales waratah, with its spidery red flowers. Just think, you could be trying them at home!

CHOOSING THE RIGHT FRUIT TREE

THE ROOTSTOCK controls the vigour of a tree as well as the age at which it starts cropping. The apples in the main orchard at Eden are grafted on M25 dwarfing rootstocks that produce trees up to 4m in height and spread. They fruit within four years of planting; on more exposed sites they need staking for the first five years. The M25 rootstock is very versatile and can be used for ornamental styles of shaping for fruit such as dwarf pyramids and cordons; because of the mature tree's small size, maintenance and harvesting are easy. MM106, a semi-dwarfing stock, is tolerant of a range of soils and is used for espaliers and cordons; they fruit after three to four years and bear heavily as the apple matures.

acres, enclosed by hedging, that also provided food and shelter for the residents of the beehives that were placed among the trees for pollination purposes, as they are at Eden. And, of course, there was an annual crop of honey. In the days before rootstocks (see Glossary) produced dwarf varieties, trees would be planted about 10m apart and pruned as standards. Trunks, at planting, would be typically about 1.8m tall, with a large productive crown.

Although you can buy trees in pots that are partially shaped (trained) in garden centres, the cheapest way to buy them is dug straight from the ground as 'bare root' specimens – these are available for planting between leaf fall and bud burst. Specialist nurseries offer a huge choice, particularly early in the season. Apples need an open, sheltered, sunny site protected from cold winds and frost. Varieties range from those you can eat straight from the tree in late August, to those you can store until the next May, with flavours ranging from spice to strawberry, pear drops to banana, and many more.

Fruit trees should be planted at the same depth they were planted in their pots and no deeper, and in a hole slightly larger than the pots. A gardener should always respond to the soil conditions he or she is working with. Dig a large hole in clay and it acts like a sump, filling with water, and in long wet periods the tree could drown; prepare the soil around the hole too well, and the tree establishes rapidly but then suffers from shock once it discovers the state of the soil beyond. This is not a problem for the Eden apple trees – the soil is so rich and free-draining that when the wires supporting the espaliers were tightened, despite being at the recommended depth (60cm in the ground and 1.8m above) the stakes pulled out of the ground. To keep them in place, rocks were put around the bases of the stakes, then concreted, and a piece of slate was put under the angled tension post of the wires. This heavy-duty device kept the posts secure.

A good mulch of well-rotted organic matter will suppress weeds and retain moisture, and the trees will benefit from feeding and regular watering until they are established. Chicken manure will encourage rapid growth, but use it cautiously, as soft growth is more vulnerable to wind damage. You can tell when trees have become established because they put on plenty of new growth and flower prolifically. Theoretically, any fruit produced should be removed at an early stage for the first three years so that all the energy goes into root growth, but in practice this usually turns out to be too difficult!

The apple collection at Eden had to sit in their pots for a long time before planting, as it took a while to find the trees a home. Several years later they are still being trained in an effort to create the best framework achievable: they started off with plenty of low branches but few at the top, and the job still isn't finished. Fortunately, unlike many plants, apples can be pruned – carefully – over several years and still retain the potential to make a well-formed tree.

The trees are first pruned in autumn or winter to create the main framework, then summer-pruned to form the fruiting spurs. At Eden, formative pruning is done in dry weather to avoid problems with apple canker; this disease flourishes in moist conditions and is a problem for apple growers in Cornwall. Pruned hard, apples will respond with a lot of strong stem growth; prune lightly and they produce more fruit. This is why it is better to regenerate by pruning a little over several years. Always remove dead, dying and diseased branches as well as those that cross and rub or spoil the shape.

The orchard at Eden has been sown with a wild-flower mix to encourage pollinating insects and to make an attractive ornamental feature. The ground was rotavated several times that first spring, raked to

LEFT: 'Roundway Magnum Bonum' (back), deep crimson 'Ben's Red' and 'Blackamore Red' (left) all flourish in Eden's damp Cornish climate.

SUPPORT YOUR LOCAL VARIETY

THE CORNISH Apple Collection, planted at Restineas Farm on the Eden estate (and not currently open to the public), holds almost fifty varieties including cookers, dessert, dual-purpose and cider apples, with names like 'Cornish Aromatic', 'Cornish Pine' and 'Cornish Gilliflower'. In west Cornwall some are even grown for pickling – a local delicacy eaten with cream for Sunday tea.

Received wisdom would have it that attempting to grow apples in the south-west must be pointless. The mild, humid climate is perfect for canker, scab and mildew, not for healthy apples, and aphids and codling moth must surely reach epidemic proportions too. Add the salt-laden winds and the shallow acidic soils, and it's no surprise that this belief holds true in one respect. For in fact, few introduced varieties have been able to cope. Only 'Golden Noble', 'Beauty of Bath' and 'Blenheim Orange', which is traditionally planted in every Cornish orchard, have stayed the course. By contrast, though, there are around eighty named 'Cornish' varieties, and almost another sixty that remain unidentified.

Local varieties of any plant are part of our horticultural heritage. They have been selected and conserved because they perform well under local growing conditions, provide good regular crops and have a distinctive flavour. Many, like the Cornish varieties, are disease-resistant, reducing the need for chemical control. There are almost certain to be varieties in your own area that possess similar desirable characteristics, with potential for use in future breeding too. Allow them to become extinct, and their unique attributes vanish for ever!

Embothrium coccineum is one of the most spectacular garden plants for cool temperate climates and is grown as a shrub or small tree.

a fine texture, marked with string lines to ensure even seed distribution, then sown with a combination of 75 per cent grass and wildflower mix to 25 per cent sharp sand – the sand acting as a 'carrier', helping to disperse the seed. Wild flowers in a Cornish orchard – can conservation be more beautiful than that?

■ The Chile collection

The Chile collection at Eden originally grew where the Core now stands, but was moved to a new location near the perimeter of the pit just before work on the building began. Now covering a hectare and still expanding, this priceless collection of one of the world's most endangered floras nestles securely in the Cornish countryside.

Chile contains 5971 native species, around half of which are found nowhere else in the world; and over three hundred are endangered or rare. The temperate Valdivian rainforest in central Chile is still one of the world's top biological hotspots, yet much has already been devastated by agriculture and forestry, firewood collection and intentional forest fires. Ninety different species are featured in Eden's display. A surprising number of our familiar garden plants originate in Chile – hardy fuchsias are probably the most recognizable; *Berberis darwinii*, a glossy-leafed evergreen with golden-orange flowers, is the mainstay of municipal landscapes; and *Chusquea culeou*, an elegant bamboo covering hectares of land in the Chilean rainforest, is popular for container-growing and as a specimen plant (it grows less vigorously in the British climate).

A wide range of Chilean species can thrive outdoors in areas of Britain that are blessed with a warm, moist climate. You often see *Crinodendron hookerianum*, the Chile lantern tree, with its hanging cherry-red flowers, and the rich red, yellow-tipped trumpets of *Desfontainia spinosa*. Add choice tender specimens such as the delectable red-flowered *Berberidopsis corallina* and pink to red *Lapageria rosea* (the national flower of Chile), and it's easy to understand why some of the temperate world's must-have garden plants come from Chile. *Embothrium coccineum*, the Chilean fire bush, is a spectacular plant that is engulfed in flamboyant, swirling orange-red flowers in late spring, and is one of few members of the *Protea* family suitable for growing in the milder parts of Britain. Given acid soil, it is perfect for sheltered gardens or woodlands; the selection 'Norquinco' is the most ornamental.

Eden's Valdivian rainforest collection forms a 'natural' landscape; it was created with advice from staff at the Royal Botanic Garden Edinburgh, who donated the plants. These have been planted in the same species groups as they would be in the wild, with the types of plant changing according to the altitude, following the Andes pattern. At the base of the slope, in a boggy area prone to flooding after heavy rain, an impressive and rapidly expanding clump of *Gunnera tinctoria*, the giant Chilean rhubarb, asserts its right to roam. Usually grown in large British gardens as a specimen plant by pond margins, in Chile it is found in damp habitats in shingle behind beaches, by forest tracks, on cliff faces where water seeps, and at the sides of waterfalls and deep, damp ravines. Very tolerant of

CONSERVE A PIECE OF CHILE

IT'S IMPOSSIBLE for one garden to keep all the threatened plants in the world, so small collections are vital, whether in botanical gardens, at Eden, or even in domestic gardens – all can contribute to their conservation. Plants like *Lobelia bridgesii*, of which there are fewer than 1,000 plants in the wild, and the endangered *Berberidopsis corallina* could be propagated in specialist nurseries and returned to their native habitat if necessary. By accommodating a few such plants in your garden, you can do *your* bit to perpetuate some of the world's most spectacular plants.

the British climate, the plant just needs protection from frost – all you have to do is cover the crown with removed leaves laid upside down – and water.

It took a dozen of Eden's outdoor team about three weeks to lift the original Chilean collection by hand from the site of the Core and move it by tractor and trailer to its new home. Small plants are easy to move, but if you are thinking of shifting larger trees and shrubs, they need preparing the year before. In early autumn, mark an area around the main stem about one-third of the height of the plant and dig a 30 × 60cm trench around the outer edge. Undercut the rootball as far down as possible, to avoid severing any thick roots, mix the dug-out soil with organic matter and refill the trench. This encourages the growth of small fibrous feeding roots that will keep the plant going while ensuring that it can be moved easily the following year.

When transplanting, move trees and shrubs between leaf fall and bud burst when the soil is not waterlogged or frozen. It's best to plant in autumn when the ground is often moist and warm so that there's some root growth before the onset of winter. If you plant later in the season you may encounter problems with spring drought. Newly planted trees and shrubs should be watered thoroughly throughout the first growing season; little and often only encourages roots to head for the soil surface, where they are more susceptible to drought. Ridging the soil in a circle a few feet wide around the main stem will cause a pool to form when you water, stopping the water from running away. Alternatively, put a piece of plastic tube vertically into the ground when filling the planting hole so that you can direct the water straight to the roots; kits are available from retailers – the tube is often supplied with a cap at one end to reduce water loss. Mulching around the tree with bark chippings also conserves moisture and suppresses weeds.

THE MONKEY PUZZLE

ANOTHER INTERESTING EXAMPLE of a vulnerable plant is the monkey puzzle tree (*Araucaria araucana*). Most British monkey puzzles descend from seed introduced by William Lobb, one of two Cornish plant-collecting brothers who grew up at Egloshayle near the Pencarrow estate not far from Eden, where their father was the estate carpenter. A mature avenue of monkey puzzles, thought to have been grown from his original seed collected in Chile, still forms the drive. The story of how the monkey puzzle got its name goes like this: when one Charles Austin, a parliamentary lawyer, staying at Pencarrow in 1834, first saw the plant he exclaimed: 'That tree would puzzle a monkey!' His comment caused great mirth – there are no monkeys in Chile – and the name stuck! It's believed that the brothers collected their seeds from a coastal monkey-puzzle population that's now extinct, so British specimens could be used to repopulate areas where their ancestors once lived.

CHILEAN CHALLENGES

RABBITS ARE OFTEN a problem for gardeners in rural areas. At Eden the fence around the Chilean collection is made of chicken wire, with the base buried some 15 cm below the surface and with no gaps where rabbits can enter.

Ideally, the ground should be cleared of weeds before any planting is done, to avoid having to use chemical herbicides that might check growth or scorch leaves. If you do have to spray among your plants, do it on a still, dry day – ideal conditions for the job – protecting nearby foliage with a piece of board to prevent the spray drifting on to the plants. Sprayers can be fitted with guards for spot-treating individual weeds. As in domestic gardens, at Eden the desire to be environmentally aware has to be balanced against practical needs; selected chemicals are used only as a last resort and strictly according to the manufacturer's instructions for use and disposal.

Bracken in the Chilean collection and the orchard was rampant so was sprayed with 'Asulox', a herbicide used for controlling docks as well. It was applied in July and August when the leaves were fully extended; they started to discolour after a month; a second spraying the following year controlled any regrowth; dead rhizomes rapidly rotted in the ground.

brambles, willowherb and other plants that have a tendency to dominate and restrict the space available for the other species to colonize. At Eden, even the walls are weeded to control rampant species like St John's wort; some plants are dead-headed, leaving just a few seedheads for the birds. If you are planting an area similar to the wayside flowers display at Eden, you will need to strim it once or twice a year after flowering, and rake over the grass so as to keep its fertility low and stop it overwhelming the flowers.

If your garden is in the country and you are creating a wildlife corner, it's a good idea to mimic the local landscape and environment and include species that are native to your area. The Wild Cornwall display aims to showcase the county's familiar flora. Two nationally rare specimens are represented among the collection: Babington's leek (*Allium ampeloprasum* var. *babingtonii*) and the Plymouth pear (*Pyrus cordata*).

Babington's leek is found only in parts of south-west England and in two locations in Ireland but there are several hotspots in Cornwall where it grows prolifically. It is a pretty allium, with wand-like stems about 1.2m long, topped with a 'drumstick' flowerhead of dark buds which open into globes of lavender flowers. The early-flowering Plymouth pear with its pink and white blossom is probably an English form of the wild pear found in Brittany, western Spain and Portugal. There are fifteen small trees left around Plymouth where the first was discovered in 1865, and five around Truro. It's uncertain whether they are native or not – they could be ancient trees established before the English Channel was formed or they could have originated as bird-sown seedlings. And, of course, there have long been links between the

The wild teasel, found in woods and fields, is a British native that is attractive to many different birds and insects.

LEFT: *This glorious Cornish hedge contains a wide range of plant habitats and provides protection for all sorts of animals.*

NATIVE PLANTS

PRIMROSE (*Primula vulgaris*) – provides nectar for early butterflies, its leaves are food for caterpillars, and birds eat the seeds. Thrives in dappled shade and self-seeds freely.

HONEYSUCKLE (*Lonicera periclymenum*) – provides nectar for butterflies and moths, autumn berries, and nesting sites for birds. Prefers organic-rich soil and plenty of moisture.

HAWTHORN (*Crataegus monogyna*) – a medium-sized tree valuable for its flowers and fruit, nectar for insects and nesting sites for birds. The form 'Biflora' is the unusual Glastonbury thorn, which flowers during warm weather in winter and produces a main flush of flowers in spring. Tolerates any soil, and even cold, windswept sites.

ROWAN (*Sorbus aucuparia*) – has white flowers that are an invaluable nectar source for insects, and the bright-orange fruit provides birdfood in autumn. A compact tree ideal for gardens, it tolerates most soils and exposed conditions.

HOLLY (*Ilex aquifolium*) – an invaluable source of winter berries for birds, and happy on chalk soils. If you only have room for one, plant 'J.C. van Tol', which needs no companion tree in order to produce berries.

IVY (*Hedera helix*) – provides roosting and nesting sites and winter fruits for birds, plus late-summer nectar for insects. Grows in any soil.

MEADOW CRANESBILL (*Geranium pratense*) – a good nectar source for insects, and happy in damp conditions.

Bretons and Cornwall. The Plymouth pear makes an attractive ornamental tree, hybridizing happily with cultivated pears, and may well be of value for breeding in the future.

Wild-flower displays

There's room for wild flowers however small your garden, whether you want to create a display in a lawn, in a border or even in a pot. Suppliers offer seed or small 'plug' plants for a range of habitats, from the species-rich meadow and chalk-and-limestone terrain to bogs and butterfly borders.

Where space is limited, you can create an area of wild-flower lawn by first mowing the grass with the cutting height of your lawnmower raised to 12–13cm. If you want a mini-meadow, let the grass grow longer. Whether in the lawn or in a border, any effort on your part will be appreciated by visiting insects and butterflies as a possible nectar source and egg-laying site.

One of the easiest ways to create a larger-scale wild-flower meadow in a lawn is to do it the Eden way. First to spray the grass with the herbicide glyphosate. Then, after a few weeks, cut the dying grass as short as possible, almost scraping the soil. Hire a lawn-rake and -slitter, then rake and slit the top few millimetres. Sow with wild-flower seed in autumn or spring, and no weeds will appear as they germinate.

At Eden, wild flowers are usually sown over very large areas, so the seed is mixed with fine dry builder's sand to bulk up the volume and ensure an even spread of seed; because the sand is visible on top of the soil, it helpfully indicates where seed has already been scattered. Wild flowers are best sown during warm conditions in April and early May; by late May and early June it's too late, and sowing should be delayed until autumn. Plug plants, however, can be planted in spring or autumn. If the garden is also a play area, restrict clover to the areas where children don't play, so they are less likely to be stung on the feet by bees in summer.

If you don't want to give over a corner of your garden, and if you have a flat or shallowly sloping roof on your home, your garage or even your shed, you could try planting that up. There are a number of roof plantings at Eden and they are becoming commonplace throughout Europe and North America, incorporating anything from designs inspired by landscaped gardens to simple mats of succulents such as sedums, which can be bought already planted for laying out. Roof plantings have practical effects too, preventing flash-flooding by absorbing rain, forming an insulating layer that reduces heat loss, and even absorbing noise and air pollution. They can make highly successful wildlife habitats – one of the first, created in Switzerland in 1914, is now home to a population of rare green-winged orchids. Thorough research is advisable before developing a large-scale green roof on your home – consult a structural engineer before you start!

Wild-flower habitats are constantly under threat, so even a small contribution makes a difference; they are not only beautiful, but part of our heritage – and making a display couldn't be cheaper than from a packet of seeds!

PURE CORNWALL

THE MAJORITY OF plants in 'Wild Cornwall' came from a specialist Cornish nursery that has permission to collect seed from local landowners, while others grew from seeds and spores blown in by the wind, colonizing the display as they would in a natural habitat; introduced turfs lifted from Eden's own fields brought with them several plants too. And there's a log pile that makes a wonderful home for insects, which are protected by a 'no-spray' policy.

PESTS AND DISEASES

In the global garden we all battle with pests and diseases; no one is exempt, though some, like our fellow gardeners in the developing world, suffer from their impact more than others. At Eden, the displays are affected by many of the common horticultural and glasshouse evils that disfigure plants but are rarely life-threatening. This may well be the case in your garden too, but if you grow your own produce it's doubly problematic, since you may find that your yields are reduced. All the same, although it may be disappointing, it isn't catastrophic: there are always alternative supplies to be got from the supermarket, even if they lack the home-grown flavour. But in the developing world there is usually no such alternative – pests and diseases can mean famine and death.

In the early Eden days a Science Team was created – similar to those at the Botanic Gardens at Kew and the Royal Horticultural Society's headquarters at Wisley in Surrey – with the aim of combining the scientists' analytical view of the world with the more practical one of the horticulturists, though in practice these roles can often overlap anyway. The team's brief was to look at problems to do with such things as plant nutrition, root stability, the propagation of rare species, and rampant pests such as white-footed ants, then to carry out experiments, make observations and find solutions, which the horticulturists would then implement.

Common sense, the first rule of gardening, tells you that you want to bring only healthy plants into

your garden. Plants suffering from some pest or disease must be isolated, to reduce the risk of allowing the villain to take hold and infect all your other plants. When the Eden Project was in its infancy, attempts were made to create a quarantine system in order to be able to do just that – to isolate, then diagnose the problem, before it affected the wider area of the Biomes; but the sheer volume of plants arriving daily and the pressure of deadlines made this almost impossible. However, now that time is less of an issue, all the plants entering the covered Biomes, from the smallest shrub to the largest tree, are isolated and subjected to rigorous checks to ensure that they are pest- and disease-free before they reach their destined Biome.

Commercial nurseries have their own control programmes in place in order to produce high-quality, good-looking plants for their customers to plant in their gardens at home. The idea is to maintain such a rapid turnover that no problems arise in the garden centre itself; but, inevitably, because of the sheer volume of plants being transported in and out of the nursery, the difficulty of identifying some pests and diseases, especially in their early stages, and the invisible nature of spores and so on, problems do arise from time to time. A new greenhouse soon acquires the common scourges – some are blown in through the door from outside, but many arrive on the plants themselves.

THE ISOLATION UNIT

RIGHT: *The ghostly forms of quarantined plants, shrouded in fine mesh to prevent pests from escaping.*

As increasing numbers of plants are being transported around the world, quarantine is becoming a vital insurance policy – particularly for gardens such as Eden which import many non-native plants. Eden's isolation houses provide an even stricter level of quarantine than that required by the law.

Before new plants arrive, a risk assessment is carried out by the Science Team. The assessment will give an idea of which hazards to look out for and how long the isolation period should be. Sometimes the assessment might indicate that the risk of the introduction of pests or diseases is so great that an alternative plant or source of material is recommended. Eden have created their own isolation system so as to ensure that new and potentially disastrous pests and diseases are not accidentally introduced into Britain – and certainly not into the Biomes!

Imported plants and seeds are checked for viruses, using pocket diagnostic kits bought from the CSL. A leaf from the plant under observation is crushed, then analyzed in what looks and performs rather like a pregnancy-testing kit, changing colour if it registers positive. There are several kits of this kind available for identifying such common problems as impatiens necrotic spot virus that are often to be found in plant collections and in commercial horticultural outlets.

▆ Vetting new plants

New plants are still cleared of common greenhouse pests such as whitefly, scale and red spider mite before they are planted in the Biomes, even though the pests are already established there. It may seem over-cautious, even futile, to try to control problems that are endemic to the plant community in the Biomes, but as a result of careful monitoring and introducing various biological controls (living predators) into the Biomes, the gardeners have now brought many pest populations under control. Introducing masses of plants with whitefly, for instance, would upset this balance that has taken several years to achieve. As greenhouse gardeners know well, it takes less time and money, and fewer controls, whether chemical or biological, to eliminate problems in one plant than to treat plants en masse.

At Eden, the vetting process starts even before the plant reaches Cornwall. When they are considering bringing plants or seeds into the country, the Biome supervisors contact one of the plant health staff, giving them information such as type of plant material and its specific source, the country of origin, previous plant health treatments given and the potential delivery date. This is followed by a risk assessment, which takes into account all the potential pest and disease hazards. All relevant information about a plant and its location can be

ADVANCES IN PEST CONTROL

SAFEGUARDING plant health is a complex and vital operation. It involves Eden staff as well as external organizations including the Central Science Laboratory (CSL), the Department for the Environment, Food and Rural Affairs (DEFRA), and its offshoot the Plant Health and Seeds Inspectorate (PHSI).

found in scientific literature and on the internet, especially on the Crop Protection Compendium website, so the plant health team will know all there is to know before the plant arrives. Needless to say, plants from countries and institutions where pest- and disease-controls are strict are less likely to harbour problems; those bought from European nurseries or introduced from botanic gardens are generally free from major problems, too.

This is a wise example for home gardeners to follow. Always buy seed or plants from a reputable source: the major seed companies in particular have to abide by strict governmental guidelines for plant health and germination, so you can be fairly certain that you are not going to be introducing problems into your garden if you buy from them. Seed or plants from unregulated sources will carry slightly higher risks. But unfortunately, whether it comes from a garden centre or a botanic garden, there is no way of absolutely guaranteeing that any given plant is totally pest- and disease-free – unless you have quarantined it yourself using some of the techniques applied at Eden.

However, there are a few precautions you can take to keep unwelcome visitors from your garden:

- Always inspect plants carefully before buying. Don't give just a cursory look – for yellowing leaves or new buds – but check them closely for pests or evidence of pests having been there or just arriving, and turn the leaves over and scrutinize their undersides. Remove the plant from its pot and check the rootball for damage that might indicate vine weevils or similar compost-dwelling pests.

- Once you've bought your healthy plant, put it into quarantine for six months before introducing it to the greenhouse, just as they do at Eden. (Not always practical, but highly desirable all the same!) You can make yourself a net-curtain cage, rather like those in the nursery, to isolate new plants in your greenhouse.

- If there is some problem, when you've located your culprit or culprits, remove any dead leaves and prunings from the affected plants, as they may have the bugs or the bugs' eggs on them.

- Use an organic winter wash – a spray used to kill over-wintering pests – on fruit trees, and scrape loose bark off vines to expose any hidden mealy-bugs before treatment with an environmentally friendly spray. Spread newspaper under the vines to collect what you're about to scrape off, then burn or dispose of the scrapings away from the garden.

- Spray colonies of scale insects or aphids with soap-based sprays or vegetable oils, giving each plant several applications.

- Buy plants of fruit such as strawberries that are certified virus-free, and check any new plants for leaf mottling, which can be a sign of virus.

At Eden, cut flowers from the Visitors' Centre on the outskirts of the pit have very little chance of mixing with plants in the Biome and therefore little chance of introducing problems. However, if they were to be used as part of a temporary display in the Humid Tropics Biome, where pests and diseases flourish, they would become very high-risk indeed.

LEFT: *Plants from retail outlets, like this* Zantedeschia elliottiana, *will already have been subjected to stringent plant-health checks. Even so, check all purchases carefully.*

Strawberries can suffer from grey mould but pick off affected material immediately and your crops will remain healthy.

Even plants that are apparently healthy, like these phragmipedium orchids, are quarantined before they are allowed on to the main site. You could follow a similar practice at home.

Orchids are a particular problem, as they can carry several pests that could be disastrous in the Humid Tropics Biome. Seeds carry the lowest risk and larger plants the greatest, as their size and complexity provide a habitat for a wide range of undesirables.

The lifecycle of a pest depends on the host plant and the temperature in which it is growing. In many cases increasing the temperature speeds up its lifecycle. The isolation period is calculated from the time of egg-laying to the point when a newly emerged female can produce offspring. Most of this information can be found in scientific literature, but for unusual pests the length of quarantine required has to be worked out from the lifecycle of the closest member of its genus or family. Some pests can lie hidden inside a plant for several years and can't be controlled with insecticides.

The length of the isolation period of a plant under pest- and disease-control will normally range from three to six months (in special cases this can be longer). The size and species of the plant are also factored into the decision on the duration of the quarantine. Some quarantine cases concern notifiable or potentially catastrophic problems.

▬ Quarantine

On arrival at Eden, each consignment goes into a separate bay to avoid contact between plants at different stages of isolation. There are two isolation greenhouses at Watering Lane Nursery, one maintained at Warm Temperate Biome temperatures (sometimes used for cool temperate plants too), and the other at Humid Tropics Biome temperatures; the interiors of both are, of course, spotlessly clean and kept locked, with restricted access. Within each greenhouse, there are thirteen bays with partitions covered with thrip-proof netting (see p. 297). The entrances to each bay are sealed with zips and they each have independent drainage systems to prevent cross-infection. The plants stand on metal grids so that water drains down gullies, to be collected in tanks below – again, so as to prevent infestation spreading to neighbouring bays. The greenhouses have concrete floors which are easy to clean and don't harbour pests – a simple and cheap measure worth considering for some home greenhouses (but remember to leave space for beds and pots).

Staff don white coats (pests are easier to spot against a white background), which are kept in a freezer when not in use to kill any pests that might be sheltering on them. They are changed regularly to prevent cross-contamination from one bay to another.

During their stay in quarantine, the plants are cared for daily by Tim Grigg, one of the nursery horticulturists, then checked weekly by members of the Science Team to assess progress. The aim is to ensure that plants leave isolation as quickly as is feasible, but also in the healthiest state possible.

Without a plant isolation unit, Eden would be regularly exposing itself to potentially catastrophic risk. Considering that a substantial number of large plants were introduced directly into the Biomes during the early days, and a huge number of potential hazards – including termites and fire ants – have been intercepted, Eden has been very fortunate indeed not to have had many more major outbreaks.

ISOLATING TEMPORARY EXHIBITS

SOMETIMES plants have to be isolated when they leave the Biomes. The Titan arum (*Amorphophallus titanum*), after featuring in a temporary display in the Humid Tropics Biome, when returned to the nursery after flowering was found to be carrying Surinam and Australian cockroaches, white-footed ants (part of the only population in Britain!), and sugar-cane Borer. The tuber was disinfected, then cleaned in a large bucket of water, and the compost put in a skip and disposed of at a specialist facility away from the site. The tuber was then quarantined for six months in the isolation unit before being allowed back into the nursery. Plants are returned to the nursery on individual trays – again, so that potential problems are not spread to other plants or areas.

RIGHT: *Checking plants for pests and diseases during routine maintenance is an essential part of Eden's passive plant-health policy.*

■ Keeping the Biomes problem-free

Starting with a sterile site and 'clean' soil is one of the most effective ways of keeping the numbers of common pests and diseases at a minimum, but over time numbers do increase, as has happened at Eden, and low-pest populations bocame a distant memory. However, not all introductions are bad: in the Warm Temperate Biome several beneficial soil fungi, for instance, absent in the manufactured soil, have now been brought in with some of the plants. In the Humid Tropics Biome an as-yet-unnamed species of tropical earthworm came in via the same route and has begun to improve the soil.

All parts of the site are checked for problems at least once every ten days. The Eden staff use two monitoring methods. The passive method involves checking plants while watering, feeding and pruning; active monitoring is a deliberate search for problems by thoroughly checking leaves, stems and even roots. Follow the Eden example in your garden.

Because they have a wider range of hosts, pests tend to be more of a problem than diseases at Eden. Many of the control methods used are familiar to home gardeners – as always, simply implemented on a larger scale. The key is to prevent problems from becoming established, by use of chemical sprays, biological controls or cultural methods. As mentioned elsewhere, at Eden sprays are used only as a last resort. Quaranteening plants at Watering Lane Nursery has kept many problems at bay. But unfortunately, pests can hitch a ride on a visitor's coat, shoes, or anything else they bring with them.

FACT!

The scale and complexity of planting in the Biomes means that widespread problems cannot be eradicated easily and are therefore just controlled by reducing unwanted populations to a manageable level – in fact, in 'natural' areas like the rainforest display, some damage makes it look more realistic!

CONTROL

The key to good pest management is constant close monitoring, speedy action to treat hotspots before they get out of hand, and making optimal use of bio-control agents.

An integrated pest management (IPM) system, combining several different methods, is used successfully at Eden. It includes the use of cultural controls, such as removing heavily infected plant material immediately and cleaning secateurs with methylated spirits after pruning to prevent cross-contamination. It also means using biological controls in the form of natural predators – ironically, there are some that would see off some of the pests, such as thrips, in the Biomes, but are not registered for pest control in Britain even though they are used in other parts of the EU. And then there are sprays made from environmentally friendly materials such as white oil, which destroy pests but have little effect on the natural predators.

The IPM approach can be very effectively employed in your garden. Outside, you can erect physical barriers made of such materials as horticultural fleece to thwart carrot fly; by winter digging you will expose pests such as wireworms to birds, or slugs to chickens and ducks. And in the greenhouse you can apply biological controls like those described above.

There are other simple measures that can help prevent the spread of infection: mulch with a thick layer of well-rotted compost or forest bark to smother fungal spores resting in the soil; choose pest- and disease-resistant plant varieties; rotate your crops – this will prevent the build-up of unwanted visitors. Delaying sowing so as to miss the egg-laying seasons can work, as can deciding not to grow alternative hosts, plants particularly favoured by the bugs you're keenest to zap. If you want to say goodbye to slugs or greenhouse whitefly, try traps; and nematodes will work discreetly without any fuss. If you look around garden centres and nurseries, you'll find there are plenty of options available that are effective *and* environmentally friendly.

■ 'Compost tea'

'Compost tea' is a new variation on an old idea that has caught the attention of Eden's staff. It's an organic tonic that claims to improve growth, disease resistance and the overall health and well-being of plants. Commercial growers have recently been searching for alternatives to orthodox fertilizers, as EU legislation removes more and more horticultural chemicals from use, and many think that compost tea might fit the bill. Interest recently began in Holland and is gaining considerable momentum throughout Europe.

The first thing you need to know about compost tea is that the recipe is a secret. Organic solutions have been used for plant nutrition and health problems since biblical times, when crops were irrigated and fertilized with vegetable and animal manures, and they were also used during the Roman occupation of Britain. This holistic approach to well-being offers plants all the nutrients they need, plus disease-suppressing micro-organisms that are commonly found in soil and compost. In material carefully composted from rich humus, or green

LEFT: *Prone to whitefly like so many greenhouse plants, cotton is kept in good health by sound horticultural practice and natural predators.*

BELOW: *Horticultural fleece is an invaluable barrier – it allows water and sunlight in and keeps pests out.*

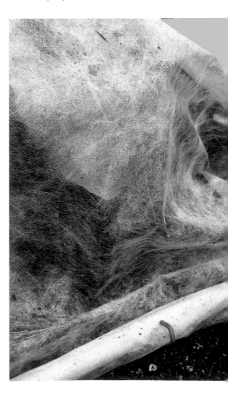

waste, there are millions of beneficial bacteria, fungi and nematodes, which 'compost tea' aims to utilize.

There are two types: 'passive' and aerated (or 'activated') compost tea. To the basic substance are added extra ingredients such as molasses, charcoal, seaweed extract and assorted herbs said to be a source of micronutrients – plus, of course, water. Passive tea is an infusion of all these components. You leave it to 'brew' just like a tea bag. The aerated sort is similar but air is bubbled through it to introduce oxygen which increases the range and effectiveness of the soil-improving micro-organisms.

Ingredients for compost tea are becoming available on the retail market, so it can be made at home using a similar technique to that used at Eden (see below). Brews deteriorate rapidly and must be used within twenty-four hours of mixing, but unused 'tea' (unlike its chemical counterparts) can be safely poured down the drain. Some nurseries run compost-tea clubs, advertising brewing days so that customers can come and buy freshly activated 'tea' and take it home for use in their own garden.

Eden's brew is made at Watering Lane Nursery in an improvised fermenter based on a Dutch design. The liquid is prepared in a recycled chemicals drum (well scoured!) containing about 50 litres of water, and the ingredients are put into a giant 'teabag' made of nylon netting, then lowered into the water. The infusion is then left to do its work for 18–24 hours while a pump forces air bubbles through it. A Dutch company supplies the secret compost recipe, plus all the other materials such as those listed previously. There are enough ingredients in each package to produce 100 litres. Because compost tea is still being trialled, it's only being made in small quantities. This specially prepared compost is preferred to any that Eden might make on site, because its secret formula manages to limit the population of undesirable bacteria like *E. coli*.

Eden's researchers' only concern is that the compost tea may continue to 'brew' and deteriorate if applied through irrigation lines, so it's essential to flush the system through with fresh water after each application. More experimentation is needed to assess its long-term potential, but the prospects look good. All the same, there's a long way to go before it can be scientifically proven, registered and used widely at Eden. The trials demonstrate the Project's eagerness to research and develop new ideas and techniques.

PEST CONTROL IN THE TRICKY SPOTS!

LIGHT TRAPS AROUND the Biomes catch moths and other insects, so their populations can be monitored and the impact of the pest and disease controls assessed. One of the most difficult areas to view is high in the canopy, so a cherry-picker carries a member of staff up to 11.5m above ground; beyond that, a tiny 'camera on a stick' – like those installed in cricket stumps – is attached to an even longer pole and inserted among the branches. The image is then transmitted to a TV screen or video camera below so staff can survey potential problems. Controlling pests in higher trees is difficult too. In the Humid Tropics Biome, the solution is a mini-pulley system that delivers biological controls – natural predators – into the canopy, which then go on seek-and-destroy missions in inaccessible places where spraying is less effective.

THE HEALING POWER OF 'TEA'

S TAFF AT EDEN, like plant pathologist Tim Pettitt, are approaching compost tea with slight scepticism but believe it shows great promise – especially if it lives up to its extraordinary claims! It's the disease-control potential that is most interesting, but it's not obvious how this is achieved or what the key active constituents actually are. A number of organisms have been identified in the brew made at Eden, including bacteria with potential disease-suppressing properties and members of the genus *Trichoderma*, a fungus which feeds on other fungi and which is well known to plant pathologists for its biological control potential.

Interestingly, when the compost tea was put on lettuce leaves during experiments, after the application the leaves would always show higher levels of *Trichoderma*, even when it *wasn't* present in the brew; so it may be that the brew operates partly by changing the conditions on the leaf surface or in the soil actually encouraging beneficial organisms. Carbohydrates in the brew can thereby have a massive impact on changing the microflora present on the leaf surface. In theory, this could have a negative effect by stimulating the spores of diseases such as grey mould to develop and infect the plant; but generally this doesn't seem to happen. Reports from some large-scale commercial growers suggest that regular foliar applications in their propagation units have significantly reduced the incidence of grey mould and almost removed the need for chemical spraying.

Laboratory cultures at Eden using lettuce leaves have shown that two out of every three compost teas trialled so far are quite good at treating botrytis, but the others don't seem to have any impact at all. Trials on the tea's effectiveness against tulip fire and box blight are being considered.

THE RICE–FISH PROJECT

AN EXHIBIT in the Humid Tropics Biome demonstrates that fish, as well as providing food for the local population, can also play a role in that same population's rice fields. Staff at Stirling University are working on schemes in Bangladesh and in other countries to stock rice fields with fish as part of an integrated pest-management project. The fish disturb the mud in which the rice is growing, thus stopping weeds from germinating; eat mosquito larvae, fertilize the ground with their faeces; and eat the older, outer rice leaves which are more likely to be infested with pathogens. This interaction creates the ideal basis for their fish–rice culture and farmers are less likely to resort to harmful pesticides, too.

■ Biological control

Biological control is the natural use of predators or bacteria to control a pest or disease. Over thirty different biological controls are used in the three Biomes, of which many are available to the public for their own gardens, and all are very effective. Parasitic nematodes are used to control such pests as vine weevil and scarid fly (whose larvae nibble roots) in the indoor Biomes and slugs in the Outdoor Biome, where they have been more effective than slug pellets.

Eden also use environmentally friendly 'soft soaps' (a more scientific way of applying washing-up water to plants), and starch sprays, both of which make common greenhouse pests such as whitefly, mealy-bug and scale insects stop breathing. When sprays are being used on plants that are new to Eden, a few leaves are treated to gauge the reaction before treating the whole plant – a bit like doing a strand test on your hair before dyeing the whole lot, and well worth taking the time to do if it saves a disaster!

■ Chemical control

When chemical sprays are used at Eden they are applied by high-volume sprayers (fogging) or as spot treatments. The greatest challenge with fogging is targeting the infected plant, particularly when the pest is located very high up. Smaller plants can be treated by hand.

Many plants in the Humid Tropics Biome are sensitive to chemicals in sunlight, so pesticides are tested on small areas of foliage on sunny days to see how they react and to assess potential problems with scorching. A rigorous treatment programme has reduced pest numbers so significantly that biological controls now suffice in the winter and only heavily infested areas now need to be targeted during the rest of the year. In practice, as many gardeners know, greenhouses provide ideal conditions for pests to reproduce, so this control is a long-term project! As in a domestic situation, whenever it is necessary to spray in the Biomes, care is always taken to ensure that it does not harm birds, animals – or visitors!

■ Eden's main bugbear

The indoor Biomes suffer most from pests, because life is more abundant and fast-moving in warmer climates – particularly the tropics. In the Humid Tropics Biome there are about 25–30 different pests in residence at any one time. There are at least ten species of tropical scale insect, including the black-olive variety that grows up to 5mm long, mealy-bug, red spider mite (or two-spotted mite) and ants: these last were introduced – unintentionally! – on some of

BIOLOGICAL VERSUS CHEMICAL

THE DEBATE amongst gardeners continues as to whether to use chemical or biological controls in their gardens. At Eden, chemicals are required for a successful IPM programme but they are very carefully chosen and used only when absolutely necessary. What you use is your decision, but the argument seems pretty clearcut:

- Biological controls are 'natural' and no threat to the environment; chemicals can build up in the soil, in the water and in the food chain.

- Biological controls are safe to use and have no side effects; most chemical concentrates are toxic to humans.

- Biological controls spread naturally over an area but affect only their target, and are easier to apply; chemical sprays aim to target the affected plant, but don't always manage to be selective.

- The impact of natural predators as biological controls lasts longer; chemical controls need regular applications.

- Pests have no defence against organic controls; they can build up resistance to chemical sprays.

- Biological controls do not affect plants adversely; they can be sensitive to chemical sprays.

- Biological controls do not affect the appearance of plants: sprays can leave unsightly deposits on the leaves and flowers.

White-footed ants feed voraciously on liver pâté mixed with sugar and borax.

the plants' roots. The white-footed ant, originally from Sulawesi in South-East Asia, is now pantropical, and the most successful pest in the Biome. These beasts 'milk' scale, aphids and mealy-bugs for their honeydew, just as ants milk aphids in your garden. The white-footed ants have moved these other pests to inaccessible locations, which has made biological control more difficult and spread the problem further.

Sometimes the ants make 'tents' full of eggs and their pupae appear on the leaves next to an infestation of scale insects, which furnishes an easily accessible supply of food. The only benefit these creatures offer is that they are excellent pollinators, and by crawling over the flowers of plants, including cocoa trees, they have set masses of fruit, saving hand pollination.

One large and several satellite colonies have been identified. The ants are not aggressive, don't bite or sting, and make love, not war (a high reproductive rate being one of their greatest advantages). Spraying with insecticides kills the foragers rather than the egg-laying population, and therefore increases reproduction rates – the more you spray, the more ants you get! More alarmingly, they don't have just one queen like many ant species, but up to 50 per cent of a colony can be egg-laying females, so numbers build up rapidly. Some of the eggs they lay are sterile, simply serving as an extra food source for the rest of the colony. Unsurprisingly in such circumstances, most traditional ant control methods, such as borax in honey, are ineffective. And most annoying of all, these creatures have no predators.

When they die, white-footed ants may produce a pheromone warning other ants to keep away, thus removing the possibility of trapping large numbers of them at once (cockroaches produce something similar). Little else is known about white-footed ants, so staff are learning from experience. Tim Pettitt, horticultural scientist and plant pathologist, and Mike Pyte, Eden's pest control expert, are fast becoming authorities on the subject. Most available information on control of these ants recommends 'removal of all plants' – which is not much help at Eden!

Several methods of delivering the bait have been tried: they ignored little bamboo 'cups', but were more interested in wicks dipped in bait and laid across the trails in the Biome. One of the most lethal concoctions so far is puréed liver pâté or corned beef mixed with sugar to which borax, a traditional control, has been added. The literature suggests that the ants prefer sweet substances, and changing the bait from peanut butter (low protein) and honey to sweetened meat (high protein) – favoured by many other ant species – reaped its reward. Techniques yet to be tried include soaking fragments of dried wood in the bait and scattering them around; any baited fragment that is not taken rots away and becomes part of the mulch.

The only way to find out whether control methods are working is to count the ants. Various methods have been tried, including standing next to an ant trail and collecting all the ants in a square metre, then counting them! Bear in mind that at any one time there can be more than a thousand in that small space. Collecting them on sticky traps has been the most effective so far; at least they are unable to move! Sixty-two such traps are set twice weekly and the victims counted. This provides a detailed record of activity and, hopefully, even when the number of traps is reduced, will prove a useful monitoring and control method.

COMMON PESTS

The Warm Temperate Biome initially had pest problems that read like a *Who's Who* of the pest world, including whitefly, red spider mite, scale insects, thrips and mealy-bug, as well as some common aphid species blown in through the ventilation system, and a few unusual ones. With an integrated management system like the one used at Eden, most of these problems can be kept under control.

Aphids

No gardener really needs a description of these horticultural horrors. They affect plants worldwide, from the cool temperate zones to the tropics, and can travel hundreds of miles on air currents to land in your garden and greenhouse, where they will suck sap, excrete honeydew, encourage black sooty mould and introduce viruses to your plants.

Outdoors they are a particular problem on sweet peas and vegetables, and not least at Eden. Aphids come in a range of colours from traditional green to pink and whitish grey, and in sizes from 2mm to more than 4.5mm – that's the giant lupin aphid resident in the Outdoor Biome. Most aphids can be found in ever-expanding colonies, clustering on young shoots and under leaves, which they distort. Some tricky species have learned to protect themselves by making leaves pucker and curl, others by producing a woolly coating or by hiding on plant roots. One good approach is to avoid using high-nitrogen fertilizers on plants prone to aphids, as nitrogen encourages soft, aphid-friendly growth.

If you discover small infestations on your plants, squash them between finger and thumb. Remove colonies on strong growth by blasting them off with a jet of water, but beware of damaging your plants. Or, if you have a keen eye and a steady hand, make it more fun and more of a challenge by using a high-powered water pistol. If you prefer something stronger than water, use an organic contact insecticide containing pyrethrum, rotenone (an insecticide made from the roots of a tropical vine), fatty acids or vegetable oils. If the worst comes to the worst you can also use chemicals, occasionally and sparingly, as a spray or drench. To prevent ants 'farming' aphids in woody plants, smear a band of grease around the stem or trunk to stop the ants climbing up.

If the infestation is in your greenhouse, you'll find that a biological control is always effective. For aphids, order one of the *Aphidius* species – you can find adverts for suppliers in gardening magazines or get information from good garden centres. This small parasitic wasp, occurring naturally in the British Isles, lays eggs on immature aphids. Or use the larvae of *Aphidoletes aphidimyza*, a small midge which will eat them.

Ladybird and lacewing larvae feed on aphids too, so encourage them into your garden. Ladybirds love to hibernate in dry plant debris, loose bark and hollow stems, so don't tidy up too much in autumn, and lacewings will overwinter in your garden if you buy or make nesting chambers for them (examples of these can be seen in and around the 'Plants for Cornish Crops' exhibit at Eden). Place the chambers at least 3m from trees or buildings, and bring them into a cool shed from early winter (by which time the lacewings should be in residence), returning them to the garden in spring. Make sure you replace the straw and the

Fennel flowers, a rich source of nectar, attract hover flies and other beneficial insects into the garden. The foliage makes a great flavouring too.

SUSCEPTIBLE SPECIES

SOME PLANTS seem to be susceptible to certain pests: mealy-bug thrives on ericas in the Fynbos and on oleanders (*Nerium oleander*), and woolly scale insects on stone fruit in the Mediterranean orchard, including olives. One ancient olive tree at Eden is over a hundred years old and a magnet for scale insects, so it's sprayed every three months with a soft-soap formulation to keep the problem under control.

attractant in shop-bought purpose-built chambers annually. Hoverflies also like to munch on aphids, and can be attracted if you plant their favourite food sources: they prefer the small, simple flowers of such plants as fennel and dill, and members of the daisy family, as well as the poached-egg plant (*Limnanthes douglasii*), *Convolvulus tricolor* and buckwheat. Put down old tiles as a hiding-place for ground (or rove) beetles and centipedes, which eat the larvae of cabbage root fly and lettuce root aphid.

If you want to pre-empt an infestation, sow lettuce varieties that are resistant to root aphid, such as 'Avoncrisp', 'Lakeland' and 'Little Gem', or grow your crops under horticultural fleece. Alternatively, you can plant 'sacrificial crops' such as nasturtiums nearby, to attract black bean aphids (as they do in the 'Plants for Taste' display at Eden). Once the plants are heavily infested, lift and destroy them and all of the pests will be destroyed at the same time.

Natural predators are encouraged at Eden, and spraying with different soft soaps has also been tried. However, Kevin Austin, the crops supervisor, believes that continued use of such sprays can be detrimental to the plant. A weak milk solution and squashing by hand has brought some success, but the aim is to encourage the robust growth of the plant so that it can withstand the attentions of the aphids – then to let nature take its course.

Caterpillars

Both the small and large cabbage white butterflies feed on the leaves of cauliflowers and cabbages, and the plants in the cropping area at Eden are

The larvae of daddy-long-legs can nibble away the roots of your grass causing parts of your lawn to die. Nematodes can be used to control the problem.

BENEFICIAL INSECTS

INSECTS LIKE *Cryptolaemus montrouzieri*, an Australian ladybird, and the predatory wasp *Encarsia formosa* are often introduced to control glasshouse pests, but there are many native insects that eat garden pests. It is often the larvae that are the most effective, and many of them enjoy aphids. Each ladybird larva can eat up to fifty per day; lacewing larvae, too, are effective; and about a third of Britain's 275 hoverfly species produce larvae that suck out aphid innards, then discard the husk before moving on to the next victim. The violet ground beetle relishes small slugs and ground-dwelling caterpillars, while glow-worm larvae (if you are lucky enough to have them around) dine exclusively on snails. Dragonflies and their larvae eat mosquito and gnat larvae, making gardening just that little bit more comfortable. These are just a few of the many beneficial insects that patrol the garden in search of tasty pests.

regularly attacked. Both varieties are easy to spot: large cabbage white caterpillars are pale yellow with dark stripes and eat the outer leaves, while the green caterpillars of the small cabbage white butterfly usually feed inside the heads of brassicas. There are two generations a year, but numbers increase from late spring until early autumn, so the damage is worst in late summer. (Be sure, then, not to plant out your spring cabbage and broccoli at this time.)

If you do fear an attack, you can protect your crops with horticultural fleece or micromesh, which the butterflies can't get through. But this is not an option for Eden's display beds. Instead, the gardeners pick off or squash the clusters of pale-yellow eggs; in addition, the biological control *Bacillus thuringiensis* is watered on every two weeks, or more often if it rains, to keep the caterpillars at bay. Several chillies in the Warm Temperate Biome have been damaged by the caterpillars of the light-brown apple moth (a species introduced from Australia that has spread throughout the British Isles and other parts of the world and that you may find in your garden) – it came in through the vents. This caterpillar weakens and disfigures plants by nibbling irregular holes in the leaves; at Eden it was controlled by checking the plants daily and picking off the caterpillars by hand.

Cabbage root fly

Brassicas such as turnips and broccoli are vulnerable to onslaught from cabbage root fly from spring onwards – it's usually detectable when the plants grow slowly and wilt, particularly on sunny days. The main egg-laying period normally coincides with the flowering of hedge parsley (worth noting, if it grows near you), and most attacks take place between April and July. Crops are especially vulnerable just after planting – the tiny maggots nibble away at the fine roots, leaving nothing but a rotting stump; however, established plants are usually robust enough to survive.

You can follow Eden's example and protect any seedlings or transplants by putting squares or circles of corrugated cardboard (carpet underlay or roofing felt can be used too) about 10cm in diameter on the soil around the stems of the plants. The flies then deposit their eggs on the barrier instead of on the soil, and so will dry out before hatching. Sometimes the root fly manages to avoid the cardboard – to pre-empt this, fit it around the brassicas as you plant them out. Affected plants should be removed and rapidly replaced – plant a few extra ones (otherwise, any new plants you put in will not have time to form a head). Thorough digging of the plot in winter and removing plant debris will also help reduce the fly population the following season. Placing moth balls around plants is said to help, too.

Flea beetles

Flea beetles are tiny black beetles about 2mm long that leap from leaves like fleas when they are disturbed. They caused some problems in the 'Cornish Pasty Story' display at Eden, as they are particularly partial to swedes! These beetles hibernate under piles of leaf debris and under hedges, in grass and under loose bark on trees, so an effective deterrent is to keep the vegetable plot free of debris – but be warned that the adults can fly

up to a kilometre from their hibernation sites in spring in search of tasty morsels. These beetles are also found on turnip, radish, rocket and ornamentals such as stocks, aubretia and nasturtiums. Their handiwork is identifiable by the fact that the leaves they've attacked are left covered in tiny holes that don't always go all the way through, and the damaged tissues are pale brown; massive incursions can kill seedlings and check the growth of older plants.

Most of the damage is caused in April and May during dry weather, so sow when it's warm and damp – such conditions shorten the plants' vulnerable seedling phase. Water well during dry spells, dust the leaves with derris or rotenone, or do it the ingenious Eden way . . . Attach a greenhouse 'sticky trap', folded to form a hood, to a cane and walk slowly up and down the rows of seedlings; the beetles will jump up when the shadow falls on them and stick to the trap. Alternatively, they use a technique often recommended for whitefly control, which is to remove the beetles with a portable vacuum cleaner! When willow flea beetle is the target, the narrow suction head used for cleaning tight corners is attached to increase the suction. Remember to regulate the suction carefully and don't put the nozzle too close to the foliage or the seedlings! The disadvantage is that both these methods are time-consuming: at the height of an infestation you need to take action every three or four days. (A similar vacuuming technique can also be used on whitefly in a greenhouse.) Finally, the beetles are squashed by stamping on the cleaner bag.

BELOW: *Flea beetles (top) are removed using a simple technique that is recommended for whitefly but rarely used – suck them up with a vacuum cleaner!*

The advantage of dense foliage is that it suppresses weeds, but it can also provide sheltered spots for pests to lurk in.

Slugs

The bane of every gardener's life, these little thugs are a problem among the crop displays at Eden too. Most of the damage is caused by 'keel', 'field' and 'garden' slugs living just below the soil surface. Vulnerable areas are given an early application of parasitic nematodes, then the treatment is repeated every six weeks through the growing season. As you no doubt do at home, the gardeners keep the displays tidy, hoed and cleared of debris and dying leaves so as to reduce the slugs' food sources and favourite places to hide. Slug pellets containing ferric phosphate have also been very effective (though they are quite expensive): these contain a stomach poison that stops the slugs from feeding, and they die within three to six days. Any unused pellets eventually degrade into plant food.

Copper barriers, usually in the form of sticky copper tape or rings, give the slugs an 'electric shock' when they touch them, so they won't pass over the barrier and soon learn to steer clear. These have proved very effective in gardening trials, and are also used at Eden. One staff member at Watering Lane Nursery, keen to protect his propagating benches, went one step further and attached a very small battery. It increased the shock impact considerably, and was therefore effective (and satisfying!). Picking the slugs off by hand also works well.

Snails

Effectively slugs carrying their houses on their backs, snails love eating soft tissue and it's the common garden snail that causes the greatest damage to plants. Protected by their shells, they are less dependent on high levels of moisture; and because they need calcium to form their shells, they are less common on acid soils. Snails often hibernate over winter in upturned flower pots or crevices in walls. At home, try providing an 'anvil' stone for thrushes so they can smash the shells and eat the contents. At Eden they have tried biological controls for slugs and snails, as well as salt barriers, and garlic granules, barriers and sprays – all with varying degrees of success. The most effective control is removal by hand.

Vine weevils

Most often found munching on rhododendron, primula and evergreen euonymus, the adult vine weevil gives herself away by being about 10mm long, matt black with pale-orange spots, and with antennae that bend at an angle. These unwelcome visitors appeared, along with the slugs, from the second year at Eden. They hide in the dark during the day and move slowly over the leaves at night,

EDEN'S PEST PATROLS

THE ANIMALS and birds that serve as biological controls at Eden are small, well camouflaged and rarely seen, but the increase in their populations is improving their effectiveness. When Eden was first opened, reports of the Humid Tropics Biome brought offers of hornbills, giant African snails, quails, fruit bats – even snakes! But plants are the Project's focus, and from the beginning the plan has always been to introduce fauna only for biological control.

In the Warm Temperate Biome there are avian pests too: blackbirds eat grapes and finches eat the seeds of sorghum and other grains.

The Biomes are successfully managed using a combination of plant quarantine and an integrated pest and disease control programme.

Mealy-bugs

These white, wax-covered insects, like tiny woodlice, are found in clusters on indoor plants in the Biomes and the nursery and attack some garden plants too, particularly ceanothus and New Zealand flax (*Phormium* species). They hide in the most inaccessible places, including leaf joints and between twining stems, where they suck sap and reduce plant vigour by excreting honeydew that produces the inevitable sooty mould. Heavy infestations may cause early leaf fall.

If you have found mealy-bugs in your greenhouse, use the biological control *Cryptolaemus montrouzieri* (predatory ladybirds) – as used at Eden – because both the adults and the larvae feed on them. *Leptomastix dactylopii*, a tiny wasp, parasitizes citrus and grapevine mealy-bug.

Whitefly

A familiar sight on ornamental plants and vegetables, indoors and out. These tiny, white, winged insects are usually found underneath leaves, where they suck sap and excrete honeydew. As mentioned earlier, foliage becomes sticky and coated with a black sooty mould, particularly in moist conditions.

To control whitefly under glass, hang yellow sticky traps above or among the plants (insects are particularly attracted to yellow). You can also introduce the predatory wasp *Encarsia formosa* (which has been used extensively at Eden); or *Delphastus catalinae*, a type of beetle (but try to reduce the whitefly population levels using traps before introducing predators). If you want to continue the non-chemical approach, use organic sprays based on vegetable oils or fatty acids, which will control greenfly and blackfly too.

Scale insects

Glasshouse pests often hide in cracks and crevices and under dense foliage. There are more than twenty-five species of scale insect in Britain. The sap-sucking adults, found on the stems and leaves, often along the central spine, of a range of indoor and outdoor plants, hide under protective shells that vary in shape and colour. The plants are weakened as the honeydew secreted onto the leaves is colonized by sooty mould, particularly in damp conditions. The adults stay under the protection of their shell, motionless, but the newly hatched nymphs crawl over the plant in their search for a new home, so this is the time when they are at their most vulnerable and you need to act – fast! Indoor scale insects breed throughout the year in the Humid Tropics and Warm

Temperate Biomes; whereas, outdoors, a single generation will hatch in mid-summer.

To control scale insects on fruit trees and roses, treat the affected plants with an environmentally friendly winter wash on a mild, dry day in early winter. Treat ornamental plants with organic fatty acids; vegetable oils can be effective, although several applications are needed, but their advantage is that they can be used safely on fruit trees and bushes in leaf. Wiping smooth, leathery leaves gently with a soft soapy cloth will also dislodge scale insects. Biological pest controls include the parasitic wasp *Metaphycus helvolus*, useful against soft and hemispherical scale insects in the greenhouse.

At one time scale insects were such a problem in the Humid Tropics Biome that trees lost their leaves and struggled to recover – some branches died off completely. Scale is a particular problem on palms, which retain their large leaves for a long time before they drop off. Because the lifecycle of scale insects is so rapid, the Biome is also sprayed weekly with fogging machines blasting insecticide up to 10m high into the canopy.

Thrips

More commonly known as 'thunderflies', thrips are minute insects with narrow bodies that feed by sucking sap, usually from the upper surface of leaves, leaving a silvery-white pattern. There is a range of species that affect a huge number of indoor and outdoor plants, including peas, gladioli, roses and onions. Western flower thrips are a variety usually found in the greenhouse; these pests, which produce many generations each year, distort flowers.

Biological control can be achieved by the use of a predatory mite, *Amblyseius cucumeris*. But act only if the problem is serious – ignore small infestations, or destroy badly affected plants. To halt the spread, you can make isolation boxes for moderately affected plants, using plastic piping, plumbing joints and horticultural fleece or micromesh; old cold frames or propagators can be converted too. Isolate any plants you think may be affected and check them for thrips using blue sticky traps.

■ More eco-friendly pest management

Take advantage of Nature, and encourage birds into your garden – they are extremely good at pest control. Blue and great tits eat large numbers of pests, particularly in spring and summer when they are feeding their young. In fact, one study found that blue and great tits removed between 10 and 80 per cent of the caterpillars on every cabbage of a cabbage patch; and in another garden, one pair delivered fifteen hundred meals of apple sawfly and blossom weevil larvae in one day. Blue tits eat more aphids than any other garden bird – one family eats as many as 100,000 in a year – so invite them into the garden with bird-feeders and nesting-boxes.

Frogs and slow-worms eat slugs, toads eat large numbers of insects. Leave a few flower pots in damp places, or log piles, where these garden friends can hide from predators. Or create a wildlife pond.

Only onions, garlic and shallots that are blemish free are suitable for long-term storage. They will last for months if stored in a cool, dry place.

THE GREAT WINE BLIGHT

WHEN PHYLLOXERA was introduced into Europe from North America in the 1860s, it devastated over two million hectares of vines in France and became known as the 'great wine blight'. It has now spread to most vine-growing areas of the world and is a notifiable disease in Britain.

The first vines that were planted in the Warm Temperate Biome suffered from phylloxera in the first year. It's a small sap-sucking aphid-like insect which causes the plant to produce galls. Root galls block the sap flow and the roots start to rot, taking between three and ten years to kill the plant. The insects can be spread on boots and machinery, or may crawl through the soil to infest nearby plant roots.

At Eden the affected plants were removed and destroyed and the soil completely replaced (digging 75cm down to the original clay); any roots that had spread under the path were severed and a plastic barrier was installed. The whole job, including digging out, resoiling and replanting was completed in just two days.

There are root and foliage feeding phylloxera within the same species.The European vine (*Vitis vinifera*) is particularly susceptible to root phylloxera but since American vines are more resistant, the pest has been controlled in Britain and elsewhere by grafting plants on to resistant – or at least phylloxera-tolerant – American rootstocks.

■ Eden's neighbourhood watch

There are many pest-control animals at Eden. They are working reasonably well, but their impact could be improved by introducing greater numbers to deal with specific problems.

The Humid Tropics Biome is home to one species of bird, the Sulawesi white-eye from Indonesia, which is green and yellow with a white ring around its eye, and slightly larger than a wren. It holds the record in the bird world for hatching its eggs in the fastest known time – only ten days – and its numbers are controlled by the amount of food available. It feeds on insects and fruit and drinks nectar, thereby helping with pollination and dispersing seeds around the 'rainforest' floor. Twenty birds were introduced initially. As they live only for about two to three years, by the time the babies are mature, the parents have died, so the population is stable but not increasing. The only way to build up the numbers will be to introduce more. The Sulawesi white-eye eats anything from worms, ants and aphids to mealy-bugs, thrips and cockroaches, stripping scale insects off leaves while hovering underneath like a tiny hummingbird. Despite such a varied diet, twenty birds have little impact on the pest population of the Humid Tropics Biome – it's estimated that the Biome could easily support at least two hundred.

Exotic animals introduced as part of the biological control programme in the Biome include lizards and tree frogs, and four species of praying mantis from the Philippines, New Zealand, Africa and Madagascar that eat only live prey. Praying mantises are very efficient pest controllers, demolishing cockroaches, aphids and snails. The mantises are introduced when fully mature, usually into the warmer areas of the Biome, such as the Malaysia, West Africa and Amazonia sections. Alarmingly, if the female is hungry during mating she bites off the male's head, but he carries on regardless! Females lay egg sacs containing 300–400 babies, but numbers usually plummet after hatching, because young mantises, too, have cannibalistic instincts. They

hang underneath a leaf that's the same colour as themselves, so that the only time they can be seen is when the sun shines through the leaf and you see the creature's outline on the underside.

The three species of beneficial lizard in the Humid Tropics Biome are the green anole and the brown anole which are active in the day, and the tropical house gecko which is nocturnal, so between them they provide twenty-four-hour cover. The green species lives in trees, controlling the high-rise pests; the brown, on lower branches and on the ground; and the tropical house gecko covers all levels in between. The anoles are particularly welcome because both species feed on ants, aphids and scale insects – some of the most prolific pests in the Biome.

There are also bright-green White's tree frogs (or dumpy frogs), found in parts of South America, Africa and Asia. They are 5–10cm long (some females are occasionally larger). They spend much of their time in the canopy, the part of the Biome that is not easily reached by spraying. They need only a few inches of water to breed in – the same as most tree frogs – and are nocturnal, rarely seen, and insectivorous. Two other frogs have been suggested as possible residents of the Humid Tropics Biome: the golden Mantella frog, which feeds on ants and aphids, and the tomato frog, which turns over leaf litter in search of pests.

The Moorish gecko and the meadow lizard are the only pest-control animals in the Warm Temperate Biome. The meadow lizard can often be seen basking among the stones in the Mediterranean section, but only in winter when the sun comes out. The nocturnal Moorish, or crocodile, gecko – it looks like a tiny crocodile – is insectivorous, feeding on earwigs and woodlice. The flat-tailed day gecko, which prefers tiny insects such as aphids and ants – could be the answer to the white-footed-ant problem in the Humid Tropics Biome – while the Madagascan day gecko may be introduced to feed on larger pests.

COMMON DISEASES

Diseases are a problem in every garden, affecting vegetables, flowers, fruit, shrubs and trees, and Eden suffers from many of those that you find in your own patch. Powdery mildew is the most widespread; the lack of air movement within the pit, aided by the Cornish climate, adds up to ideal conditions for it to take hold. The Warm Temperate Biome and Watering Lane Nursery are most affected. Other fungal diseases like downy mildew and potato blight cause localized problems throughout the site too.

Powdery mildew

Powdery mildews are a fascinating group of fungi, as each is attracted to a specific host. They are very cunning, using peg-like drinking straws to suck nutrients from the host's cells; this rarely kills the plant, but it controls its metabolism, ensuring the long-term survival of both plant – even if unhealthy – and pathogen. Some plants are more prone to powdery mildew than others; at Eden, it's the members of the cucumber family, fruit trees, roses and the grape vines that are badly infected.

This particular mildew manifests itself by coating upper leaf surfaces with a dry, whitish powder that can spread to the undersides, the shoot tips and the flowers. Any growth, especially the young shoots, is stunted and distorted, and fruits split and crack. Yellow patches appear on the upper surface of rhododendron leaves, with corresponding felty brown blotches below, and as rhododendrons are evergreen there's plenty of opportunity for the disease to spread. As a result, the common rhododendron (now regarded as a weed) is being eliminated on the Eden estate; it's a sump for many

wilts as well as for powdery mildew, and can readily infect and spoil ornamental rhododendrons on site. It is also a host for sudden oak death – a disease with disastrous potential for several species of trees (see p. 310).

Look out for powdery mildew on shrubs and herbaceous plants like roses, clematis, apple trees, sweet peas and hanging-basket plants; the leaves of vegetables such as spinach can succumb too. To reduce the threat, keep plants well watered and ensure free air movement.

Improving air circulation around the plants by pruning and by opening vents, or installing fans in the greenhouse, also helps to alleviate the situation. Don't plant too densely, and avoid high-nitrogen fertilizers that encourage vulnerable sappy growth. Grow plants in their preferred position so that they are stress-free, and if possible choose resistant varieties.

Prune out infected parts immediately and ensure that white patches on stems, evidence of the disease's resting stage, are removed from your roses during winter. Once you have collected all the infected debris, burn or dispose of it carefully. Many local authorities now compost domestic green waste, like the material used at Eden, at temperatures high enough to kill pathogens, but don't do it at home unless you know that the temperature created on your compost heap is high enough to kill spores and prevent re-infection (see p. 45).

Alternatively, try the Eden way and spray with food-grade sodium bicarbonate or fatty acids. If you are resorting to chemical controls, check the label carefullly as they can only legally be used on the range of plants specified. For most vegetables there are no fungicides available, so you will have to use alternative methods there. And if it's any consolation, if you wipe mildew from gooseberries they will still be edible!

Downy mildew

Downy mildew is caused by a family of fungus-like organisms called *Peronosporaceae* fungi that are relatives of the potato blight fungus, *Phytophthora*, and affects a range of garden plants from roses to peas and grapes. It is found regularly on hops and onions at Eden, and in the nursery, and is worse in all of the Biomes where it's humid or damp.

Yellow patches appear on the top of the leaf and a greyish-white fungal growth, sometimes with purple tints, below. The leaf veins act as a barrier, the infestation forming tell-tale angular edges, but if a patch is rubbed it doesn't disappear, as most powdery mildews would. If the infection spreads, the whole leaf may die, and it is particularly common on soft, young plants.

Remove infected leaves promptly, improve air circulation around the plants and avoid overhead watering so as not to wet the leaves. Copper-based fungicides provide some control. When grape downy mildew first reached Europe some time before 1878, probably from the United States, within five years it nearly destroyed the wine industry in France and the rest of Europe too; but it resulted in the chance discovery of the first modern fungicide, Bordeaux mixture, still in use today.

Root and stem rots

These diseases in various forms appear occasionally at Eden and are usually introduced via plant material

MANAGING POWDERY MILDEW

A SOLUTION OF food-grade sodium bicarbonate at 2.5g per litre has controlled powdery mildew effectively at Eden. Researchers in Brazil discovered that milk solution was effective on courgettes, and boosted the plant's immune system into the bargain. A weekly spray of 1 part milk to 9 parts water reduced the severity of infection by 90 per cent, but if milk concentrations rose above 30 per cent fungus grew on the plants. In New Zealand, researchers found skimmed milk to be as effective as full-fat, with reduced chance of odours. The whole plant needs to be sprayed thoroughly, as it is a 'contact' control.

NB According to pesticide legislation, neither bicarbonate of soda nor milk are approved in the UK for powdery-mildew control, so they cannot officially be recommended!

from nurseries. Rots that appear in the garden also take many forms: there are narcissus basal rots, bud blast on rhododendrons, parsnip canker, and damping off and grey mould are classed as rots too. In the Humid Tropics Biome, one type of rhizome rot has caused considerable damage to plants in the ginger family, particularly cardamom. As soon as the disease was diagnosed (it was a *Fusarium* fungus) the badly affected rhizomes were rushed into the isolation unit at Watering Lane Nursery, the rotten areas were cut away and disposed of, and the remaining material was sterilized with 10 per cent bleach. The rhizomes were then grown in isolation until staff were certain that the disease had been eradicated. Those specimens that survived were replanted in the Biome and are now flourishing.

A similar technique can be used at home to prevent or control rots that sometimes afflict rhizomes after they have been divided. The cut surfaces of iris rhizomes, for instance, can be dusted with sulphur powder.

For improved performance and larger crops, keep your apple trees free of powdery mildew.

When rot set in at Eden, the bed where the gingers were growing was cleared of plant debris, and about 5cm of the topsoil was drenched with the systemic fungicide carbendazim. Then the whole area was treated with another fungus isolated from another part of the Humid Tropics Biome, *Trichoderma viride*, which had been found in tests carried out at the laboratory at the nursery to be antagonistic to *Fusarium*. *T. viride* is a parasitic fungus that feeds on *Fusarium* and other fungi in the soil. It is hoped that this will provide an element of protection against future outbreaks.

A fungus that has caused problems in heliconias also attacked some varieties of banana at Eden. It is not known if all of this fungus came from the same source, but it caused a rhizome rot similar to the disease in gingers. In bananas it produces the classic symptoms of Panama disease, which has been a major problem in banana production over the years and caused the demise of favourite old varieties such as 'Gros Michel'. The current main dessert banana, 'Cavendish', is resistant to most races, or species, of the fungus, apart from a new one, race 4, which is very aggressive (not present in the Eden banana collection). A control programme, similar to that used during the cardamom trouble, has been set up.

As the fungus develops, discoloured patches appear, the leaf and stem tissue deteriorates and sinks inwards; it spreads rapidly and is fatal or seriously damaging to crops if it's not stopped. The spores are spread on pruning tools, during handling or by insects. Infection spreads so rapidly that control is difficult.

Fortunately, the hardy bananas that can be grown at home are rarely affected. But if the disease *does* strike, remove infected material immediately and disinfect gardening tools like secateurs by wiping the blades with meths and allowing it to evaporate before using them on new plant material. Disinfecting tools with meths is a standard practice throughout Eden that can be used at home and helps prevent the spread of diseases – any diseases – from plant to plant.

Fusarium wilt

Another disease caused by *Fusarium* that has been a problem at Eden is wilt. This has been particularly problematic in the Outdoor Biome where the pinks are affected. The fungus invades, blocks the water-conducting tissue and releases a poison, causing the leaves and stems to collapse as if suffering from drought. Cut the stems or upper roots, and the water-conducting tissue shows dark brown or black. Plants either die immediately, or over several seasons. The fungus stays in the soil, so remove and destroy infected plants straight away and don't grow related plants in that spot for at least five years. Different forms attack different plants, including sweet peas, peas, asters, tomatoes, sweet potato and cabbage.

LEFT: *Some species of banana are prone to Fusariam rot, which also affects heliconias.*

BELOW: *Crocus bulbs can suffer from several types of rot; make sure growing conditions are good, improving the soil when necessary.*

Potato blight

This is becoming an increasing problem for gardeners, attacking tomatoes as well as potatoes. Brown or black patches appear on the tips and margins of leaflets, which curl up and wither. The disease spreads rapidly to the stems too, and finally the plant collapses. The spores of the fungus (*Phytophthora infestans*) are washed down to the tubers, which become discoloured, and a reddish-brown rot appears (in tomatoes, patches of brown rot appear on the fruit). This, together with possible secondary infection, reduces the tuber to a stinking, liquefied mass. Potato blight rapidly devastates crops, whether stored or in the ground. It is an ugly disease that has had disastrous consequences: the sight of it must have struck terror in those affected by the Irish potato famine in the 1840s.

Potatoes are usually infected first so, if your crop is affected, follow all the recommended controls so as to reduce the chance of the blight spreading to your tomatoes. Spores are spread by wind and rain in warm, humid conditions from mid-summer onwards, when temperatures exceed 10°C. Remove infected foliage immediately, to slow its spread and prevent spores reaching the tubers; don't harvest the crop for at least three weeks after removing the infected foliage, to allow time for the skins to thicken up and spores on the surface to die.

Tuber infection can be reduced by 'earthing up' (see p. 000) or mulching with a thick layer of organic material like hay or straw as the stems and foliage develop. Don't leave blighted tubers in the soil; lift every last one, and dispose of them away from the garden. Always buy tubers from a reliable source.

Early main-crop varieties are more prone to blight, so plant early varieties, which will have more time to mature before the disease has a chance to take hold; planting alternate rows of different resistant varieties can improve cropping. Check any tubers you have in store regularly, and remove any that are rotting.

There's one particular pre-emptive strike you can make: before your plants become infected, apply Bordeaux mixture. In addition, listen out for any mentions of blight infection or of the 'Smith period' (which is related to temperature and humidity). Farmers' programmes on local radio are the best source of useful warnings, and *Farming Today* on Radio 4. This information can also be found on the internet. Cultural methods that can be employed to avoid blight are many: as well as planting alternating rows of resistant varieties, grow a crop of second earlies that will bulk up before the high-risk period, use healthy seed potatoes, avoid sheltered sites, widen the spacings in and between rows, plant into the prevailing wind, maintain good hygiene, look out for early signs of blight in neighbours' gardens and in nearby fields, apply copper fungicides. Dry, sunny weather stops blight from spreading.

Damping off

This most commonly appears in the greenhouse, but at Eden it has affected cabbage seedlings in the Outdoor Biome. Seedlings become discoloured, particularly around the base, and collapse. Infection spreads rapidly, patches of seedlings die off in their trays, and fluffy white *mycelium* appears on the surface of the dying plants. If it occurs before germination is complete, seedling emergence is patchy.

BLIGHT-RESISTANT VARIETIES

To INCREASE your chances of ensuring a good yield of potatoes, grow varieties that show some resistance to blight: these include 'Colleen', 'Premiere', 'Cosmos', 'Lady Balfour', 'Pomeroy', 'Orla', 'Remarka', 'Cara', 'Milva', 'Valor', 'Verity' and 'Arran Victory'. 'Sarpo Mira', the first to score 100 per cent against blight, and 'Sarpo Axona' are ushering in a new era of blight- and virus-resistance, and have been used successfully in displays at Eden. More varieties are to follow – roll on the blight-resistant revolution! At Eden, blight control is helped by growing early varieties that are harvested before the main infection period in July, then planting later with resistant kinds – mainly Sarpo varieties such as 'Axona' and 'Mira', plus 'Eve' and 'Lady Balfour'. Be warned, though, that even the 'resistant' ones may be attacked in years when potato blight is severe.

Spray your outdoor tomatoes with Bordeaux mixture before any problem appears, to protect against attack; keep the greenhouse well ventilated, and don't save seed from sick fruit. Remove and destroy infected plants immediately. The cultivar 'Ferline' shows some resistance, but not always. Smaller-fruited varieties are less susceptible. Tomatoes grown under glass are less prone to infection, but are still vulnerable.

Damping off is caused by *Pythium* species, which are close relatives of *Phytophthora*. It is encouraged by overwatering and prolonged high temperatures; seedlings that are given poor light or sown too densely are particularly prone, and it often appears when hygiene is poor in pots and trays, when tools aren't scrubbed and disinfected, or when unsterilized compost is used. Always sterilize your equipment when sowing seeds and use water from the mains, not from the water butt that has been standing for a while. Sow the seeds thinly, ensure they get enough light and aren't kept warm for longer than needed. Any compost you are using can be drenched with a copper-based fungicide like Cheshunt Compound, or you can treat the seedlings themselves with fungicide.

Never plant out seedlings from infected trays, or they could contaminate healthy land.

White blister

Sometimes known as crucifer white blister, this disease is caused by *Albugo*, a member of the same family of organism as the downy mildews. It is most often seen on the weed shepherd's purse, so make sure that doesn't grow in your garden. At Eden the condition affects brassicas, particularly cauliflowers.

The discoloured white 'blisters' become fluffy with fungi, while the upper surface of the leaves turn yellow and they may become distorted. You can avoid this at home by rotating crops or by allowing at least two years before planting brassicas in the same location. Spores are spread in air or water, so the disease is worse in humid or moist air, but it can sometimes be checked by spraying with Bordeaux mixture fortnightly

and up to a week before harvesting. However, it's better to do it the Eden way and immediately remove and dispose of the affected parts.

Phytophthora root rot

The organisms that cause this disease are closely related to potato blight, and are generally spread in water or plant debris ('splash and trash'), whereas potato blight also produces spores on the leaf surfaces that are dispersed when it's wet and windy.

One of the greatest challenges in the Outdoor Biome has been to establish shrubs in the poorly drained soils, and in the past many plants have suffered from phytophthora root rot, though conditions in most areas are now improving. Rotting at the roots and base of woody plants causes poor growth, foliage becomes sparse and discoloured, and stems show signs of die-back, so gradually the whole plant is killed. The disease has taken hold if, when you lift the plant, you find the fine roots are dead and the larger roots discoloured black and brown; or you can identify it when, removing bark from the trunk, you find a reddish-brown discoloration and a faint smell of seaweed.

Phytophthora is now regarded as one of the most common causes of death in ornamental trees and shrubs in Britain, and is believed to have reached epidemic proportions. It's worse on heavy, waterlogged soils and following wet winters. After the fungus has killed the roots, decay organisms of other wood-rotting types rapidly invade them. The infection also tends to flourish in warm, wet conditions, and where farmyard manures and mulches, which increase water retention, have been applied.

ABOVE: *One of Eden's cauliflowers – mercifully free of white blister and caterpillar damage.*

LEFT: *All holding bays at Eden are kept spotlessly clean to halt the spread of pests and diseases.*

Sadly, there is no cure available to gardeners. Infected plants should be removed along with the soil from the immediate vicinity, and poorly drained soil improved to inhibit the spread of the disease.

Narcissus leaf scorch

This disease is evident when the tips of young shoots turn reddish-brown soon after they emerge. In damp conditions, the symptoms will spread down the leaves, and lens-shaped brown spots will appear before the leaves finally turn yellow, shrivel and die. The fungus is spread by rain splash and will rapidly transfer on to neighbouring plants. Storing bulbs at low temperatures, particularly if combined with late planting, can increase the likelihood of damage, though the bulbs don't show signs of rotting or discoloration. Other plants such as amaryllis, nerines and snowdrops may also be affected. The fungus survives on the papery outer scales of the bulb.

Some narcissus varieties are more susceptible than others, and they should not be grown where this disease is, or has been, a problem. The usual treatment at Eden is to remove the scorched leaf tips before the disease gets seriously established, which reduces it to acceptable levels. Alternatively, you can spray with Bordeaux mixture every two weeks. However, be aware that this preparation can cause unsightly deposits on the blooms if applied during flowering.

RIGHT: *Tulip fire is a disease that cannot be easily controlled. Although it has appeared in some beds at Eden, luckily it has yet to spread.*

Tulip fire

Tulip fire, caused by the fungus *Botrytis tulipae*, is the tulip grower's nightmare. Leaves emerge from the ground grotesquely distorted, scorched and spotted with brown. In conditions of high humidity and rainfall they can be covered by a fuzzy mass of grey-green spores, which are easily spread by wind and rain – so, almost literally, the disease spreads like wildfire. Plants may flower, but there will be bleached spots on the petals and the stems will topple over. If it's humid, the plants may be engulfed by the fungus, then rot. Symptoms are more severe in heavy soils when the plants are stressed.

Buy your bulbs from a reputable supplier, but choose carefully, as there are different levels of resistance among tulip varieties. *Tulipa fosteriana* and its cultivars, for instance, are to be avoided, as they are prone to tulip fire. Remove infected plants before high humidity forms the fuzzy fungus on the leaves, and burn them immediately. You can try copper-based fungicides, but no treatment gives complete control, and the resulting flowers will have a sprinkling of light-brown spots, like burnt patches. Infected plants will contaminate the soil with resistant overwintering structures called sclerotia that can survive for long periods, so don't grow tulips in the same soil for at least three years.

Tulip fire is a disease that cannot be controlled, only managed. At Eden management will call for some creative thinking beyond rotations and soil treatments. Temporarily growing the tulips in crates or aquatic plant pots is one option as this reduces soil contamination and prevents cross infection.

Grey mould

Grey mould, caused by another form of *Botrytis* (*B. cinerea*) isn't fussy – it attacks the flowers, fruits, leaves and stems of many different plant types. The

most obvious signs are soft brown rot, followed by a fuzzy grey fungus and pale spots forming on the flowers. The spores are spread by water (including rain), and the fact that they go through resting stages in the soil only exacerbates the problem. Remove all dead or damaged material as soon as you notice it, cutting back into healthy growth, and dispose of it immediately. Spray the plant with fungicide. Grey mould thrives in cool, damp conditions, so in the greenhouse raise the temperature and improve the ventilation.

Box blight

This fungal disease can defoliate a plant in a few weeks; the infection starts from the top and spreads all the way down to the base. Dark-brown spots appear on the leaves, which eventually fall, and black streaks appear on the stems.

Control at Eden has so far consisted of removing the worst-affected plants and drastically pruning the less badly diseased areas, followed by a spray programme concentrating on the affected areas. There are no fungicides currently recommended for domestic use, however, so at home you must buy good quality plants and prune out infected stems. Another good preventive is to alter your husbandry habits and water your box plants around the roots rather than from above, to avoid wetting the foliage.

Sudden oak death

Otherwise known as SOD(!), *Phytophthora ramorum* is a disease that has reached epidemic proportions along the California coast, infecting many species including the Californian black oak (*Quercus kelloggii*) in its native habitat (a tree that can be found in the Californian displays in the Warm Temperate Biome). It can attack a wide range of plants and has been found on many in Britain, including rhododendrons, viburnums and camellias, which are the ones of greatest concern at Eden (the disease is established in parts of Cornwall). Consequently, the Biomes are strictly regulated as far as plant movements are concerned, and any plants on Eden's suspect list receive special attention. SOD is most likely to come into Eden on car tyres, via puddle splashes, in wind-driven rain or on a plant. In an effort to reduce the proliferation of the fungus, as much susceptible material as possible is being removed from areas where cars are liable to splash. Plant pathologist Tim

A NOTIFIABLE DISEASE

A CAUSE OF GREAT worry is that a new species of sudden oak death, *Phytophthora kernovii*, has been found in the rhododendron-rich woods of Cornwall. This one seems more likely to attack our native trees (although the evidence suggests that it still likes to 'practise' first on a plant like the rhododendron, to build up its reserves). What is even more sinister is that it can survive in the soil in a dormant state for long periods.

SOD has been found in plants quite close to Eden. DEFRA are doing their utmost to contain it, but if plants at Eden were affected, then drastic action would have to be taken, such as lifting and burning affected specimens, setting up exclusion zones, and removing, treating and disposing of affected soil.

Although both species of SOD are potentially less aggressive than Dutch elm disease – SOD is spread by people and commerce so it is easier to control than Dutch elm disease, which is spread by flying insects – they are still vigorous diseases that pose a threat to our flora and need to be rigorously controlled.

Pettitt is constantly looking for symptoms wherever he is on the site; none have been recorded so far.

The red oak (*Quercus rubra*), which is sometimes planted as a specimen tree on estates, can be affected, but SOD will only attack the English oak (*Quercus robur*) if there are large amounts of spores present in the atmosphere. The problem is that *Rhododendron ponticum*, a common weed species that is found on the Eden estate, suffers badly from the disease and so provides a mass of material for infecting other plants. In the more domestic setting, plants such as viburnums, especially *Viburnum tinus*, which have little resistance, can be contaminated over winter but not show symptoms until spring.

EDEN'S SOLUTION

Eden's philosophy is that there's room for some tolerance of pests and diseases, providing they don't pose a threat to the local flora and aren't killing or badly disfiguring individuals or whole displays. And there's an emphasis on eco-friendly controls, as this chapter has made clear. If a plant looks reasonably healthy, it doesn't really matter if its growth is slightly stunted or suddenly slows down. Some pest damage is often seen as an advantage, making areas throughout the Biomes look more natural than the real thing! We could do worse in our own gardens than to follow these simple guidelines for environmentally friendly gardening.

CONCLUSION

A visit to Eden should change your life. It's gardening with a message, a chance to be inspired, to reassess your values and to learn fascinating things you didn't know about plants both familiar and exotic. It will tell you a lot about the origins of the plants that you grow at home and increase your understanding of their importance in the wider, global context. You may be surprised to discover that some of those you can buy from nurseries and seed catalogues are actually endangered species from Chile; that the bulbs you want come from Mediterranean cork pastures, or those perennials from the South African Fynbos. You may not know, until you come to Eden, that some vegetables started out as seaside weeds; that some fruits were only recently wild plants; that the pot marigold, the sunflower and the willow have great potential as economic crops. And if you return home with a better understanding of the natural habitats of the Mediterranean herbs you use, and of the hardy palm in your garden, you will be able to provide them with better growing conditions, and you will certainly enjoy them more.

If you ever feel downcast about the growing conditions you have to contend with in *your* garden, let Eden be your inspiration. What began as a soilless – some might say soulless – reclamation site has been turned into an innovative landscape, a wonderful garden – living proof of what can be achieved with determination, imagination and optimism, not to mention a lot of hard work. It is not the location or the conditions in which you garden that counts, it's how you respond to them!

There's very little at Eden that can't translate to the domestic setting in some form or other. Tree ferns may be beyond your budget and *Victoria amazonica* too tropical for your pond, but there are many large-leaved hardy plants, palms and vigorous climbers that can make your garden more exotic than you may ever have dreamed possible; or if you want to create a low-maintenance desert, there's even several hardy cacti to choose

from. Via the internet you can acquire the lost crops of the Andes – and much more besides. We can all do it the Eden way: the myriad plants available, together with the techniques described in this book, are all you need to transform your own plot. Gardening is for everyman.

The Eden Project is a work in progress – it will develop over time. But stop that process, and it will decline. When visitors return they expect to see something new – and they are rarely disappointed. But there's a delicate balance to be struck. Change is inherent in the Eden concept, but changes have to be made with care. Much thought and discussion precede any innovation: the site must be developed with sensitivity and with an eye to the future. A visit to Eden will make you look, and look again; it will teach you a great deal, but it will also be enormous fun. From an idea that germinated in the back room of a pub, Tim Smit and all those who dared to share his dream are creating in microcosm their vision of how our world could be.

So let the vision of Eden enter your mind, and open up to the challenge it offers. Value the plants that beautify your borders and decorate your home; relish the food that your garden can put on your table. The Biomes change with the seasons, reflecting on a larger scale what is happening in gardens around Britain. We can all learn from the Eden Project – from its failures as well as its successes. We can make the artificial appear 'natural', challenge tradition with maverick alternatives, modify old techniques to suit extraordinary situations. Eden is a reminder of our dependence on plants, the fragile nature of the Earth and its finite resources. We must all contribute by recycling, and gardening sustainably and responsibly, and as we each do so we add our own infinitesimal contribution to the well-being of the planet, to the global environment. The least we can do is to cherish and conserve the plants in our care, they are our past, present and our future.

GLOSSARY

Key words from Eden

Biome: A Biome is a community of interdependent organisms, both plant and animal, whose habitat is characterized by a particular location and climate, e.g. desert, tropical rainforest, grassland etc.

Sustainability: The ability to carry on, taking the environment, people and economy into account, minimizing the impact of our actions and maintaining things at a steady level without exhaustion.

Waste neutral: This is achieved when the weight of introduced products made from recycled materials is equal to or greater than the weight of materials sent for recycling or disposal. This concept can be applied to any organisation, community or even individual household.

acid soil – having a pH less than 7.

alkaline soil – having a pH greater than 7.

alley-cropping – a system in which trees, usually members of the pea family, which produce nitrogen from the roots and respond well to pruning, are planted in wide 'alleys' with crops grown in between. The trees provide firewood and stakes, and fertilize and stabilize the soil.

architectural – describes plants with bold foliage, or with smaller leaves that combine to form a dramatically shaped plant.

biomass – a renewable energy resource derived from sources such as plant material including willow and cardoon, other food crops and raw material from forests; such resources absorb the same amount of carbon when they are growing as they release when they are burned, so they don't add to the sum total of carbon dioxide in the atmosphere.

blanch – to block out the light, thereby turning green plant tissue white; done with vegetables such as leeks, endive, cardoons and celery to make them more tender and sometimes to remove natural bitterness.

brassica – a member of the plant family known as *Brassicaceae*, formerly (and often still) referred to as *Cruciferae*. This includes plants with edible leaves such as cabbage, Brussels sprouts, broccoli, kale and kohlrabi.

bulbil – a small bulb or tuber developing at a leaf joint, or occasionally on other aerial parts of a plant.

canopy – a dense population of closely spaced tall trees whose upper branches intermesh to form a covering over the flora and fauna below.

capping – the formation of a hard crust on the soil surface, usually due to the impact of raindrops or irrigation; mainly found on poorly structured soils or those with fine particles like silt and sand. The 'cap' reduces the penetration of water and air into the soil and forms a barrier that emerging seedlings find difficult to penetrate.

cherry-picker – a hydraulic platform used to gain access beyond that which can be attained by ladder.

chitting – the sprouting of potato tubers or the germination of seeds so as to advance development or to check that they are alive before sowing.

companion planting – the practice of growing plants that have beneficial effects on their neighbours, primarily by enhancing growth or controlling pests.

contact action (or contact) – used to describe herbicides (weedkillers) or insecticides that only kill by direct contact.

cordon – a plant restricted to one main stem with short flowering and fruiting sideshoots, which is usually grown at an angle of 45° but can also be trained vertically. Normally used for training fruit like apples, pears and redcurrants, but can also be used with shrubs such as pyracantha.

crown – **1** the upper part of a rootstock from which the shoots grow; **2** the branches of a tree.

cultivar – a plant selection maintained as a clone in cultivation.

earthing up – raising a mound of soil around the stems of a plant, used to increase potato production, to blanch leeks or to stop the wind from rocking tall brassicas.

epiphyte – a plant that grows on the branches of trees but does not take nutrients from it, using the branches only as a means of support.

ericaceous – describes a plant that only thrives in soils with a pH of less than 7.

espalier – a method of training fruit trees by creating a vertical central stem with three or more horizontal tiers of branches coming from it in the same plane.

F1 hybrid – the first generation of offspring from inbred parents, exhibiting uniform growth, vigour and flowering and fruiting capacity.

family – a category of plant classification, such as *Liliaceae*, which is divided into genera, which in turn are divided into species.

fatty acids – also described as 'soft soap', used as an insecticide.

genus, genera (pl.) – a category of plant classification, e.g. Canna, Agapanthus, Musa, which is then subdivided into species.

glyphosate – a type of herbicide (weed killer) that moves around a plant in the sap system (hence 'systemic').

grain – used to describe the seeds of e.g. wheat and barley, but also the seeds of other edible plants that they replaced as seed crops in South America such as 'Inca wheat' (amaranthus) and quinoa.

green manure – a crop that, once it is mature, is dug into the soil to improve fertility, add nutrients and protect the soil surface. Such crops, which include winter field beans, mustard and grazing rye, take up nutrients that would otherwise be washed out by winter rains.

green waste – efficiently rotted-down organic matter, which forms the basis of Eden's soil. It comes from organic waste collected by the local authority from domestic gardens around Plymouth.

Growmore – a balanced general fertilizer containing equal parts of nitrogen, phosphorus and potassium.

hard landscaping – the paths, walls and any other element constructed from 'hard' materials like stone, concrete and gravel. Plants are described as 'soft' landscaping.

herbaceous – describes non-woody perennials whose stems and leaves die down in winter and regrow from underground storage organs each spring.

horticultural fleece – a finely woven material which forms a physical barrier over the plants but allows sunshine, air and rainwater to reach them. It also protects plants from pests and raises soil and air temperatures around them.

humus – a mixture of compounds formed by the breakdown of organic matter in the soil. It improves the soil structure, helps it to retain nutrients and is a slow-release source of nitrogen and phosphates.

hybrid – the offspring of two plants that are not identical.

internodal – describes the length of stem between the leaf joints.

interplanting, intersowing, intercropping – the planting or sowing of a fast-growing crop amongst one that is slower-growing.

mediterranean – describes areas of the world where there is a Mediterranean climate, typified by hot, dry summers and cool, wet winters, including parts of California and the Little Karoo in South Africa.

modules – small compartmentalized trays filled with compost and used for plant propagation. They can also be formed from the composting material alone.

mulch – a layer of material laid over the soil to retain moisture, suppress weeds, protect from the cold and keep the roots cool in hot weather. It can be organic, like shredded bark and straw, or inorganic like gravel or grit.

nematodes – or eelworms, can be beneficial and used in pest control, e.g. for suppressing vine weevils; or can be pests themselves, such as the potato cyst eelworm.

neutral soil – having a pH of 7 which is neither acid nor alkaline.

node, adj., nodal – the point on a stem at which a shoot or leaf arises.

offset – a young plant produced asexually alongside its parent, usually a bulb or a rosette-forming plant, and easily detached for propagation.

peat substitute – a material that is used instead of peat, e.g. coir, worm compost, leafmould.

perlite – a material formed from crushed and heated volcanic rock; it is added to potting composts to increase air capacity and improve drainage, or scattered over the compost surface when seed-sowing.

pH – a measure of acidity or alkalinity: 7 is neutral, above 7 is alkaline and below, acid.

photosynthesis – the manufacture of complex chemicals by green plants from carbon dioxide and water, using energy from sunlight.

phytosanitary – refers to legal controls or legislation relating to plant hygiene which prevent the introduction of pests and diseases into countries or into gardens like Eden.

potting on – transferring a plant to a container larger than the previous one it was planted in.

rhizome – a horizontal underground stem bearing buds, leaves and roots, e.g. many kinds of iris.

rootball – the combined mass of roots and potting medium found in a container or in open ground.

rootstock – the part of a budded or grafted plant that supplies the root system, also known as a stock.

Root-trainers – a type of seed-sowing system first patented in Canada. Each module has grooves to direct the roots straight downwards, and hinges to allow opening for easy plant extraction, thus minimizing root damage.

rosette – leaves or flowers radiating from a central point.

scarification – **1** the removal of moss and dead grass from a lawn using a wire rake or machine created for that purpose (lawn rake or scarifier); **2** the treatment of seeds before sowing to encourage germination, e.g. by rubbing thick-coated seeds with sandpaper.

selection – a plant chosen for its desirable attributes.

sets – usually, immature onions or shallots that will be grown on to maturity.

shrub – a plant with many woody stems formed just above ground level.

spadix – a type of fleshy flower spike enclosed by a large leaf-like structure, the spathe.

spathe – a large leaf-like structure encircling a flower spike (see above).

species – the group into which genera are divided, and the smallest category widely used; e.g. in *Pelargonium echinatum*, echinatum is the species.

stamen – the male part of a flower, made up of a thin stalk (or filament) with pollen producing anthers at the tip.

stigma – the female pollen-receptive part of a flower.

subspecies – a smaller unit into which species can be divided; usually geographically isolated populations of the species.

taproot – a root system where the main root remains dominant, though smaller fibrous roots may be present, e.g. carrots.

tuber – a stem tuber is the swollen end of an underground stem that produces buds and that grows a new plant, e.g. potato; a root tuber is a swollen root acting as an underground food store, e.g. dahlia.

variety, var. – **1** A unit of classification into which species are divided. **2** General definition of a type or cultivated form of a plant.

vermiculite – a naturally occurring mineral mined in several locations around the globe including South Africa and China; it expands to many times its original size when heated, and is used to improve the drainage, air capacity and density of composts.

INDEX

'To my Father, Ivan, who loved creation.'

Acknowledgements

I'd like to thank the following for their invaluable help when writing this book:

All the staff from Eden's Green Team who gave of their knowledge and time so willingly, particularly Adrian Lovatt, Tom Keay, Kevin Austin and Glen Leishman who retained their good humour over several months when constantly bombarded with questions. The Science team, particularly Tim Pettitt and Alistair Griffiths who delivered science in a form for everyman, all the staff at Watering Lane Nursery, particularly Roger Wasley for his friendship, enthusiasm and irrepressible sense of humour, and Chrissie Dew and Hilary Duckett the great organisers in the office who arranged my appointments. I'd also like to thank those who wrote the information labels at Eden for allowing me to use their work.

Caroline Hughes for her friendship, calmness and magical images, to Sue Minter for checking my facts on the gardening at Eden, and to Jo Readman for mentioning my name – again!

At Transworld Publishers I'd like to thank Susanna Wadeson for her patience, Sarah Emsley for her persistence and meticulous attention to detail, Helena Caldon for her editorial skills, Sue Phillpott for her enquiring mind and command of the English language, and Isobel Gillan for her fantastic design.

I'd like to thank Sonia Clyne at Boslowen Guest House for her cheerful hospitality, Sarah Weller for her help in a time of crisis and my wife Gill, who often transcribed the interviews in the early hours of the morning. Finally I'd like to thank Jessica, Henry and Chloe for tolerating the stress at home.